Sail Easy in Peace and War

An Autobiography

By Sherman Elias Walgren

ISBN 0-7414-2724-9

Cover design by Margaret Bucklew

Published by:

INFINITY
PUBLISHING.COM

1094 New DeHaven Street, Suite 100
West Conshohocken, PA 19428-2713
Info@buybooksontheweb.com
www.buybooksontheweb.com
Toll-free (877) BUY BOOK
Local Phone (610) 941-9999
Fax (610) 941-9959

Printed in the United States of America

Printed on Recycled Paper

Published August 2005

Contents

Sail Easy in Peace and War

An Autobiography

By Sherman Elias Walgren

This book primarily for my family will be captioned "General Reader" in other words, there will be certain topics not mentioned. Keep in mind I was a sailor.

Not knowing the right procedure in grammar, language, etc. I most likely will violate all rules.

The chapters, if I can refer to them, as chapters will cover first memories, grade school, junior and senior high.

After graduation, jobs and activities up until my joining the Naval reserve and volunteering for active duty in 1940.

Life after the service and rejoining the Naval reserve and called back to active service for the Korean War.

Read on...

Chapter One

Memories

"In the beginning" as the Good Book starts. I was born in the front bedroom of the family home at 3048 10th Avenue in Minneapolis, Minnesota. My mother was Josephine Emily Walgren Nee Loberg. My father John Meyer Walgren. By decent mom was Norwegian, my grandmother from Toten, Norway. My grandfather died before I was born. My other grandfather was Swan John Walgren and also died before my being born. I have a genealogy of my father's side dating back to, Ulfanus Johannes generation one, 1549 in Sweden. Swan married a Norwegian girl named Andrea. She died when my father was 12. They lived in a log cabin in Kandiohi in western Minnesota. Swan hired an Indian woman to take care of the children. He was busy with a 100-acre farm, plus he had the first sawmill in the area. I'm loaded with relatives and would take another book to tell you about them. Mom was born in Minneapolis. At 2717 18th Ave. South. There were her brothers and sisters. Josephine, the eldest, born July 11, 1884. Then, Aunt Mabel, Arthur, Pauline, and George. My father was born August 6, 1883 and had two brothers, Elmer and William.

That takes us to my family. My brother Lawrence, the eldest, next Dorothy, Louise, Gaylord, Marjorie, and I'm the baby of the family born October 21, 1918. I must add, it was a great family. Every single night was supper and the eight of us present until the passing of years and they disappeared because of marriage. They were good years.

The house was three stories, built by my grandfather and my father in 1907. We lived on the first floor. Eight of us in a two-bedroom floor. When we boys grew older, we slept on the third floor. No heat in the wintertime. When it was below zero, we had flannel sheets and blankets and old coats. Anything to try and keep warm. When I was old enough I had the front bedroom. It was painted with calcium paint. The ceiling had clouds and stars. Quite nice. In the summer tho it was hot. Would put a little mattress in front of the window. As I said, in the beginning I would ramble on with anything that came into my mind. Right now I see the neighbors houses. The Elm trees making a canopy or tunnel over the street. Minneapolis was a city of trees, lakes, and parks. What a wonderful place to live until I found out there were places that saw the sun more often. We lived in South Mpls., abbreviation. One block away was Powderhorn Park. I've always thought how lucky we were to have such a park so close. I grew up in that place. Downtown was three miles away by streetcar, plus or minus. It figured a lot in my life. We had 11 lakes within the city. They were not puddles. Calhoun was about a mile or more across. Tho it was fairly round. Lake Harriet also large, Nokomis, Lake of the Isles, where I almost drowned except for a buddy swimming along side to bolster my will to live. And Cedar Lake. Those were the main lakes. Powderhorn was shaped like the Powderhorns of the colonists for their long rifles. When I was about seven years old they dredged it to make it deeper and then the dredgings formed the Hollow, as we called it for baseball, football, skiing and sliding. Sure was fun. I will elaborate on it, as I get farther into this "epistle".

The first things that I can remember and I don't know how old I was, I remember a metal bed, maybe they called it a cradle. The sides went up and down. It was white with most of the "leaded" paint maybe chewed off or something, I think all of us kids had the bed. It was located in the back bedroom with my three sisters. There came a a time when Dr. Withem wanted to give me a shot. I locked myself in the bathroom and don't know how long I evaded him. I seem to recall Lorry (Lawrence) trying to come in the window. I must have come out, but I don't recall that part. Another memory was in northern Wisconsin at Bayfield. My father's uncle was a fisherman on Lake Superior. The island was 18 miles from the mainland. He had a fishing boat, the Mildred B. named after his daughter. The whole family was there I guess, and my great uncle Charlie even remembers I fell off a keg. Also, I went to sleep and when I woke up I guess I caused such a fuss on missing the boat ride, he had to take me out again. These things I remember, not thinking it because some one told me about it.

In the early days I went walking with my mother and grandmother. This was well before I went to kindergarten. Usually thru the park and out to my Aunt Ollies. Uncle Art's wife. Then they moved into my grandmother's house. I had two first cousins, Norman and Robert, or Bobby, as I knew him. When he was six years old, we were the same age, he contracted lymphatic anemia. We went to see him often but he died. The first traumatic thing in my life.

I was around four when I first went skating. With supervision of course. I had clamp on skates with four runners like a tiny sled. I doubt if what I did was skating, but more like walking. As time passed, I got a sled. It was a "Rosebud", this sled was the same as was in a famous movie about Hearst, the publisher. It got tossed into the fire at the end of the movie. By this time I had neighborhood friends, Gordy Moe, or Gordy. And Johnny Santrizos. We went sliding at the park, we couldn't wait for winter. We lived at the park. I'll use that phrase many times. The sled ended up tragically, however. I was jumping with it. Would sail thru the air for maybe six, seven feet and that last time both runners flattened out and that was the last of Rosebud. Am going back in time again. I remember clearly my mother taking me to Horace Mann School for kindergarten. Going into the school, up the stairs to Miss Raider's room. All the kids to play with. Miss Raider broke her arm and we all wrote letters doubt if anyone could read them, but we did it. I can still remember the greatest part of the class. One reason was most families did not move away. I graduated with many of the kids who were in my kindergarten class. First grade was Mrs. Porter, it was there most of us learned to read a little. I recall mom there for PTA and Mrs. Porter holding up cards like cat, pig, hen, dog, etc. the one that said it first got the card and at the end, whoever had the most cards was the smartest???

Second Grade was Miss Kelley. I really don't remember a great deal, but I must have passed cause I ended up in the 3rd grade. That was Miss Lindberg. Two things happened there, the first was the death of Jean Bruce, my first love? She was a nice girl. Died from a burst appendix on their kitchen table over on 12th and 11th Ave. The other event, Miss Lindberg flunked Janet Selveig and I and we had to go to summer school. I've always felt she needed pupils, as when I got there she was the teacher. Gay, George Santrizos, and Johnny came to visit at recess just about everyday. Another neat thing about it was, I was the only one of us kids that went to the same grade school as my mother.

On the way home we'd walk the Milwaukee Railroad track to 11th Ave., then stop on the hill on Lake Street and watch Sears and Roebuck being built that was around 1927. 4th, 5th, and 6th grade we had Miss Chalgrin. She was the kind of teacher you could fall in love with. Everyone liked her. Once a week in all grades Miss Winter came for music lessons. How to read music and tap rhythm with your forefinger over the notes. Every Christmas all classes would form outside the classrooms and sing Christmas carols. The school had four floors, but the 4th floor was just a mystery place for we kids to explore. Mr. Hansen was the janitor, darn nice man with size twelve shoes, or so it seemed. He shoveled the snow in the winter, mowed the grass in the summer. All the schools had their own power, big steam turbines to turn generators. We never lost power. All thru grade school we had paper sales. Going to all the neighbor's collecting paper. That was a big event. We had clubs in 6th grade. Went to the park bird watching. We had very many different species. Also study trees and berries and bugs. Darn it was good kind of life. Wish I could do it again.

At this time I was about eleven or twelve and moved onto Bryant Junior High. It was around two miles from home. At this age we all had bikes and sometimes rode to school. In the winter, Johnny and I would wait for Mr. Bertelson to take Arthur and then we would leave Johnny's house and be invited to ride to school, we were not dummies. I forgot to mention, Gordy Moe. He lived with his grandmother, my second grandmother. Anyway, Gordy got TB and had to go to a special school called Lehman's House. He ended up a half year behind me, and Johnny by his own admission said he was skipped a half grade because Mr. Moss, the principle of Horace Mann was his mother's first cousin. Pays to know someone. Bryant had a swimming pool. That is where we learned to swim. Always sans swimsuits. Think of just coming out of a pool and a shower at 3:15 pm, walk home from school with the temperature 10 degrees below zero. It happened and sometimes worse. The lowest temperature I ever saw in Mpls. Was 45 degrees below. When you talked the words froze and in warmer weather all those words would fill the air????

It was in junior high we took shops. The kids today should do the same. I had printing. The teacher was Mr. Bolinger. Electric shop with Mr. Busies, he had halitosis bad. Mr. Labarge was wood shop. Wonderful teacher, I still have a plant stand I made in 8th grade with a lot of important dates under the bottom. Mr. Shimmely was the mechanical drawing teacher, still have a lot of my drawings and I'm amazed at how good they were. My mother saved a lot of my drawings in science class. Got a lot of A's and B's. Some are darn good. Mr. Trafser was the sheet metal class where we made cups, cookie cutters, mud scrapers and the like. All of this helped me pretty dang good at a lot of things I've done in my life.

Johnny and I were in the Glee Club when I tried out Miss Angel had me sing "The Last Rose of Summer". I was a fair country singer. I also had Miss Angel for study period and she caught Johnny and I playing "battleships" she took it pretty good tho and sat down with me and showed me how to fold a paper into a little four-legged bowl. I still know hot to do that at 86. All in all, it is too bad schools are not the same now with computers and all the things. Kids are not playing sandlot baseball, playing marbles in the spring and fudging at it. Using steelies and agates and mibs, playing pie in the snow, flying kites (at which I was a master) and spinning tops. We had "spikes" that was a top with a spike end and if you hit the other guys top you could split it in half. Also the red, white and blue, Hummer. That had a ball tip, you could swing it down with all your might and it would hum like crazy. God, what a life. It was good. It used to be a privilege to clap the erasers after school after the days use on the black boards. They were full of chalk.

When I was about six or seven the whole school marched down Elliot Avenue to Lake Street. We all lined up on the hill between Elliott and Tenth and waited for President Coolidge to go by. That was the first time I saw him. Somewhere around 1926 or so we went to Willis Island in the Apostle Islands of Lake Superior. It was just my father, mother, Gaylord, my brother, and I. While there we took a boat trip, in my uncle's boat, to Devil's Island. There was a lighthouse there and a Captain Christeinson was the light keeper. President Coolidge was in the area as many summers he fished for trout in the Bule River in northern Wisconsin he came, with all his aids, on the motor ship Nautilus out of Ashland, Wisconsin. My great uncle Charlie showed him lake trout and I have pictures of that. In the picture also is great Aunt Fredrika, my cousin Howard, actually my father's first cousin, and my brother Gaylord. I spell his name because in now days they use the name Gay as something else, but that was what we always called him. Back to the president, Gaylord was at the time a second class boy scout and had his uniform on: he got to shake the President's hand. Quite an experience. On our trip to the island that time we had a 1924 Hupmobile touring car. My oldest brother Lawrence drove. We had about three flat tires and a blowout. Had to buy a new tire, also. Rubber tires were not like the tires we have now. Lorry had to take the tire rims off and get the tube out and put an a patch on. It was a lot of work. It took us six hours to get to Duluth, a distance of one hundred and sixty miles. When you come to the top of the hill overlooking Duluth you could see quite a panorama. The iron ore docks, the arial bridge over to Minnesota Point. Now it reminds me of the view of Kaneoha on Oahu from the Pali. Anyway, here we are in Duluth. Every year we picked up my cousins? (first cousins once removed) and they went to the island with us. Len was Gay's age and Howard was closer to mine. We stayed at Charlie Benson's home in Bayfield. A beautiful house, lots of gingerbread and a porch that went from the front and around the side. I think it was the best house in town. The next day Pa and Ma, our terms then, would go to Senses grocery store and buy up food like crazy. I know they did not want to impose on Aunty. We would go down the hill to the Booth Fishery Dock where we boarded the C.W. Turner, the boat that went around to all the fishermen on the islands and collected the catch. They did this every three days. The Turner would first stop at Sand Island, then on to Rice Island where later Benson would move. From Rice it would come to each of the docks on Willis. Willis is also known as North Twin and Rice is known as South Twin. Willis is about a half mile in circumference. Many times I would go out with uncle when he set the gill nets. They were in gangs of three and stretched quite a long ways. Usually one of my cousins (?) was with him. Either Art or Fred. Uncle always took care of the setting and the other took the helm, which consisted of a long bar connected to the rudder and they steered with their feet. Standing up in the stern, this went on in almost all kinds of weather. The nets were hauled in with a lifter; it was geared to the engine. As the nets were coming in one had to put the net in boxes, one had to take the fish out of the net, and my job was to hit any trout that was still alive with a little club that had a spike in the head. That was so the fish would not tangle the net. An average catch for the day was around 600 pounds. Lake trout could go up to 60 lbs. but the best size I liked for eating were five to ten pounds. After coming into the dock at Willis, the net boxes were taken to the drying racks, or reels, and they were spread on the reels. Uncle and his hired man, or Fred or Art would repair the net. There were two sizes of gill nets, one for lake trout and one for white fish. They had a much smaller head so the size of the

The shack on Willis Island. Len, Me, Howard, Iley, & Wendle. 1929

net was small. What a lucky kid to have had that experience. The other fishermen on the island were Lenus Jacobson, who later bought the island, and nobody liked him, old man Doofy who had an open boat and a one Lung engine, the Edwards, who were darn nice people had two daughters around our age and the Frieds, they were from Finland had two nephews Wendel and Iley. Gay and I, len and Howard, Wendle, and Iley built a clubhouse. It was neat, had a porch and enough bunks for all of us to sleep in. All the material we got on the island, pine cedar and fir were plentiful. One year they were lumbering over on Rice Island. More than once we rowed the mile over there and got cookies from the lumber camp cook. How many kids can say that. On the way over and back Howard had a chromatic mouth organ and played. He was good at it. Much better than I, tho I think I was better than most. At times we would go to the clearing. At little area that had less trees. No one could see us and it was there we went swimming. The water temperature in Superior is around 45 degrees, all summer; it took a lot to dive into that. You could lose your breath for a moment. If you were thirsty just drink the water. At that time superior was considered 99.9 tenths pure. It was a self-purifying lake. You could see the bottom 40-50 feet down. I don't think that is the case today as when the iron ore in the Mesabi Range petered out they built some plants north of Duluth that took the weaker ore and produce taconite pellets that were sent to the big mills in Cleveland and New

York. The by-product was tailing they discharged into Lake superior. It was a type of asbestos and ruined commercial fishing. This happened however after World War Two. Also they opened the Weland Canal where ocean ships could come in the St. Lawrence River and into the Great Lakes. They did not foresee that the sea Lamphry, a suckerfish, would be on the bottom of these ships and they came into the Great lakes and propagated like crazy. Many trout and white fish would be caught with the blood sucking fish attached. After many years of electrifying creeks and rivers, they depleted the sea Lamphry but I don't think fishing ever came back as good as it was in the early years. It wasn't all just fun we had to work too. Aunty had a cow on the island for milk. It had a bell on so when we were ordered to get the cow we had to scour the island for it guided by the bell. There were many paths through the wood so it was not all that hard. We also took a skiff and went around the island getting pulpwood. It was hard work, but easy to find that too. Big tugs from the north shore of Minnesota would take huge rafts of pulpwood in gangs. Some of them would get pushed under the gangs and wash up on all the islands. They were about six feet long and around eight or ten inches. We gathered them in the boat and back to the dock. After they dried out a bit we had to saw them to length and then quarter them with an axe. The saw was a big go tome and from me about five feet long and one of us on each end. Through the years we cut enough wood to fill a barn at the Benson house in Bayfield. My brother Lawrence visited the house after the war and said it was still full. They both died leaving a legacy in firewood. I mentioned Lenus buying the island. He had the best fishing tug in the islands named the Polaris. When he bought the island he tried to make the other fishermen pay him rent so they all moved over to Rice Island leaving "King Lenus" alone on Willis. Eventually the government made a national park of all the islands and kicked King Lenus off. Around the fishing shacks as they were called, was a smoke house. Uncle made the best-smoked white fish you ever ate. The fish house was connected to the dock. Inside and outside everyone painted their initials. The C.W. Turner took tourists with them and they awed at all the initials and words on the walls. Not any like on rest room walls around the country, all general audience. I'm told the parks commission left all of this stuff intact. The main shack, our clubhouse and all the buildings that were on the island. I have no idea how they may look now, if at all. As I never got back to the island after the war. Mell, Carleen (as a little girl) and I. and my dad and mom drove to Bayfield to see Aunty who was laid up in bed. Fredrika wore glasses as thick as the bottom of a pop bottle. She did knitting and crocheting holding the work about four inches from her eyes. But at that time she was just bedridden. It was the last time I saw her. Was the end of the island. I can still hear her hollering on Sunday, "Sondag Idag" you better not work on Sunday. Every one of my cousins are gone now, I'm the last one of those wonderful years inDuluth and Bayfield and the island.

My next adventures took place in the same years as the island. I had more cousins than I could count. I spent part of summer vacations at times on cousins farm in Kandiohi. I stacked wheat and cleaned barns with the best of them. There were two farms, the Felt farm and the Joe Bjornberg farm. My cousin, real second cousin, who lived in Willmar, Minnesota, and I stayed on the Joe Bjornberg farm. Usually for two weeks we did chores every day and then we would ride Maude. Most every farm had four horses named King, Queen, Prince, and Maude. At that time many still used horses for the farm implements. Not too many tractors. There was a depression at that time. One late afternoon, Stanton, my cousin, and I were riding Maude. The only way we could get on her was one of us would hold her and the other get on the platform at the pump. This was about a six inche or more platform so you would keep clean. Without the platform on the pump spilling water on the ground it would have been a muddy mess. These early folk were no fools. Anyway, I'm holding the reins for Stanton to get on, we had no saddle, and it was all bareback. I was wearing tennis shoes. Horses have a way of snorting and then taking one leg and stomping it down. The only thing wrong with this was my foot was under the hoof that came down. I thought the foot was smashed. It wasn't but it hurt like crazy. I'll get to the Felt farm later. Now my brother Gay and I went with my parents and my uncle George and aunt Margaret to Willmar in a 1922 Hupmobile. It was about an eighty-mile trip to Willmar. We were outfitted with cloth goggles to protect us from the dusty roads. Highway 12 had yet to be paved. We stayed at Stanton's house. His father Burdick Bjornberg right now I can't think of his mother's name. While there we were taken to some little carnival. I remember colored lights and we went into one sideshow I guess. There was some nut with an IQ of 2 sitting among chickens, snakes and whatever. Then he would grab a chicken and bite it's head off. That blasted scene has stayed in my mind forever. There was a small lake close to their house and Stanton and I built a raft and poled around in it. No thought of falling in the water. I've got to admit all the things I've done it's a wonder I'm here to type it. At this time I think I was five or six. My father's uncle was a beekeeper. We went over to their house and he looked like Methuselah and his wife very frail. I can remember some of this well as I have pictures of this trip. These people were in their seventies. They were old I guess from hard work. He put on a head mesh and got us a bunch of honeycombs. Burdick Bjornberg had a Buick. I think it was a 1920 model. We were going to a big IOOF meeting in Northfield, Minn., that stands for International Order of Odd Fellows. This was a place south of Minneapolis and I can hear Stanton hollering at his father "faster dad" we were maybe doing 45 miles an hour. The manifold was red hot. You could see it as the motor and hood was narrower than the front seat. Gawd what memories. Now Stanton is gone and all those people. My other farm, the Felt farm, was my favorite. Tina Felt was my father's aunt. Her husband, Louie was a gambler and played a lot of poker and had huge debts. When the depression started in may of 1929, the bank took the farm. I think that is what got old man Felt. He had a heart attack and died. Rubin and Harold got advice from my father and went to the bank and bought the farm back. In those days banks suddenly found themselves in the real estate business and readily sold it back at a price much less than was owed. They promptly bought three other farms and had one of the biggest farms in the area. Both cousins went to the Minnesota Agricultural College of the University of Minnesota and learned modern farming. Rubin became a state representative not long after, Rubin died and Harold had to buy off his widow to about 180 thousand dollars. That was quite a sum in those years. Harold did well. The farm was clear and prosperous. After the war and Mell and I were married the farm was my personal hunting place. That will come later.

Chapter Two

Grade School

Junior High

Back to the city kid. I enjoyed school. In senior high school I took chemistry, biology, cabinet shop, civics, Shakespeare that was also, English and Norwegian. There was more but like math and etc. were not elected, I was on the chess team for a while I was an alternative on the tennis team but my main thing was the stage crew. I asked Maylon Hep if I could be on it. He was my cabinet teacher. He said I had to count the prop screw holes in the stage floor. It was a joke. I became the flyman. My place was a metal grating balcony on the right side of the stage. We had a stage and auditorium that would put a lot of stages to shame. We had outside shows that rented the place but they had to use us and pay us fifteen bucks. Sidney H. Morris was the director of music and every year put off a Gilbert and Sullivan opera. The three years I was there we had "Dorothy", "The Mikado", and "Pirates of the Penzzance". Think that is right. Wouldn't bet on it tho. With all the rehearsals I thought I could have taken any part including the girl's parts. Learned all the words. We also had assemblies and good ones. I was promoted to stage carpenter with Rollie Halstad; we had our own room so we didn't need lockers. In my senior year I was stage manager. I had the wheel. We put off a stage show one Friday I had the crew set up a bunch of baby spots on the cyclorama, hung some pants and with the folds of the curtains and pants with red and blue, the school colors, it was a knockout. While this was going on the crew would bring out scenery and set it up and take it down and bring out an old English cottage set that I had made, but professional scenery artists painted. It was a good set. While all this was going on "Curly" a good janitor was reading Edgar Allen Poe's poem "the Raven" even Miss Thomas the assistant principle liked it. In the fall during football season we had a pep assembly on Thursday. Central was a big school. The student body was so large that we had to have two assemblies. That meant the whole crew missed first and second period. In my senior year I had Byron T. Emerson for chemistry. When report cards came out I had an "A" the first time. The second session he gave me an "F". Fail. I went to see about this and he said, you do good work when you're here but your not here all the time. You see I missed first period and that was chemistry. The same thing happened in English but I composed a poem titled "the Seagull" and made a book of poems from magazines and she was happy. At the end of the semester Byron T. gave me an “A” with a “B” average. Besides missing class on Thursday I missed it on Friday as I was in charge of putting up canvas around the chain link fence that surrounded the football field. Just the same on that report card I had made all “B’s” and “A’s”. They weren’t all that way but I did pretty good. Had some “C’s” and even a couple of “D’s”. However in my senior year I just missed the honor roll. I should also mention I got a “C” in Norwegian. I saw Absolom C. Erdahl, my teacher, and told him it ruined my good card of “A’s” and “B’s” and darned if he didn’t change it to a “B”. My mother spoke Norwegian, well I tell everyone I took two years of Norse and my mother got straight “A’s”. That not really true but she helped me a lot. When I was very little, my grandmother, aunt Polly and my mother spoke Norwegian all the time. I knew more Norwegian almost than English when I started school, but it was not like it is today when very many emigrants can’t speak English. More about the high school. There were two terraces up to the front of the school. It was an impressive entrance. Over the front doors was a slogan in stone. Every kid that went to that school must have read it. At a reunion, which we had every five years, one person from each table was asked to speak. I don’t know why I was asked????? But I did. In my little speech I brought up the slogan over the front of the school. No one remembered it so I told them. “The commonwealth requires the education of the people as a safeguard of order and liberty”, now the whole school has been razed and the old football field named Markley Square in honor of Joe Markley our old football coach. He died in Montana on a sheep ranch. He always said he would get and made it come true, died at 99. During these years other than going to school I was building model airplanes. I always loved airplanes. In junior high I was working on a Howard racer the plane Howard Hughes set a record across the country. My dad was working on plans at the round table in the dining room and I had all my stuff on a card table. He finally went to bed and I had to finish this model to take to Bryant the next day. Actually it was already the next day. I was using a banana oil spray to tighten the paper when I guess I went out like a light. I had breathed too many fumes. Guess it was my first and last “high” but I got it done. But I didn’t win. Carol Carmichael a boy that went all the way thru school with me won it with a model of a Boeing Bomber 1935. They only made a couple in real life. Carol and I were the best craftsmen in the cabinet shop and Mr. Labarge chose us to receive a kit from General Motors for a Napoleonic Coach, it is a trademark for Fisher bodies. To tell the truth, we were both too young for it. I got the Tonneau seat and the body made but not the doors; the top itself was a job. I never finished it and it ended up under the bed in the front room. My folks most likely put it in the basement and I guess the Greek boy ended up with that also. Anyway, I lost a lot of things I was saving when I went into the Navy in 1940. I had quite a collection of old buttons, presidential ones from the 1900’s, “Remember the Maine” etc. also an old Edison phonograph. It used cylinder records and I had some of those. It was all there except the big horn. Also had an electric contraption that was supposed to help arthritic conditions. It had a metal plate to put your hand on and induce electric shock. I'm sure it was a stupid invention for suckers.

I was about twelve when I buried my treasure. I put a note, a couple of toy cars, a little wooden speed boat my brother Gay carved out of pine. Had a collar button for a horn, all in all, it was neat. I remember those things but I know there were more these I put in a Mason jar and sealed it. I dug a hole five feet deep, it seemed, so then, but was most likely more like sixteen inches. It was right in front of an access door to get under the porch. I don't think anyone ever went under there. It was just sand and stones and no room to crawl. On either side of this I always planted corn. Was just what we called pig corn I got from the farm. Back to the treasure. I always planned to someday dig it p, the Mason jar. Alone would have been worth something. To finish this tale I have to go forward to the time I was in California. I guess I was in my sixties. We lived in Arcadia at the time. For some reason I had to go back to Mpls. I got Gordy Moe, at that time he was the city accessor, Dick Hubrig from high school days and I went up to the front door and rang the bell but there were no owners. A woman renter answered the door. They had turned the whole house into rental units. My old home that was so stately was going down the drain. A beautiful stained glass window at the landing to the second floor had been broken and replaced with glass. The carbon filament light bulb over the front porch was replaced with a 60-watt bulb. The mirrored address was gone and replaced with just black numbers. I'm sure the Greek took them for souvenirs but then he owned the house so I can't complain about that. To continue, the woman gave me permission, but said to be sure to leave

Cat & Myself about age 12. Buried my treasure right behind me.

The area as I found it. So around to the back we went. My heart was pounding and I had a lump in my throat to think, I was going to retrieve my treasure after all these years. I had to remove a square of cement that was in the way. Gordy and Dick were looking on in anticipation too. I started digging. I got down about a foot and kept making the hole bigger in circumference and no treasure. I was careful, as I did not want to break the Mason jar. I dug deeper and deeper. I got down far enough that I had to admit to my self someone had robbed me of my treasure. Maybe the little Greek kid. I just had to admit defeat. It was hard to take. My treasure gone, Life is not always happy. So much for that.

Back to earlier times again and how Powderhorn Park played a big part in my early life. Many summers I would fish for red horse carp. Actually they started out as gold fish that people put in the lake. They propagated like crazy. In the winter after the ice was shaved you could see hundreds of them swimming just under the ice. Back to summer. I made bread balls. Fresh bread was easy to form into little balls. I fished the bottom, as they are bottom feeders. Always caught three or more and kept them in a pail until I got home then I put them in the bath tub to keep them alive. I sold them to Zinzmaster bakery for their outside pool. Got a dollar for each one and two bucks for fantails. They bought all I could catch. I didn't care for bullheads but a lot of people fished for them for food.

We played tennis all summer. Dave Berdahl, Jimmy Knudson, Bob Orfield and I. We kept one court for hours as we always had someone to play the winner. There were four courts anyway so we didn't have much trouble with other players. These courts were on 32nd and 10th, there were four more on 34th and 10th and eight courts on 15th on the other side of the hollow. I felt I was a good tennis player. I started with Lorry's, my oldest brother, Top Flite racquet. Made by Spaulding Co. I wore that one pretty well out got another and here is how I got it. I was swimming at the main beach at Calhoun, diving for stones and such on the bottom when I found a nice opal ring surrounded with diamonds. I put it on my finger and when I got home I couldn't get it off. Ma put soap, ice and grease on the finger and we finally got it off. I traded that ring to Mig, my sister Marjorie, for a 15-dollar Davis Cup racquet, which was the top of the line then and strung with the best gut of the day. I knew it wasn't an even trade as the ring was worth a bunch of money. I was happy tho. Back to the tennis.

Arzy was the high school state champion and I won a set from him. There was no way I could do it again but that made me feel pretty good. I found out from him how to restring racquets and repair broken strings. That saved me some money and in those years it was important.

The park also had band concerts every Monday night. A city band, in band uniforms played for about two hours. Harry Anderson directed the community singing. He went from park to park and it was a contest to see which group sang the loudest. Powderhorn won most of the time. Being a natural amphitheater a good crowd always came with punk to keep the mosquitoes in check. We used to take ordinary grocery string and light the end with a farmer match. It smoked little but I managed to get my share of bites. They say only the female's bite so there must have been a lot of them. On 33rd and 10th there were always about five popcorn wagons whistling. Little steam whistles. They sold popcorn and ice cream cones. A Greek owned every popcorn wagon. There was a couple of trucks sold hot dogs, candy bars etc. One year my brother Gay built a little wagon with a top and heated wieners in a pot with canned heat for heat. He and Myron Orfield were partners in this operation but Gay did all the work. You haven't lived until you hear a few thousand people sing row row row your boat starting first on the left side then after a couple bars the second group come in and then the delayed third group. You think you could get a bunch of people to do that today?????

The big bash at the park was the fourth of July. To us kids it started at least a week before the 4th. We could buy "lady fingers" at Curtis Confectionery Store on 32nd and Chicago Ave. To get the real stuff we had to have Lorry, Lawrence, my brother, drive us out to xrxes ave. That was out of town then. We got rockets, 1,2,3, inch firecrackers, flash crackers. Son of a guns you scratch on the sidewalk or twist under your heel. Torpedoes you could throw at walls or sidewalk and the most powerful cherry bomb. We once blew the seam open on our garbage can. Tin cans blew completely apart. It's funny nobody got hurt. I did one time. Dick Patrick and I were down by the tennis courts. I had a sling shot. Made out of a tree y. I had the idea that if Dick would lite the fuse I could count to ten and let it reach the apex of its flight into the air.

That was the plan. Call it plan "a" Dick lit the fuse, I drew back the pouch with the cherry bomb was counting to ten, got to about nine and the rubber broke. Then Dick and I used plan "b". That plan was to run like the devil after I dropped the slingshot and bomb. Didn't get far enough as I got a little piece of the casing embedded in back of my ear. Lucky I didn't get lockjaw or something from that episode.

Meanwhile down at the warming house there was lots of activity. They held all kinds of races for kids and grownups. Legs tied together, Gunny sack races, Blueberry pie eating, and doll buggy parade. My sister Mig was in it about three years. The buggy was all decorated with poppies we had them like crazy in the back yard. The warming house was surrounded with concession stands and red white and blue bunting all over the place. They had horseshoe tournaments soft ball games in the hollow. Also hardball games. All in all it was quite a day. We looked forwards to this every year. It was sponsored by the Lawrence Wennel post American legion on Bloomington and Lake Street. All day the veterans would be placing the fire works for the evening on the island, it was just right size for it. Then at around nine o clock in the evening the would start with some dago bombs to get the crowds attention. There were ooh's and ahh's with each burst of color. One year something went wrong and all the fireworks started going off all at once. The guys lighting them off all dived into the lake to get away from them. One rocket burst in the crowd by the warming house and a woman was burned badly. That was the only accident I ever heard of in all the years I went to the 4th of July celebration. The evening ended with the star spangle banner being played over the loud speakers and the Niagara Falls between two lamp post on the island. Magnesium flares real bright.

Johnny Santrizos, Gordy Moe and I spent many a summer afternoon just lying on the hillside grass looking up at the billowy white clouds, seeing animals, faces and all kinds of formations. It was lazy dazy days of summer. Later as a teenager Bob Berdahl, Nick Nachicas, Dick Hubrig and I laid on the same hills. Not looking at clouds but just dreaming. One time we talked about who would get married first. The general consensus me as I was the oldest. It didn't work out that way however. Bobby was first, Dick second, I was third at 26 and Nick waited a long time.

I forgot to tell about the paper route Gay and I had. The Minneapolis Journal route 160 from 35th St. and 4th Ave. North to Lake Street. Just five blocks but a lot of apartments so it was a lot of papers. We would get them right after school for the afternoon papers but on Sunday morning we had to get up about four in the morning. We'd have a bowl of Campbell's soup with the letters in it. In the winter we pulled a sled to carry the papers. We waited on the corner by the library at the above place. 4th Ave was a streetcar line and we would put our ears to the track and listen for the roar of the paper truck. We could tell about how far it was. When it came roaring into sight they just slowed a little and threw our papers out. Then we delivered. When we finished at Lake Street we went back to 31st street and would wait for the team of horses and sleigh that was going to Powderhorn to clean the snow off the lake and shave the ice. Later they had a little tractor do it but that was after we were no longer peddling papers. We road the sleigh to 10th Ave where we lived.

Winter was a time of fun. My first sled was "Rosebud" that was the same sled that was in an Orson Welles movie about William Randolf Hearst. In the end they thru his sled "Rosebud" into a furnace that was the end of the movie. Mine ended up a different fate. I used it for a few years. When the snow turned to ice we could slide down the hill and coast all the way to the other side of the hollow we built little jumps and my last ride I jumped about six feet and on landing both runners went flat out. That was the end of "rosebud" I never got another sled but got a six-foot toboggan. Had a nice mat to lie on. Dave Berdahl had one too. One night we took the toboggans up the ski jump. Both of us had jumped from it many times but never belly flop on a toboggan. We did it that night.

Dave and I also played on the park hockey team. Addition to us there was

Hal linger and Rica Lampman. They were from south high and Evy Carlson. We were the first line. Hockey really was my favorite game. Fast and furious tho it isn't all that much fun to watch I don't think. I lived a half block from Dave so I would go to his house and then we'd go to the toboggan slide on 33rd by the water pump. Every winter they formed a slide a little wider than the width of the toboggan. The sides were slightly slanted up about a foot and a half. They were pure ice when they hosed water on them. Well Dave and I would put on our skates tie our boots together and hang them on our hockey sticks and skate down the slide.

We never fell but had we it would have been disastrous. The top ice on the slide was rough and jagged. We just sailed on to the lake and ended up pretty close to the hockey rink. Fun fun. Later in life when I was working at Sears Roebuck I would go skiing late at night. At times I would ski with a fellow from Norway who liked to tell me about his skiing there. I envied him. He was middle aged and named Haggard. The same guys I played tennis with in the summer would be skiing together. We would build a little jump and sail thru the air for about fifteen feet. After they built the ski jump we sailed for about fifty feet. Not everyone tried the ski jump. As for jumping I'll jump ahead a few years when Russ Lee, he'll appear again later, went out to the Bush lake slide near Shakopee south of Minneapolis. This was a big one. I watched Berger Ruud, Sigmond Ruud, Alf Engen, Casper Oiman and Rieder Anderson all famous Norwegian jumpers. They had jumps of 250 and more feet. I was not in that class but that day I jumped at least one hundred feet. Russ who was not a good skier but would try anything damn near killed himself. Head over heels. I also jumped at the Glenwood slide in Theador Worth park. That was a little higher then the Powderhorn Park slide. I saw Anders and Lars Haugen do a forward summer sault hand in hand. They were Olympic champions around 1918. They also invented or thought of the first indoor ski jumping. Their first slide was in the Minneapolis auditorium. The start of the chute was at the top seats the jump was from the balcony to the main floor. Was quite a thing to see. Lots of guys did it but not this kid. The last time I saw this was at the Pomona County Fair in California. I forget if it was Lars or Anders that was there one had died. Whichever one it was had to in his seventies but he still jumped. That's it for skiing in my teens. I could write about more but it would be for my benefit of memories. It was in my teens I met Jim Holt. He was four years older than I but we did a lot together. Remember this was in the depression. Jimmy's dad had the Otto C. Holt Coffee Co. Downtown and he worked there and also got an allowance I think. Anyhow Jimmy paid for and supplied the golf clubs for play at Columbia Golf Course. We went target shooting west of Minneapolis and he supplied the ammo and a Winchester 22 rifle. Jim had a 1924 model "T" to get around in. One day going down tenth ave. The motor started to run on pre ignition. This happened to "T's" carbon builds in the cylinders and glows red and the motor runs on it's own. You can't stop it with the ignition switch, there were no keys, wouldn't do it. Had to shut off the gas and brake. Kind of scary. He also took me on a few airplane rides. Jimmy was a neighbor lived on the corner of Elliot and 31st.

About that time Gay got into the picture. He was interested in radio and Jim and he were the same age. Jimmy got interested in radio and the other stuff stopped. They both got ham licenses. Gay was w9kwg and Holt was w9kwl. At that time I wasn't interested in radio as there were more exciting things to do. But when all the neighborhood guys were around like Jud, our Nickname for George Santrizos, Johnny, Gordy, Jim, Gay and I, Jimmy would give me money to go to Curtiss confectionary and get popsicles for everyone. I got a dime for going. Sometimes it was a pint of ice cream for each. We all went to movies with him and maybe a malted milk after the movie. Holt was just a darn good friend and knew none of us had money for all of this.

This brings up Curtiss's confectionary store. To anyone remembering Harold Teen in the comics there was a character called Pop Jinks. Clarence Curtiss was our Pop Jinks. It was there we got our penny candy and ice cream cones. Later when Bob Berdahl, Nick Natchicas, Dick Hubrig and I hung out there we would just walk in and not say a word, sit down in the front booth and with out a word spoken Clarence would bring us a dimes worth of Nickel malted. Gosh that was good. A couple of times we brought sandwiches and just ordered water. Anything for a laugh. A fellow named Jerry Dibble worked part time for Clarence. Jerry had an orchestra and played at the Marigold Dance Hall on Hennipen Ave close to downtown. He was red headed. One night he was working and I was alone there I watched a fly. Then I asked Jerry what kind of aerial maneuver the fly made when landing on the ceiling was it a half loop. An immelmann or straight up and grab the ceiling. Later he told me I was driving him nuts over that. Good humorly tho.

Chapter Three

Senior High School

Finally I graduated in January 1937. It took place right after new years so we were really the class of 1936. I got a two pants suit, coat and vest for 19 dollars. We had no caps and gowns in those days. I had helped put up the stands on the stage as a last thing I did on the stage crew. We lined up in the front hall. Half on the right side and half on the left. There were about 250 of us. Then Sidney H. Morse directing the orchestra started to play "Pomp and Circumstances" and we paraded down the aisles to the stage and I was near the end having Walgren as a last name I was always last for a locker and a seat in the classrooms. But I was first in the hearts of my countrymen. After the ceremonies my mother, who was the only one of the family that came for the graduation services, and I walked home in the snow. At home my father was busy drawing and I don't know where the others were, I went to bed. Other grads went to parties and dances but I wasn't into that at that time. Monday morning I went to work at Sears and Roebuck. I didn't work for my father as he felt the money was in the family and on the books. I wanted a check at the end of the week. It so happened that my brother Lorry worked for my father. My dad needed Lawrence as he could not drive, but Lor was paid maybe five dollars a week. In time Lorry had met a girl and wanted money on a Saturday night for the date. Pa wouldn't give him what he wanted and Lorry went to pieces and ran out of the house and down the alley to Lake Street. Mom said, Sherman goes after Lawrence, I ran down the alley and caught up with him right at the end of the alley. He was crying and trying to get away from me. I had to sock him one, lights out, and I carried him on my shoulder all the way home. Mom called Dr. Withem and he said Lorry had a nervous breakdown someone got hold of his girl friend and she was mad at me because I hit my brother. I talked to Pa and told him he should pay Lorry just like the other carpenters and he got mad and called me a "young pup" and kicked me out of the house. I called my sister Legs, Louise, to see if I could live there. Then Russ Lee sounded the horn in front and Russ and I went to a dance. Getting home to Louise's house there were a bunch of cars in front. My uncle George came out and said my dad wanted to talk to me. This was about one thirty a m. I went into the house and all was straightened out. My dad said come home and after that Lawrence was paid a check every Friday. Lorry was ten years older than I and I was eighteen but I was still able to carry him one Might think I was the black sheep of the family but I knew I was right. I was the only one that stood up to my dad. I also was the only one that wanted to travel. And do something.

When I was still in high school Gay wanted a motorcycle, something that was also in my dreams, I drove our 1931 Hupp to places Gay found in the Sunday paper. He found one he liked; it was a Henderson super X45 cubic inches. The guy wanted one 100 dollars. Gay agreed so we went home. On Monday the guy rode it over to the house. It also had a sidecar. Gay and the guy went to the bank to transfer title and I'm standing in the back yard looking at the cycle. Then I sat on it. Then I turned on the key and kicked the starter. Boy that felt good. The motor running. The sidecar was not attached.

That was brought in a pickup truck I revved up the motor and then turned it around. Looked at the shift, moved it into gear let up on the clutch with my left foot and I was moving. I turned into the alley and rode to Lake Street. I was in the mode of turning it around by foot power when I let it drop on its side. Lo and behold that was when Gay showed up after the bank. He was a bit angry with me but he wouldn't ride it home. I had to do that. He learned to ride it after work. At the time he was working downtown at the market for Star Distributors. They sold canned goods and such. Now he didn't get home until about six o clock. I got home from high school about three thirty and I would look at the cycle in the garage. Would back it out and take it around the block and a little farther and before Gay got home I would put it in the garage and take a broom and cover the tracks in the drive. I never thought about the heat of the motor. I think he always knew I did that but never said anything. Gay and I never had a big fight we always got along well. The only fight in the family was between Lorry and Gay. Gordy and I were in his back yard when Gay came running over with a pail. He would fill it up and run across the alley where Lorry was with a hose. Lor squirted the hose at Gay and Gay would throw the pail of water at him. That went on until both were sopping wet. I never did find out what they disagreed on but it couldn't have been important.

Eventually Gay sold me the cycle for fifty bucks as he got a first class commercial license in radio and went to the SS Colonel an ore boat on the Great Lakes. And from the Colonel to a newer self-loader iron ore boat named the SS George F. Rand. So now I have a hack, a heap that is what we called motorcycles then. Even a pile of junk. It wasn't until years later they called them bikes. To us those were bicycles. When I got working at sears I was packing wallpaper on the fourth floor. I got to talking to a fellow named Russ Lee and found he also had a motorcycle. An old Harley Davidson. We had common interest and became good friends. Russ also drove a racecar in the fall for a promoter named Walt Klausler. He was the automobile instructor at North high school and had his students building racecars. When they found out about it he had to sell them and Russ bought number 9. Russ never smoked swore or drank

I'm in front of the race car. Russ is by the side. Circa 1938

a drop in that respect we were different but we both liked to go to dances, motorcycles and all sports. I ended up becoming mechanic and relief driver with the racecar. Walt had dates at all the county fairs around Minnesota, Iowa, North Dakota and Wisconsin. The biggest county fair was in Spencer Iowa.

Walt had two of the best dirt track drivers in the country driving for him. They were Gus Schrader of Cedar Rapids, Iowa and Emory Collings of Davenport, Iowa. Their racecars were all chromed Schrader's was red with a gold number five on the tail. Emorie's was white with a gold number seven on the tail both cars were 350 cubic inch Offenhausers. The Indy cars were limited to 275 cubic inches. A lot of horses for dirt tracks. Russ's car had a Winfield flat head with two carburetors. Most of the heads mounted on a Ford model B block. Doug Audett had a Frontenack dual overhead cam and that mounted on a model T block. Billy Snyder had a two port Riley and I think his brother Hank had the same. In the fall of 1937 we raced at the Minnesota state fair. That was a mile track. The promoter was John Sloan and all the big drivers came for this fair. Billy Arnold, an Indy racer, drove a twelve-cylinder Liberty, an aircraft engine. It was also a two seater as at the Indy 500 they used to have two men in the seat. The crazy thing about it all was years before I used too go to the races with Lorry. We saw Sig Haugdal who was big in the early thirties. Neer did I think I would end up down in the pits and even drive the mile track. But I did. After an afternoons racing, we were getting ready to leave and my brother Lorry. Came down out of the stands and was looking at the racecar. I could see he longed to get in so I asked Russ if it would be ok for him to take it around the track. He said ok so we pushed him off to start him and he was off. The motor was roaring and Lorry was going into the back of the track. Motor really sounding and he came to the far turn over by the university of Minnesota Agricultural College. Came in to the front stretch and into the pits. Pulled on the brake and stopped. He was beaming. He asked how did he do. I told him great except for the fact he never got it out of second gear. I think it was a high light in his life. Racing was for me I know. Thousands of people in the stands all waiting for a wreck but the best racing was no accidents. It did happen however. In 1938 a good friend Hal Reinsberg was killed. He was in a race for Minnesota drivers only. Billy Donahauer his best friend owned and drove a 220 Miller, the forerunner of the Offy. Hal was also in a car with more power than he had ever driven. Racecar engines have a lot of compression and when you take your foot off the gas they immediately slow. Hal held the gas too long and his left front wheel went over Billy's right rear axle. It pushed Hal to the outside of the track into a post flipped the car; it rolled about five times into a tree so hard the motor cracked in half. When I saw Hal's wife Helen at the funeral I knew that no one should be in racing and married, tho many were.

With Walt Klausler we raced mainly at county fairs. The biggest being Spencer Iowa. Arling Lake went thru the fence there but not hurt. Billy Fenstamacker flipped there and vowed never to drive that car again. That was Arling Lakes car, it was a beauty. Maybe none of this makes sense to you who are reading it but it all flashes in my mind like it was yesterday. Like, we were on our way to a race in Iowa. It was early morning and we had been on the road from northern Minnesota. We towed the racecar and trailer with a 1937 Packard convertible. Russ was sleeping and I'm tooling down the narrow highway and passed a car at one hundred and one. Often wondered what the person in that car thought. At a race Iowa that was a two-day date. On Saturday night we went to the dance. I talked to one of the guys in the band and Russ and I got to carry an instrument case into the dance. We were with the show??? Saved the price of the tickets. Russ saw a rather buxom girl (lady) whatever and danced with her. Russ was one heck of a dancer and really enjoyed it. He came back after the dance and said "Shim you have to dance with her she is good, so off I went. She really was sharp I have to admit that. When I returned by the band they are all laughing. They said we had danced with the half man half woman with the sideshow. Just the same he-she could dance

In Menominee, Wisconsin we got to know the Richartz family and we stayed with them. He was a big farm implement dealer at the fair grounds. This particular time Russ and I arrived fairly early at the track; these were all dirt tracks at county fairs, very dusty. They usually sprayed water on the dirt before races. However this morning the track was dry. The truck looped the rope over the axle. When they pulled and the engine started you take and throw the rope and they speed up and clear it. It was just to test the car. Well I took off and was really moving. When you come to the turns you grab the brake once and hit the throttle. That gets the tail sideways. The power of the rear wheels keeps you from going around. You may have seen wheels turned all the way to the right and the rear of the car way over to the left. It's a knack. Anyhow I made a lap and then came into the turn for home and hit my own dust. I was sitting there looking rather foolish when a sergeant with the guard in the infield came up swearing like crazy at me. Seems I got dust in the beans for breakfast. I don't think he was ever a Boy Scout cause ashes and dirt made them taste good? I will end the racing bit. It was an exciting time of my life.

Thru Russ I met all kinds of interesting people. Most all of them went around in circles. I made a plaque of that out of cement and I still have it. "Blessed are they who run around in circles for they shall be known as Wheels" I met Gus and Art Larsen. They were in hydroplane racing. I had a chance to try the boat out and for a while I thought that might be fun but it took a lot of money. So forget it. When Russ and I rode motorcycles I met Paul Bjork and Jimmy Hershberg. They had Harleys and I had a 1937 Indian Chief 75 cc. Beautiful hack. One night the three of us were down town at teen hang out. My cousin Aldomary Walgren was there. We had some ice cream and then out to the curb where the hacks were. Kicked them over and all three of us retarded the sparks. A bunch of backfires must have shook up the place. I led Paul and Jimmy to the police radio station where Tommy Edmonds was working. When we walked in he was just sending out a dispatch to the patrol cars that three motorcycles were causing a disturbance and the three culprits were right there. Nothing happened however. We never hurt a soul. Another night in May of 1938 we were on our way to Chicago. We didn't get started until about eleven in the evening. Were barreling along the Mississippi River racing the four hundred, a Milwaukee Road train. The engineer was blowing the whistle like mad and later I think I knew why. At Minnesota City the was a spur track that came off the main line. Jimmy was switching tank but Paul came whizzin past me and I took off after him.

S.E. Walgren, 1938

Shim was nickname until the Navy. Circa 1938

Too late. He hit the track between the ties and locked the front wheel. I watched Paul flying thru the air. The cycle going end over end and carbon sparks making look like a fourth of July pinwheel, split second later I just missed a stop look and listen sign, I hit the a tie and went up in the air. I could see the lights of the town down below?? But I did go up about twelve fifteen feet. Then I landed on the wheels and bounced again and this time I ended up under five hundred pounds of motorcycle. Just so you know the four hundred was called that as it took four hundred minutes to get from Minneapolis to Chicago. Also I have to say why this all happened. We leaned into a curve in the highway. When it turned into a corner. We could not bend the hacks over to follow the road and it took us on to the accident.

Motorcycle don't make square corners. With Jim's help I got out from under the cycle and then he and I carried Paul up to the side of the road. Finally a car came by and Jimmy flagged it down. They took Paul and I to the hospital in Winona the next town. I just had a lot of bruises no broken bones and was released but Paul had a broken wrist and lacerations on his forehead that had to be stitched. In the morning Jim called two friends in Richfield, Minnesota Evy and Esk Carlson. They came down in a pickup and we all went back to the scene of the accident. Where Paul and I ended up were all kinds of broken foundation blocks. How we missed them I will never know. We got Paul's hack into the truck and then mine back up on the highway. One handlebar was bent a bit and the crashbar bent back and interfered with the clutch a little but it was rideable. We started out for home. It was drizzling and close to freezing. I had on Paul's wet suit so I was dry. But there were no goggle washers like on a car. We took it slow. We had to. The road was icy. This was a hundred and twenty miles from home. We made it without further mishap. Paul stayed at Evy and Eskes, Jimmy lived fairly close to them and I had five more miles to my house. I got home around nine thirty pm and put the cycle in the garage and went into the house. I said nothing about what happened. At ten o'clock the news came on with Cedric Adams and in the course of news he brought up a motorcycle accident in Winona gave the names of those involved and I was suddenly the center of a lot of "I told you so's" that was the worst accident I ever had. In 1939 I took my last ride on the Indian. Picked up Nick Natchicas and just riding around for the fun of it. Got to Lake Calhoun and I made a right onto the blvd and turned up the throttle. Not fast at all when suddenly the chain locked and we skidded on the side, thank God for crashbars and spill guards. The primary chain broke and locked the rear chain. There was oil and aluminum all over the place. It would take more money than I had to fix it. I asked a neighbor in the area if I could use their phone and called my brother Lorry. He came in his 1926 hupmobile and with a big rope tied on to the front of the hack he pulled me about five miles to Aabergs Indian motorcycle shop where I had bought it.

Back to racing. At big county fairs Walt had a thrill day. There was a pilot named Don Vogue that would buy old airplanes that could barely fly. A crude wooden house was built in the infield with two big poles inside and some explosive. Don would come in side slipping to slow the plane down and fly right into the house. Bang went the explosives and the fuselage would slide thru and amide broken struts and fabric would emerge Don. He was always so hyper his voice would be very high pitched. He did this many times. Once he rented a plane and he just made it out of town in front of the sheriff. Another thrill act was by Einer Dale. And old neighbor of mine. His brother Roy went to school with me. His act was to land the plane, a Taylor Cub, on the top of a car. It was all synchronization. The car would go clockwise around the track and in the backstretch the plane would be over the car and land on a track before the car came to the turn. This was on a half-mile track so you can see there wasn't much room for this. But by golly he did it.

Smokey Harris was a black racecar driver. Besides driving three races he did thrill acts. They would tie a rope around the axle on both sides and Smokey would sit on the tail. There would be about five gallons of gas spread on the track in front of the grand stand and burning. As the driver came around the turn Smokey would lower himself to the dirt and let go the rope and slid through the fire. He had protected clothing and face was covered. Went over big. Another thing he did and I drove a couple of times but that was the easy part. They built a board wall out of one by six lumbers and poured gas over that. . Smokey would lay on the hood of these old 1930 cars with his feet against the windshield struts and holding on to the headlights. He had a crash helmet on. Going as fast as the car would go we hit the flaming wall and his head hit it first. You had to duck down in the car so as not to be hit with wood pieces. Smokey never got hurt doing these things but was stabbed to death in a bar in St. Paul Minnesota where he was a bouncer.

When I was working at Sears I saved a little money. I don't know how as all I got was thirty-three cents an hour. I saw an ad in the paper about damaged freight at the Milwaukee railroad yards. I went to look at an eight-foot canoe. A bottom board was slightly broken but the fabric looked good on the bottom. I bought it for fifty dollars. Another toy for my mother to worry about. Sure had a lot of fun with it. It fit on top of the hup real good.

Bob Berdahl, Nick Natchicas Dick Hubrig and I would launch it in Lake Calhoun. This was about ten at night. Four of us in an eight-foot canoe. It had a fairly wide beam tho and did not tip over as easy as the big canoes. However four of us in the middle of the lake at night now seems to me a little bit risky. I had a little Hoehner button accordion with and I'd play polkas and schottisches. We had a ball. But now thinking back if the darn thing had spilled us in the lake I don't think we could have swam to shore. I rented the canoe to duck hunters and got my money back. My brother Gaylord and Johnny Santrizos borrowed it and went about fifteen miles down the Minnehaha Creek. In the spring it was fairly high, however they hit rocks here and there and the canvas-lacquered bottom was quite cracked after that. I sold it to my brother for a song.

I also bought a 120 bass accordion. Always like them. I tried to take lessons. Took one. My lesson was to play the "Prisoners Song" reading the music. I found I could play it better by ear so that was the end of lessons. I wasn't good but I enjoyed it. Even that I kept in the family and sold it to my sister Mig. My sister Dorothy and my Mom played the piano, Gay and I played at it. I played the harmonica fairly well and still do. Writing about music I'll skip ahead some years when I was able to buy a Hammond organ. Still later I traded that in for a big Lowry organ with rhythms and instruments. That I still have, tho it is about thirty-five years old.

Bob Berdahl was one wonderful friend. After Dave started running around with a bunch, I didn't care for Bob and I became fast friends. It was thru him I met Nick and Dick. Bob joined the stage crew in school and he was the projectionist in the booth. Our auditorium was huge and had a balcony. So we were together a lot. I knew his whole family. E.U. his dad was a wheel with the Mpls. Chamber of Commerce. Bob never skated skied or played sports but he had more humor than anyone I ever knew. Nick was also in this category. Some of the things we did I still laugh about. I'm proud to have known him. Bob, Nick and I went down to the courthouse to join the Navy. Bob was the only one that passed. Nick had flat feet and they said I had raised follicles on my neck and I was out too. We all were in the ninth naval battalion at the armory. All except Dick. Bob Nick and I were the real three musketeers. Bob went to boot camp, Nick kept trying to pick up marbles with is toes and finally was taken into the regular Navy. In Sept. I think it was they gave us reservists a chance to serve one year in the Navy. I went to the exec's office and applied.

Chapter Four

The Navy WWII

Nine others and myself were chosen I always liked the Navy, I saw all the Navy pictures that came to the theaters. Even tho I was still going to racing with Russ I wasn't making any money. Remember this was still the depression. Many good men joined the services for lack of jobs. I didn't go right away. They gave us shots and all but we didn't leave right away. It wasn't until July 1940 that we actually left Mpls. But we had more shots and for a while I had cat fever. Caused by serum. Not bad tho. The ten were Dave Byard, Stan Walstad, Perry Greenberg, Ralph Little, Bob "Red" Peterson. Edward Pouliet, Don Ericson John Soltvedt Russ Treanor and I. Our active duty started on March fifth but we didn't leave yet. Finally we got the word and we got ready to leave. It really wasn't easy to leave the family and friends and especially the cat. I still have a picture of him. He was what we called and Australian tomcat gray with black stripes. I remember when I first saw him. I was about four I think, and I looked out the front window and there was this cat meowing. The weather was around zero and a blizzard blowing. I must have raised a fuss because Lorry took the cat and put him in a box with blankets in the garage. It wasn't long he was in the basement. Then allowed to come up stairs and soon he owned the whole house and slept on the pillows. I fed the cat 99 percent of the time. Tho the cat loved everyone. I would go to Rings meat market and they would give me scraps trimmings. Got many a beef heart and kidneys. No market to day would give you those things. They sell them. Mom also bought canned salmon for him. He ate good and provided many happy times to my life. Anytime spring summer fall or winter if he was on the front porch when I came home I would bend over a little bit and he would get on my shoulders and ride into the house. I can still hear him coming down the hall on the third floor to my front bedroom and jump on my chest and put his claws in me and purring like crazy. He lived for eighteen years and I was aboard the USS Northampton when I got a letter from my mother that Gay had the cat put to sleep, as he could not take care of himself. When I read the letter I was sitting on the fantail of the ship in Pearl Harbor and cried like baby. You can see it was hard to leave him. When the time came to go. Jimmy Knudson and Wayne Johnson. Rode with us in our 1939 Packard. All ten of us in uniform were at the Milwaukee station. I had said my goodbyes to the family at home but mom came to the station. When it was time to get on the train I kissed my mother for the first time in my life. Scandinavians were funny. They seldom showed emotions. There was a Norwegian joke about Ole he told

Olaf "you know I loved my wife so much I all most got around to telling her one time" in my lifetime. I never saw my mother and father hold hands, hug, or kiss yet they loved each other very much and were married for 52 years. I haven't said much about family life. My father never drove in his life but we got new car every two years. When the depression happened in 1929 I was eleven years old. We heard it on the radio. Immediately all banks were closed. You could not get any money. Many of the people my father and uncle Elmer who did general contracting as Walgren brothers tried to save homes and apartment buildings they had built and were owed money. It was thought that the recession wouldn't last very long so they made payments on the loans for these people. Time went by and the depression deepened and they saw it was good money after bad. They lost $89 thousand dollars and no one ever paid a single penny back. Think what that would be in dollar value today. There were five kids still in school. Lor was working for Pa. He quit school in the eighth grade. I don't know the year but my Dad earned six dollars for framing a garage. That was his total income for the year. My uncle and he were not partners anymore as there was no work. Luckily both men had some capital in the bank.

There were the largest general contractors in the city. They had a group of sub-contractors that worked solely for them. One might say I was born with a silver spoon in my mouth. Our Christmas's were big. Lots of presents and good stuff. My mother and I were in front of Nolander's store on 17th and Lake Street and I saw Santa Clause there. I got bag of peanuts and he asked what I wanted for Christmas. I said an electric train. Christmas morning came and Gay and I were told to go down the basement by the furnace. We didn't have a fireplace. There were two boxes. Gay got the bigger one. I opened my box and found I had a wind up train that went around in a circle. Gay opened his and he had a Lionel electric train. He got my train. I didn't like Santa much after that. To this day I give Santa Clauses a bad time over that. But Augie Trujillo a carpenter I worked with many years in Los Angeles sent me and electric train. Just a toy tho. As Augie played Santa Claus to the kids in Whittier Calif where he lived. Shortly after that he died and I lost my partner. Most likely I will mention him again in future pages.

Apprentice seaman 1939

Now all this came up just as I was entering active duty in the Navy and one thought after another comes to mind so I type it.

The world was going thru change. Germany was already at war with England and taking over country by country. With these conditions I was in the Navy. When we left Minneapolis for San Pedro I, being the eldest, was in charge. We had vouchers for food and we had the best in the dinning car. When we got to Los Angeles I had vouchers for cabs to take us to the P.E Station (red cars) for transportation to San Pedro. We got off at the ferry landing and took it across the channel, about a hundred yards. where a Navy stake truck waited to take us to the receiving barracks at Reevs Field. We were taken to a supply office where we were issued a mattress, mattress covers, two, and some greenish blankets. They were world war one left overs and were prickly to the skin. Just had to get used to them. Didn't have to use them too much as we ended up in the tropics anyhow. The first night a sailor they called "China Boy" he was Asian. Gave us sentry duty. That meant white leggings, a duty belt with a piece of plywood with directions as to duties of a sentry and a thirty ought six rifle. I had never fired one in my life. I had to walk the fence between the airfield and little Tokyo that was on the other side. However at that time it was peaceful. The field was called Reeves Field after an admiral. It was funny but the v division officer on the USS Northampton where we eventually were stationed was his son. More on him later.

We spent less than a week there with a few liberties in long beach. All ten of us were together and walking around the "Pike" the big amusement park there. We were big shots. I had my cuffs rolled up so they no one could see I was an apprentice seaman. Until... A shore patrolman told me to get the cuffs down. You had to listen to SP's. One evening we had just walked Ocean Blvd in front of the fox theater and who should I meet but Christ Andrews from kindergarten to high school. A good Greek fellow. He was the manager of the theater and let us in to the show free. He was going to college in long beach. Eventually became an aeronautical engineer. Didn't know that until I saw him at a high school reunion years later.

We were transferred to the battleship USS Tennessee. We were in a gun compartment. In the corner of the port side aft was a 5 inch 25 cal gun. The bulkhead dropped to fire. They were meant only for surface to surface or to shore. When they were built there were no airplanes to worry about. So no anti aircraft batteries. We slept in hammocks. When the bos'n mate passed the word to up hammocks you had to jump to it. We also had to live out of our sea bags. All our clothes were rolled and tied together with little strings that were called stops. A sailor gave me a wooden spreader for the head of my hammock. That helped lot. Otherwise you ended up in a cocoon... We spent about a week at anchor in Long Beach harbor. Evenings there was a movie on the fantail.

So called because the hull came together like a dull point as opposed to as square stern. They played records before the movie and it was there I first heard "Blueberry Hill" now when I hear that song I'm back on the Tennessee. We finally upped anchor and headed for Pearl Harbor Oahu, Hawaii. A territory of the United States. Never having been that far out on the ocean, the only other time I was on the steamship Avalon out of Long Beach for Catalina Island in 1937. I had gone to L.A., as I wanted to go to Curtiss Wright Institute in Burbank and learn about aircraft engines. My uncle Kenneth was going to get me a job as an electrician in a sub station while I went to the school, But I got home sick and went back home. That was another story but I should have brought that up before. Too late now.

The water soon changed to a very pretty blue and all we had to do was lie in the sun and get a tan. Funny I didn't burn to a crisp but I didn't. We finally saw CoCo head but didn't know that at the time. Then Diamond Head and I recognized that. Passed the Aloha tower and into the channel to Pearl Harbor. When we were tied up at battleship row along Ford Island we were transferred to the USS Portland for further transfer to the

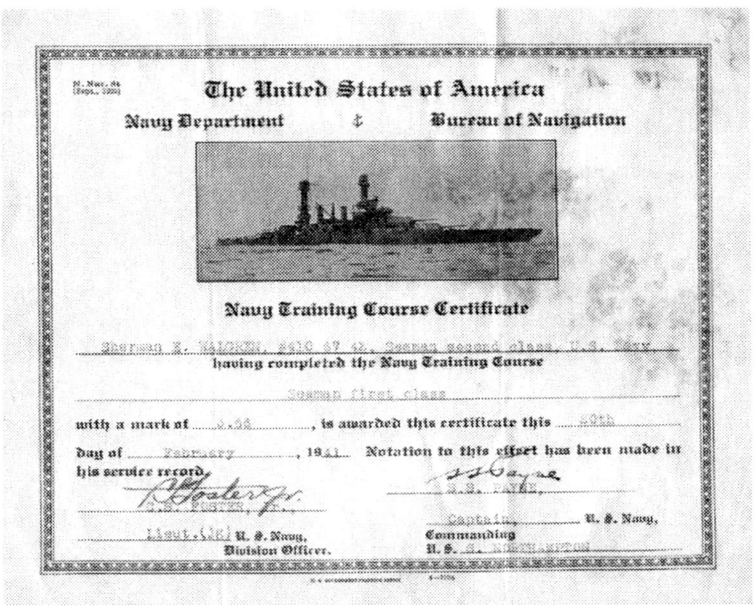
The United States of America

Navy Department ⚓ Bureau of Navigation

Navy Training Course Certificate

having completed the Navy Training Course

Seaman first class

with a mark of ...., is awarded this certificate this ....

day of February, 1941. Notation to this effect has been made in his service record.

Lieut.(JG) U. S. Navy, Division Officer.

Captain, U. S. Navy, Commanding U. S. S.

USS Northampton. She was out to sea and a day later when she tied up at cast four buoys we were sent over to it. With sea bags and hammocks lashed together we had to jump onto the gangway. Red Peterson missed it and sea bag and all fell in the drink. He was sopping wet when we saluted the officer of the deck and the flag and asked permission to come aboard.

We were the first reservists to go on active duty. The regular Navy sailors kind of shunned us at first like we had no business being there. We spent four months on the Northampton as apprentice seaman. The pay was twenty-one dollars a month and one dollar of that was taken out for health and benefits. Whatever that was. We were known as the "X" division. We ate last were paid last and went on liberty last. Finally we were put in divisions. Perry Greenberg and I went to the fourth division. We had to good boats Dutch Worthner was in charge and Pappy Breeze was leading seaman. They were the power.

Pappy had a motorcycle so we got long fine. I used to ride into Honolulu with him. I knew more knots than a lot of the sailors that went thru boot camp. I learned them in Boy Scouts and Sea Scouts. Our duties were taking care of the boats. Admirals barge, the captains gig, officer motorboat, motor launches and whaleboats. Plus holy stoning the deck, teakwood, and swabbing it down every morning. Reveille at 530 am. This was done every morning before chow. Holy stoning went out pretty quick.

It was a brick with a hole in the top. You put a pole into that and holding it a certain way you moved it back and forth eighteen times to the board the ship was just ten years old when I went aboard but all the brass fittings in the deck were raised about a half an inch. The deck was worn down that much. Our general quarter station were two five inch twenty five caliber guns on the port side. The guns on the starboard side were manned by the Marine division. We used to lay off Lahaina Roads, Maui in the evenings but no shore leave just the gold.

At that time the Nora, nick name for Northampton, was comcrudive four. We had an admiral aboard I don't recall his name. Our captain was Capt. Paine one night we had maneuvers off the island. A practice GQ. Our job was to fire star shells off the port quarter. We raced to the guns from our bunks and stuffing cotton in our ears. There were no such things as muffs etc. We were a little late getting the cotton; at least I was, when the after gun started firing. I was right be low the gun barrel. The guns have a terrific blast. Without cotton I didn't know up from down and they led me away from the guns. I didn't hear very well for a week and from that time I had ringing ears. It also cut down my hearing.

It was not for that reason tho that I wanted to transfer into the radio gang. I didn't want to spend a year as a deck ape but at least learn something. Mr. Fowler okayed my transfer and now I am a radio striker. I automatically got seaman 2nd class but had to take an "A to N" exam for seaman first. Got it on my first try. Now I got 56 dollars a month. A sailor named Kenny Gail taught me the code. Three of us were strikers. Thomas L. Young, Dick Hladky and I. It seemed to come to me rather easy and then I spent a lot of time on a radio circuit in the radio shack.

There were frequencies for beginners sending code five words a minute then ten, fifteen and on the hardest part was learning to typewrite. I took the exam for radioman third about three times. At that time they didn't give out rates all that easy. We were in contest with radiomen on the other ships in Comcrudiv four. When Admiral Taffinder came aboard we were Comcrudiv five. Same ships. The flag on the Northampton. The Portland, Salt Lake City and Pensacola. When the rates came back

The United States of America

Navy Department — Bureau of Navigation

Navy Training Course Certificate

Sherman E. WALDREN, Seaman First Class, USN,

having completed the Navy Training Course

Radioman Third Class

with a mark of 3.[illegible], is awarded this certificate this 1st

day of June, 1941. Notation to this effect has been made in his service record.

[illegible] FOSTER, JR.

Lieut.(jg), U. S. Navy, Division Officer.

Captain, U. S. Navy, Commanding U. S. S. NORTHAMPTON

maybe they went to the other ships. On my third try I was the high man in the test so I got third class. I was the first of us reserves to get a rate. Perry Greenberg was second as a signalman. In June of 1941 we were called, nine of us, and asked if we wanted to stay in the Navy or go back home. We all voted to go home. It was not to be.

That evening I had the watch copying the skeds. This was radio NPM for all ships and stations in the Hawaiian area. Most of the messages were in five letter code groups but then I got an Alnav. That meant all ships and stations. It read primarily that all men on active duty would remain on active duty for the remainder of the emergency. That meant no more discharges for anyone/ it was the first indication all was not well.

I'll go back to May. The Northampton and Indianapolis or Chicago had dual exercises close to the big island of Hawaii. Both ships had admirals and were flagships. We anchored off Kona in the evenings. There was rumor and scuttlebutt that Japanese sampans might try to ram the ships at night. After it was all over none of this made sense but the command took precautions.

We had sentries on the foc'sle with rifles. On the quarterdeck and fantail. The fifty caliber machine guns were manned on the mainmast. Also the searchlights. Every small boat that came within a half mile was challenged. It included the admirals barge, the captains gig and officers motorboats. Enlisted men had no liberty. This lasted a full week. I've only met a few sailors that remember this but I can assure you it took place. After we returned to Pearl Harbor again I had the NPM watch and copied an alnav that read. All ships in a five hundred mile radius of the Hawaiian islands would remain at sea and not anchor anywhere but Pearl Harbor. All ships at sea would darken ship, we had reflectors that fit in the porthole where light would not get thru, and would use a zigzag course. So many feet to starboard and so many to port yet keeping on a straight course. It was figured a submarine could not follow a ship with certainty.

The emergency followed in June. Every morning after that when we were at sea we had general quarters an hour before first light actually it didn't change our lives a great deal still had normal routine every day.

I'm going back to my time in the forth division. A little humor and such. My brother in law, Leo Lyons and my sister Louise had a recorder to make phonograph records. They also had a lot of gatherings of friends and relatives. They would send me records. Every time I got a record a few of the guys off duty would listen to them with me. Raymond Mc Nulty my nephew, I was his sea pappy, would sing sons for me. He sang Don't sit under the apple tree and others. We all got a kick out of that. Then everyone that was there would say their name and "hello Sherman this is Lawrence or Clara. My father and mother and then my grandmother would be given the mike. With her voice dripping with a Scandinavian accent she would say" hello Sherman this is grandma" and the whole bunch of us would laugh about it. The other sailors enjoyed my records as much as I did. Going back some more.

It was around December 1940 we went back to the states for overhaul at Mare Island. We passed the Faralong Islands in a fog. Kind of spooky and then the Golden Gate Bridge came into view. I had climbed up to the foretop and as we passed under the bridge it seemed like I could touch it. In reality it was still quite far up. We got to a berth at Mare Island Navy yard and life did change. There were cables all over the ship and many changes were made. They welded up all of the portholes in the hull. In the enlisted men's compartments they changed the bunks to four making it more difficult in fact you couldn't sit up in your bunk. Out went the dishes for chow and they put in steam tables and trays. You may see that the country foresaw conditions that were coming and making room for more crew. When I went aboard the Nora the ship's complement was 600. Later we had as many as 1200.

There was a reason. While at Vallejo, we called it Valley Jo; I went to Frisco and bought a motorcycle so I could get around. The guy that sold it to me told me he would buy it back for what I paid for it when I had to leave again. When I was buying it he said there was a hack in Oakland in pieces and he would put it together for one hundred dollars. A 1930 Harley Davidson. It turned out to be better than he had thought that was why he was willing to take it back. I rented a garage other sailors had hacks too it was like three dollars a month. It kept me out? Of the gin mills on Georgia Street. While in dry-dock all hands had to go over the side as the water was taken out. We scrapped the barnacles off. All around the ships were hanging planks 2 by 12's's hung by ropes. You had to lower them as the water dropped. By the time you got to the bottom you were a longs ways from the top. Now that was not too bad but then we had to raise the stages all the way to the top again. Now with chipping hammers run by compressed air we chipped the scale off the hull then with wire brushes run by compressed air we brushed our section of the hull. Think of coming back off a night in Vallejo and climbing on to one plank a mile? To the bottom of the dry-dock and doing this. Well we got thru it without any casualties. The only men that didn't have to do this were chiefs.

The Navy yard painters then sprayed the hull with a special paint. Also degaussing cables were installed on the inside of the hull. They would, it was hoped, demagnetize the magnetic mines. They would not take care of the ones with the thorns on them tho. They were an impact type. After the Navy yard completed all their work they would trim the ship. While in the dry-dock full of water. The ship should right itself level. To prove this all of enlisted men would move from port to starboard then back to port and keep this up until we had that 10,000-ton cruiser listing back and forth. Then stand in the middle of the ship and let it come to rest. If it wasn't level they would move ballast until it was. Seems kind of funny now but it worked. When we left Mare Island we went to the Navy dock in San Francisco on Embarcadero Street. It was right under the Frisco Oakland Bay Bridge. During the day we went around in circles while civilian electronic people calibrated our direction finder. They use a fixed signal on the beach while the ship goes in circles. This piece of gear is very important and is done by BUNAV. The Bureau of Navigation in

Washington. No one is supposed to mess with it. I bring this up as later I will write about it. When that was done we left the bay area for San Diego and a week of shakedown. That is to test all the new stuff that was added on the ship. We would operate around San Clemente Island. One day they were using a drone airplane for gunnery practice. It was an N3N or something like it. Anyway it was a biplane. It was coming in from the port quarter directly at the quarterdeck. Someone must have lost control because it almost became a kamikaze. Luckily it crashed into the water but it was close enough to splash water over the whole quarterdeck. Real exciting. I was watching it on the communication deck that over looks the quarterdeck. We had some good liberty in Diego and then back to Pearl Harbor. Now I'll forward again to June 1941.

In Pearl we again went into the Navy yard for more work. They installed a CXAM radar antenna on the top of the foremast. It looked like a bedspring. The gear itself went into the radio direction finder shack just above the bridge. You know I never knew where the direction finder went? Anyhow it was a cathode ray tube that an electronic hand went around and gave blips. It depended on the size of the blip as to what kind of ship it might be. Very crude compared what we have today. However it was the first ship in the Pacific to have radar. There was a purpose for it.

The following article was taken from "Way of a Fighter" the memoirs of Claire Lee Chenault major general, U.S. Army retired. I "Claire Chenault" flew to San Francisco on United Air Lines and met the first contingent of the (avg) in the Mark Hopking's hotel on July 7, the fourth anniversary of the double seventh, the night the Sinoa Japanese war began. Nobody that saw that odd assortment of young men looking slightly ill at ease and uncertain in their civilian clothes could have possibly imagined that in a few months they would be making history. The first group left on July 10 1941 aboard the Dutch ship Jaegersfontaine. Japanese intelligence was not fooled by the passports claiming occupations of musician, student, clerk, banker, etc. With a leader who was a farmer, the Japanese radio announced that the first group of American volunteer pilots planning to fight in China had left San Francisco by ship.

"That ship will never reach China," the Japanese radio chortled, "it will be sunk."

West of Hawaii passengers on the Jaegersfontaine spotted two warships, steaming in loose escort formation. Navy pilots identified them as the U.S. Cruisers Salt Lake City and the Northampton. The cruisers stayed with the Dutch ship as it swung far south of the regular shipping lane to avoid Japanese bases in the Carolines, in the Torres Straits of Australia a Dutch cruiser picked up the job and convoyed the liner to Singapore.

This is a secret communication to the Dutch ship on July 16 1941

From the United States Pacific Fleet, cruiser division five, scouting force USS Northampton, flagship

The master: S.S Jaegersfontine; sir: to assist in avoiding detection, it is requested that you stress darken ship from ten minutes after sundown to sunrise daily. And that during day time you run with out making smoke. Burn all burnable material if possible, puncture metal containers before throwing overboard bilges should be pumped, and garbage and other waste that cannot be burned should be thrown overboard, only once daily, at one hour after sunset. Two signal men are being sent to your ship to facilitate the reading of day and night signal if you can berth them without inconvenience until arrival at point hypo, we will recover them then. Do not stop if called upon by any vessel.

Signals regarding changes of course and changes of zonetime will be sent as required. Unless otherwise prescribed, changes of course will be in succession from ahead, rear ships turning in the same water as ships ahead. At night and during low visibility cruisers will be closer to you than at other times. Zigzag plan is enclosed and will be used if considered necessary. Signal will be made. General instructions regarding zigzagging are also enclosed.

The instructions to preserve radio silence are most important.

Respectfully... S.A. Taffinder, Rear Admiral, US Navy Commander Task Force Nineteen.

I added these two secret messages and then will tell it as I saw it. Remember we were not at war with anyone at this time so it was a completely covert mission. This was why we had the new radar put on the ship. As we cruised south our job was to sweep the horizon with the radar. If we saw anything the Salt Lake City and Nora were to get on the side of the Jaegers and shield it from view. We didn't see a ship thru the whole trip luckily. On that ship were all the pilots. Planes logistics, mechanics and nurses for the Flying Tigers. Really was an historic voyage. When we met the Dutch cruiser Java and another cruiser I forgot the name. Took over the Jacersfontaine for the rest of her trip. The Northampton turned south just outside the Great Barrier Reef all the way to Brisbane Australia. When we entered the Brisbane River we must have looked like we were really moving as when we were in the Navy yard in Pearl they painted a fake bow wave on the bow. Looked like a speedboat. People line the river waving sheets, flags anything they could. We were all lined up on the lifelines in undress blues. It was publicized as a good will visit. Nothing said about the Dutch ship. We tied up at Newfarm wharf. The city went all out for the US sailors. Hladky. Gracie Gilman. Alex Gillis and I went to the Yorktown Coffee Inn first and had a drink of milk. I kid you not. There we met three girls Mary pronounced Mahry. And Ruby McNeil. I forget the third one. Ruby's husband was killed in Africa where most of the "diggers" were sent. I rented a car for six dollars including gas and had it for our stay in Brisbane. Ruby's mother was happy, she brought us to their house for a singsong. She had a baby boy and her mother thought now she would maybe find another man. She didn't mean me but it broke the ice, as she had not seen anyone since her husband was killed in action. Ruby was darn nice. I gave her twenty dollars to buy gift for my mother and sisters, which she did, and for many years she wrote to my mother and sisters. When my mother died I sent Christmas cards to her. She out lived two more husbands. Became blind in later life and died two years ago and her daughter wrote to me.

While in Brisbane we bought a gunny sack of Belimbra beer. They drink beer warm, couldn't get used to that. There was Gilman, Gillis, Souza and Peter O' Toole. The captain of the Salt Lake City showed up a Capt Zacaharis. O' Tool laid the sack on the sidewalk and we all came to salute. When he passed O'Toole picked up the sack and threw in over his shoulder and dropped it and it crashed to the sidewalk. Broke most of the bottles. So much for that. Inside the Trocadero dance hall were big fans waving back and forth, most unusual. Music was ok but wasn't the best dance I was ever at. With the car I had to drive on the wrong side of the rode. That is to us. I came to a big circle and didn't know where to go so I asked a Bobbie and he said, "I don't care if you loop the loop" so I did. Was quite an adventure.

L to R: Gillis, Walgren, Gilman. Gillis was lost in the entine room of Northampton. Photo taken in Brisbane, Australia.

I missed telling about crossing the equator. We did that before we passed the Dutch ship to the Java at the Torres Strait. There were a lot of us Polywogs, sailors who had never gone over the equator. Also a lot of officers. Well they built a big tank on the quarterdeck. With a chair that would tip backwards into it. Also had a target sleeve on the deck. We all had summons like not sharing pogybait with a shellback etc. All crazy ones. We had to crawl thru the sleeve that was filled with slop from chows. Must have saved it for a couple days. We just had skivvy shorts on. While crawling shellbacks had flat bats they would swat us. When we got thru that they put us in that chair, bust and egg over the head, and tip us into the pool of water that was full of slop and a mess. We earned the right to become a shellback.

Back to Brisbane. After a big parade and the ambassador coming on the ship we left for our return trip. There was more secret stuff going on. We went north again to Port Moresby Papua New Guinea.

While there the admiral went over to a big British liner that I think was a gunship in disguise. He spent quite awhile there. Some of us had a chance to go to the town. The aborigines still fierce looking. Bones in their ears thru their noses and such. There were shops mostly run by Australians. I bought a water buffalo on a onyx base for a couple dollars. Eventually I gave it to my brother Lorry and Clara as a wedding gift. It would be worth a lot of money today.

While in Brisbane I bought a Meerschaum pipe and I gave that to him also. The sailors that couldn't go ashore were entertained by native girls sans bras and grass skirts. They came out in dugout canoes.

The sailors were buying the grass skirts and as they took them off there was another that kept up until they were in a cloth covering. The sailors had other images. After all this they had to turn them in to be burned. They were full of bugs.

We left Port Moresby and headed to Rabaul, New Britain. When we arrived a volcano was building in the bay. Sulfur odor was prevalent. Got to go ashore again but not for very long. Didn't get to buy anything there. Just could say I was there. Then we headed back to Pearl but first they set a course that would take us across the 180th meridian and the equator at the same time. When we went across the date line before we became Golden Dragons. When we passed over both at the sometime we became Golden Shellbacks. Really not many of them. And so back to Pearl Harbor and Honolulu liberty's.

When we returned we were once again comcrudiv five. We went out on maneuvers for a few days and back to Pearl. I think it was around August 1941 when we had a ships party in the Ioloni Palace. It was held in one end in the basement. It was in a room on the third floor that the queen was held prisoner by the U.S. and there she wrote the song "Aloha Nui" before we went there Benny Morris. Frank Souza and I think it was Bill Bronn and I. We got a fifth of whisky and by the time we got to the party it was flank speed. We didn't last long as we got booted out of the palace. How many others can say that? It was that night I started world war two. We were on our way to the USO?? On Fort Street. It had a narrow sidewalk. A young Japanese civilian was walking towards us. He stopped in front of me. Without hesitation I decked him and we walked on. I swear the devil made me do it. Shortly after that you know what happened. I'm not proud of that but it happened. Was the only time in my service career that I hit anyone.

I must now tell you about T.R. Gray a darn nice warrant officer. He made all of us radiomen learn how to operate the emergency radio gear. It was called tby3. Came in canvas bags. Had a hand operated generator. Transceiver and a couple other ways to operate with power. He made us in teams and we would get in a whaleboat and go to the marine base in Pearl and right at the waters edge put the thing together and contact the ship. This exercise would come in real handy for me later.

It was close to the latter part of November 1941 when we went out of Pearl and joined in a big fleet maneuvers off Waikiki. Some miles off shore however. I 'm sure it was planned for a purpose. Most all battleships, two carriers many cruisers, heavy and light were operating all day. The next day it was still going on and that night around one a.m.under secret orders the Northampton, Salt Lake City, Portland, Pensacola and a destroyer squadron and the Enterprise. left the fleet. We found out later that we were on the way to Wake island to deliver, I think it was fifteen f4f fighters the name of that plane was the Wildcat. We knew there were unexplained things about it but we were in condition 1 which is next to general quarters. Means watch on and watch off. There was live ammunition in the ready boxes for the five-inch guns. We were prepared for anything. It was an uneventful trip to Wake and when in sight of the island the planes took off for Wake. These were the only aircraft on Wake when later events took place. A fellow radioman on the Northampton had been transferred to Wake a couple months before. Five of us 3rd class radiomen drew straws and Marvin C. Balhorn won the transfer. You might say lost it as he spent over three years in a Japanese prison in Japan. I may as well explain that now. When the Japanese finally subdued the garrison on Wake they stripped all the Naval personnel and for three days they walked the around the perimeter of the island naked. Wake is really an atoll and the rim of an old volcano. Must have been a long walk. There were also many civilian workers there. Pan Aam had a base there. After the Naval personnel were transported in a filthy ship to Japan the Japanese put the civilians to work. When it looked like curtains at the end of the war they executed all the Americans. Some Japanese snitched on the officer that ordered it and he was hanged. Marvin got every parasite know to man I guess and when he was freed they put him in a hospital for quite a time made him a chief radioman. He went through hell.

Back to our journey to Wake. After the planes were safely at Wake task force five turned back for Pearl Harbor. We had an eta, estimated time of arrival, of ten o clock dec.6th. As we steamed east we had to fuel the cans, (destroyers), as they cannot travel that distance with out refueling. The sea was running, (rough) and as the can came along the starboard side about a hundred feet away. They shot a light line over to it, and then they pull the six-inch lines over and tie them off on the cleats. Then they shoot over the fuel line. Things were progressing as planned. The bow wash of our ship and the wash from the destroyer makes the water between really boil.

PEARL HARBOR 7 DEC. 1941
APPROXIMATELY 0800 HRS.
PICTURE TAKEN BY
JAPANESE SQUADRON LEADER OF FIRST WAVE
TO ATTACK THE SHIPS PRESENT
ORIGINAL PICTURE FOUND 9 NOV. 1945
IN YOKASUKA NAVAL FACILITIES
SOUTH OF TOKYO, JAPAN

The ship was only doing about ten knots for this operation. The aft line snapped and trailed back and wound itself around the propeller shaft and screw, (propeller) the bridge secured all engines and were dead in the water. The rest of the ships just circled the Nora while two divers, Capo. Quite a hero when the ship was sunk, I don't remember the second one. It took five and a half ours to cut all the hemp from the shaft and screw. Finally we were underway again. It was the next night around one in the morning, an electrical generator burned up and again we were dead in the water. Admiral Bull Halsey was very unhappy and by light (it can be seen many miles) sent a message not to hold up the taskforce. Now with these problems the task force changed it's eta to Sunday Dec 7th at ten o'clock. The force reduced speed to save fuel and we were about, the official log stated 2oo miles from the entrance to Pearl but written in long hand was 127 miles. I think the latter was right. Now I had the morning watch. I had just relieved the operator on NPM skeds that had the mid watch. I was copying five letter code groups when they suddenly ceased sending and then sent the letter "o" a few times, this means urgent

Edward J. August, Editor

U.S. Navy Cruisers Association
21 Colonial Way
Rehoboth, MA 02769-1220

Dear Mr. August

I have just received the fall issue of the Cruiser magazine and found the

\article on page 21 about Niihau interesting,. The article stated that the Japanese aviators were directed to land on Niihau if they could not return to their aircraft carriers. We, on the Northampton ,were told that the Plane that crashed on the island there, was the one that was shot down by the two planes from the Northampton.
I have enclosed a portion or the Northampton War Diary of December 1941. Note that the island of Kauai is in the area of Nihau .

"On December 7.71941 two Northampton planes were launched at 1115 to conduct a search for a distance of one hundred and fifty miles to the Northward. At approximately twenty minutes after launching [geographic position 15 miles west of Kauai] the section was attacked by an enemy single seat monoplane; The engagement lasting from fifteen to twenty minutes, and ending when the enemy plane broke out in smoke. The search continued until completed when the section proceed to Pearl Harbor, landing at 1527, where repairs were and the bullet holes were patched.

The Japanese plane was single place plane fighter with enclosed cockpit [kept closed during entire engagement], retractable landing gear, single radial engine, low wing and was of a grayish or light khaki hue. The fuselarge was marked with a wide band and a large red ball between the cockpit and tail. The speed was 275 mph or better. "

The article and War Diary substantiate what we were always told.

Capt Lewis Thomas USNR
Radio Officer
USS Northampton CA 26

message. In plain language, then I copied this "Pearl Harbor attacked this is no drill Pearl Harbor attacked. This was about 8:o clock Sunday morning. I Might as well explain the "this is no drill" in peace time we drilled a lot gunnery drills, fire drills, one time there was a fire and we all went to our fire stations and hooked up hoses and turned on the water and pointed the hose over the side. We would look like a fireboat. The only trouble was there was a real fire, now things happened fast. First they got me off the skeds and put Benny Morris first class radioman on the skeds. Messages were fast and furious. I knew the war had started before the admiral and the captain but then every man on the other ships did too.

This started all divisions to prepare the ship for war. One of the first casualties was our piano from the forward mess hall. I don't know if any of the boats went over the side but I doubt it. The idea being to get rid of anything that would splinter if a bomb dropped on the deck. Naturally we went to general quarters. We couldn't go anywhere, as we were short on fuel. At around ten o clock they launched two SOC's (scout, observation Curtiss) Curtiss was the manufacturer. The pilot of the first plane was Micky Reeves he was the skipper of the aviation division, Robert Baxter, now deceased, was radio gunner in the rear seat. The second plane was piloted by Ensign Covington USN and in the rear was John Melton radioman 2/c Baxter was an rdo 1/c.

About twenty minutes from being catapulted they were intercepted by a low wing monoplane. Had enclosed cockpit retractable landing gear, a red stripe on the fuselage behind the pilot and a big red circle, later called a meatball. The SOC's were flying real close to water so the Jap could only dive and pull out above them. He made five or six passes with Baxter and Melton shooting up at him. All they had was a swivel 30 caliber machine gun. They had boxes of ammo that they had to change as they ran out. They both fired about the same amount of rounds. On the last dive by the Jap the plane started to smoke and cut off the engagement. It flew west towards Kauai. The SOC's proceeded to Ford Island in Pearl. Must have been quite a sight for them as the island was devastated.

It wasn't until after the war I learned what happened to the Jap. He landed on a little island 20 miles west of Kauai called Niihau. It was a private owned island by a man on Kauai. He had a sugar plantation there. They had no radio and there were just a few Hawaiians and one Niesi Japanese man. When the plane made a crash landing it knocked out the pilot and one of the Hawaiians went to the plane and took the revolver from the pilot and when he came to they made him a prisoner. They had no idea what they had. Well the Jap talked the American Jap into joining him so now he got his gun back and the two of them made prisoners of the others.

One night one Hawaiian took an outrigger and paddled to Kauai and informed them what had happened. Meanwhile the prisoners rebelled and a great big Hawaiian grabbed the Jap pilot and threw him into a wall so hard he killed him. The American Jap then commit suicide and shot him self. Right after that US soldiers landed on the island to find it was all over.

LT. REEVES AND ME

By
John R. Melton

Early in 1941 the Northampton went to the Navy Yard in San Francisco and the aviation unit went to the Fleet Air Base in San Pedro. Lt. Reeves gave me a letter so that I could take the exam to go to flight school. I passed. He then changed his mind, said I could only have 10 days leave and he would not approve my transfer.He said we were going to war and we needed to practice gunnery. During the three months we were in San Pedro , I fired only 29 rounds at float lights. I was really pissed off.

When Reeves read Baxter's and my citations at quarters, he came to me and congratulated me for being the only slick-armed chief he'll ever know. I told Reeves that made me 1st Class. He raised hell with me for not reminding him to have me promoted after I took the 1st Class exam. On 1 July '41 I had less than 3 years in.

Baxter and I both took the exam on 1 July '41. We both missed 2 out of four questions on abstracting messages. Reeves told me that I had a very high mark and for that reason he would see that I was promoted to 1st Class.

Reeves gave me a special letter so that I could take the exam for second class without the required time in rate. He also did that so that I could take the exam for 1st class. When I didn't make 1st Class, I was determined to get out of the Navy as soon as my enlistment expired. Therefore I did not go up for 1st Class the next quarter. Baxter went up the next quarter and was promoted.

For the attack on Wake Island and the Marshalls I flew with Reeves. At that time we had 5 radiomen qualified to fly in the rear seat. Reeves could have had anyone fly with him.

When I arrived at Lakehurst, 1 July '42, the personnel officer called me in. Lt. Reeves had been his classmate at the Naval Academy. He told me Reeves had written to him and asked him to help me all he could. My picture and an article were printed in the station paper.

I was in British Guiana when the Officer of the Day left. Lt. Commander Herbert Graves came to see me and thanked me for all the hard work. He said a person from the squadron was going to be selected to go to flight school. He would see that I was selected or promoted to Warrant. I told him whichever would get me out of the jungle the fastest. Shortly thereafter. I received orders to flight school. I graduated 3 May '44 and was promoted to Ensign.

The two SOC's on landing at Pearl found eleven bullet holes in each plane. Nothing in a serious place so the were patched and Mr. Reeves plane was left at Pearl for overhaul and also Covington's plane. A big mistake. Mr. Reeves and Baxter returned to the Northampton when we returned to cast four berth and right away gave all the credit to his plane and Baxter. I think Baxter was overwhelmed by the attention and never mentioned Melton. It really was like a firing squad that shot the prisoner? It should have been called a co-kill. Baxter made chief then and there and Melton got first class.

Meanwhile back on the ship it is still Sunday. Like I said, we could not go anywhere. That night we had a Navy station on speakers and listened to a lot of bum dope. There were reports of transports landing troops at Bishop's Point. That is just to the left of the entrance to Pearl. All of it was bum dope. But they said they heard shots up by Aiea and that was the sugar mill and plantations. I don't know how true but it was said they shot a few Japanese in anger.

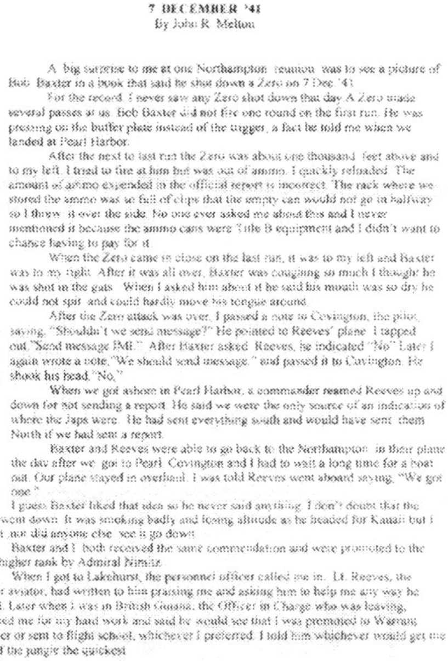

7 DECEMBER '41
By John R. Melton

A big surprise to me at one Northampton reunion was to see a picture of Bob Baxter in a book that said he shot down a Zero on 7 Dec '41.

For the record, I never saw any Zero shot down that day. A Zero made several passes at us. Bob Baxter did not fire one round on the first run. He was pressing on the buffer plate instead of the trigger, a fact he told me when we landed at Pearl Harbor.

After the next to last run the Zero was about one thousand feet above and to my left. I tried to fire at him but was out of ammo. I quickly reloaded. The amount of ammo expended in the official report is incorrect. The rack where we stored the ammo was so full of clips that the empty can would not go in halfway so I threw it over the side. No one ever asked me about this and I never mentioned it because the ammo cans were Title B equipment and I didn't want to chance having to pay for it.

When the Zero came in close on the last run, it was to my left and Baxter was to my right. After it was all over, Baxter was coughing so much I thought he was shot in the guts. When I asked him about it he said his mouth was so dry he could not spit and could hardly move his tongue around.

After the Zero attack was over, I passed a note to Covington, the pilot, saying, "Shouldn't we send message?" He pointed to Reeves' plane. I tapped out, "Send message IMI." After Baxter asked Reeves, he indicated "No". Later I again wrote a note, "We should send message," and passed it to Covington. He shook his head, "No."

When we got ashore in Pearl Harbor, a commander reamed Reeves up and down for not sending a report. He said we were the only source of an indications of where the Japs were. He had sent everything south and would have sent them North if we had sent a report.

Baxter and Reeves were able to go back to the Northampton in their plane the day after we got to Pearl. Covington and I had to wait a long time for a boat out. Our plane stayed in overhaul. I was told Reeves went aboard saying, "We got one."

I guess Baxter liked that idea so he never said anything. I don't doubt that the Zero went down. It was smoking badly and losing altitude as he headed for Kauai but I didn't nor did anyone else see it go down.

Baxter and I both received the same commendation and were promoted to the next higher rank by Admiral Nimitz.

When I got to Lakehurst, the personnel officer called me in. Lt. Reeves, the senior aviator, had written to him praising me and asking him to help me any way he could. Later when I was in British Guiana, the Officer in Charge who was leaving, thanked me for my hard work and said he would see that I was promoted to Warrant Officer or sent to flight school, whichever I preferred. I told him whichever would get me out of the jungle the quickest.

The next morning we slowly entered Pearl we saw the battleship Nevada beached in a sugar cane field. A chief quartermaster got the ship underway as most officers were ashore. At least that is what I heard. As we passed battleship row the Tennessee was locked in by the West Virginia sunk to the main deck and still burning. The Oklahoma capsized the California burning like crazy and abandoned the Arizona broke in two and burning fiercely. Smoke all over the area. Oil all over the water. The battleship Utah was sunk but it was just a target ship at that time. The Pennsylvania was in dry-dock but sustained light damage but two destroyers in front of her, the Cassin and Downes we burned up, the minesweeper Oglala was also sunk. It looked like the war had just started and we already lost it. However: the Saratoga was in overhaul in San Diego. The Enterprise was safe and the Lexington was on a mission west of Hawaii. No cruisers in Pearl were damaged. And all the heavy cruisers were at sea during the attack. We lucked out. Sad as it was with some 2300 sailors lost. The battle ships were really obsolete for this type of warfare. They were mostly built during world war one and most were coal burners converted to oil. They were slow and not too many anti aircraft guns. Most secondary battery was meant for surface to surface. The cruisers and aircraft carriers were the fast carrier task forces capable of speeds up to thirty-two knots. The

Northampton entered Pearl Harbor, Dec. 7, 1941

damaged battle ships were raised and repaired after some time. It was a physiological thing for stateside moral and also when we controlled the skies they were seagoing bombardment stations off many of the islands. They pounded them for weeks before invasions.

Orders to flight school came and I graduated and was commissioned in 1944. The former senior aviator, Admiral Reeves, retired and called me on the phone on the Christmas Eve before he died. Lt. Shipman looked me up at Lakehurst. Ensign Covington, the pilot I flew with on 7 Dec.'41, also looked me up several times and flew me to Washington several times for a weekend.

In the fall of 1941 I was in the rear seat of an SOC when Lt. Reeves hit a big ground swell on landing. We were both knocked out. When I came to, I was standing with my safety belt in my hand. I quickly unbuckled Reeves and was trying to pull him out when he came to. He had the knob of the altimeter in his hand. We both jumped from the plane and swam clear of it.I told Reeves he forgot to put down his flaps.After half an hour the Northampton came to pick us up.

Lt. Reeves asked me to write a statement of what happened. I wrote that we were coming in for a normal landing and I pulled my head inside, The next thing I knew I was standing up with my safety belt in my hand. He asked if I was sure that was all and I replied that that was all I remembered.

After seeing all this everyone was very quiet. There were bodies stacked on the Aiea landing where we used to go to catch the narrow gauge railroad for the trip into Honolulu. We got stores. And oil barges replenished the fuel and that night was eerie. At three in the morning we got under way in the dark and out the channel. Comcrudiv five and the Enterprise were task force eight. Our task was to find any Japanese ships or anything. At first light we were off the starboard of the carrier. The cruisers take stations on each side of the Enterprise. The idea is if there are any torpedoes fired at the carrier the cruisers will take them to protect the birds nest. I was at breakfast in the after mess hall when the ship made a nine turn (that is a 9o degree turn to starboard) the ship was doing about thirty knots and it heeled way over to port. All of the tables, benches, sailors, and food all gathered up in a mess on the port bulkhead. It was said someone spotted a white streak in the water and a fish went under the fantail being too deep. It was reported another went under the bow. These are pros and cons. Some say it didn't happen and some say it was true. As for my self I didn't see anything but sailor's food tables benches all wrapped up together.

After one day we reentered Pearl. We had liberty but had to be back on board by six in the evening. 2 until 6 just enough time to have a steak dinner at Loo Chi Fys in Wakakii. We had to take gas masks with us at all times. Aboard ship or ashore. On January 11 Enterprise, Northampton, Salt Lake City and Pensacola, five destroyers departed Pearl for the first offensive operation after war was declared. We patrolled west and north of the Samoan Islands to cover convoys reinforcing those island until the 25 of January when the course was set for the Marshall Islands. Aircraft from the Enterprise attacked Kwajalein and Maloelap atolls the first of February they sunk two ships and damaged nine and destroyed 35 enemy planes. Modern air bases on Tarao and Wotje were damaged. Numerous shore installations were destroyed. . At seven fifteen Northampton led Salt Lake City and destroyers in bombardment of Wotje for an hour and a half we steamed back and forth lobbing eight inch shells and five inch shells and wreaked destruction on shore facilities, coastal defense batteries and ships in the lagoon.

Our admiral R.A. Spruance was awarded a letter and ribbon of commendation for this bold and effective handling of the bombardment group. We had enemy shell landing around and over the ship but no hits. As we retired from Wotje and rejoined the Enterprise we twice helped fight off enemy bombers threatening the Enterprise. I was down in our compartment when the five-inch guns started firing and I raced up the ladder getting about half way up and concussion blew me back down to the deck. No damage and I raced up again to my battle station in the radio shack. I saw the bombers, they looked like two engine German Junkers. The Enterprise suffered one close hit that caused a serious fire in a machinegun battery. On Feb 5th we returned to Pearl Harbor with brooms up on the foretop signifying "clean sweep" and lots of cheers from ships in the harbor. At this time task force eight was redesignated as task force sixteen with Admiral "Bull" Halsey still in command of the Enterprise. On February 14 the Northampton again sailed from Pearl Harbor as flagship and screen for the Enterprise, this time bound for strikes conducted 24 Feb. Against southern Wake and Wilkes Islands. Carrier based dive-bombers destroyed runways of airfields, gasoline storage and ammunition dumps. At the same time Northampton led by Rear Admiral Spruance's bombardment group which included cruiser Salt Lake City and destroyer Maury and Balch, to rain destruction on northern Wake and Pearl Islands. After retiring from Wake the carrier task force conducted an air attack on Marcus Island March fourth. Northampton returned to Pearl Harbor March 10th 1942.

The preceding accounts I copied from official Navy texts. They tell a lot more than I can remember as to dates etc.

Before I continue with the saga of Northampton engagements I want to go back to the beginning of the war.

The radio shack was in on a lot of information the rest of the crew didn't get. But we copied news every day from KFS San Francisco. Two and a half hours usually it was Benny Morris. Our submarines were now sinking Japanese ships and the news would report, as an example. "our submarines sank 5000 tons of Jap ships, the Kabushi Maru, Yagasoi

Maru and so on,"

Maru was the designation for commercial vessels. For the U.S. it would be SS, which stood for steam ship, or MS, which was motor ship. I was up in the radio shack one morning and came up with "Nora Maru" I had one for the Salt Lake City too but will not put it in print. Tho I loved the Salt Lake City and the Pensacola. They were two of the best-looking ships in the Navy with their flush decks from stem to stern.

Now only the radio shack heard me say that and I used it from time to time in letters. But my greatest satisfaction came after the war in the mini series "War and Remembrance" with Robert Mitchum as Capt. Pug Henry was supposedly in a whale boat on the port side viewing the damage and fire and said "I'm going to miss the Nora Maru". I walked a foot of the ground for a week. Captain Chandler never heard that phrase or anyone else but it has lived on with the crew.

I was in Bora Bora some years ago, in fact my wife and I went there five times. We were practically adopted by that family in Faaa Tahiti. Now we knew a rather hefty woman on Bora Bora and she came to our fari, hotel, and said she was in a movie with a famous movie star. I asked who it was and she said Jason Nelson Robards. It so happened Jason was a shipmate.

Robards was a radioman on the Nora Maru. I made many a liberty with him in Honolulu. Jason imbibed at bit as most sailors but he was a darn good shipmate and a friend after the war. I was the only one that knew where he lived and I would phone him about movies he was in and congratulate his acting. He was a top performer.

That should take care of that. Now we go on. On the eighth. Of April we took to sea again on a historic mission. Comcrudiv five again screening Enterprise. We proceeded to Midway Island area and rendezvous was made on April 13th with the USS Hornet with sixteen B25 Michell bombers on her flight deck.

The other ships in her company were the heavy cruiser USS Vincinnes and USS Nashville a light cruiser plus a flotilla of can and an oiler. Submarines were also involved in this mission tho we never saw them. When we were a thousand miles from Japan the cans and the oiler were left behind and just the remaining force task force sixteen adding the two other ships to the force became I think the most famous task force of world war two.

We were to launch aircraft when five hundred miles from Japan but it was not to be. These planes manned by all volunteers were led by the famous aviator Jimmy Doolittle. About six hundred miles from Japan they spotted two picket craft. They surely had radioed Tokyo before the Nashville sunk them with their six-inch guns.

The weather was terrible. It was raining and quite a sea running. Bull Halsey gave the command for "pilots man your planes." From the Northampton, I was standing on the communication deck right behind the radio shack. I didn't have the watch so I could watch the action. Right next to me was a Pathe news cameraman taking pictures of the operation from a distance. We were screening Hornet off her starboard bow. As we usually screen Enterprise the powers to be had us off Hornet for the historic pictures of the bombers taking off the carrier.

When all was ready Doolittle was the first to take off. I'm sure everyone's heart was beating fast. The Hornet turned into the wind, which was brisk and would be a big help they also gagged each plane to take off when the bow was coming up. One plane came off and started losing a little altitude but then started rising. That was the only one that seemed to cause a little concern. They formed together and headed west to Japan.

Task force sixteen turned around and headed for Pearl. On the way picking up the destroyers. This was one dangerous mission for all hands. Two carriers five heavy cruisers, and a light cruiser. Had we been attacked and possibly lost it would have been a huge dent in the Navy force. But there were no problems and we returned to Pearl for stores and fuel. That was on the 25th of April 1942.

On April 30th Northampton raced south with Halsey's Task Force 16. A powerful force of cruisers and cans. We were supposed to support task force 17 in the Coral Sea in the battle of the Coral Sea. However that was over before we got there. We lost the carrier Lexington. The Japs didn't sink it but it was so badly damaged it was sunk by our own destroyers.

Carrier Yorktown with Admiral Fletcher was damaged but raced back to Pearl with the rest of task force 17 we missed that battle by one day. We were returning to Pearl fast, as they already knew that the Japanese were going to attack Midway Island. The night after the Lex was sunk, that was on May 8th, I had a mid watch. There were about eight of us doing nothing except the operator copying NPM skeds I had a frequency that was under radio silence so nothing to do unless things happened. I decided to write a poem. I worked on it for a couple hours plus or minus and came up with this. It was really about the lonely side of the Navy.

"Sailing Home"

What is it the billowing waves impart?
And repeat and repeat with each dash
What is the pounding in my heart?
I'm sailing home at last.
The salt spray stings on the naked cheek
And the wind sings in the mast.
But it only sings because it knows
I'm sailing home at last.

Was it centuries since we sailed away
Out of the harbor there?
Or was it only yesterday?
I don't know nor care.
For gone are the lonely nights and the days
Mid tropical isles alone
And gone is the hunger countenanced there
At last, I'm sailing home
And tho the sailor sails the seas
And in distant places roam
There is no "call" that's quite so sweet
As the call "I'm sailing home"

The poem has been published and tho it started out, as a lonely sailors poem as time passed it became somewhat of a funeral poem like sailing home to heaven. It has been read at Arlington Cemetery. The wife of a chief gunners mate from the Nora asked if she could have it read. I was pleased and happy she had asked. It has been read at my close friends Bob Berdahl and Russ Lee in Minneapolis and I expect it to be read a mine if I have to record it. Because I have recited it at Northampton reunions and other poetry some good some bad. They made me "poet laureate" I'm honored.

When we returned to Pearl for stores and fuel we lost our Admiral R.A. Spruance. He was a regular fellow when one on one. There was a night when I was standing, tho we sit down, watch in flag plot. That is right over the radio room on the bridge. It was late at night and it was peacetime. The ship was underway zigzag course darken ship and Spruance said to me, when do you think we will be going to the states? I told him if he didn't know I certainly didn't and he said. "Well when we do I'm gong to light this ship up like the Matsonia" that was one of two passenger liners that came from the states. Now the reason we lost him was that Admiral Halsey had a bad case of the hives. They even had to send him to the states. Before he left he put Admiral Spruance in command, per him, of the Enterprise and task force 16. There was one unhappy admiral, that being Fletcher. He thought he should be in command of both carrier force 16 and 17. Said that Spruance was not an aviator, which was a requisite for a skipper of a carrier. Halsey won that debate but there was one concession. Fletcher would command the aircraft on all three carriers but Spruance had control of the surface craft of 16 only. We were the bigger force of the two. Now the Japanese code had been broken and they knew there was going to be an attack on Midway. They put out a false message that Midway was short of water and immediately the Japanese informed their fleet that the target was low on water that gave the US notice that they were headed to Midway. They knew this when we were in the south pacific. We had been observed there and reported by Tokyo Rose of our presence there. It was good, as they had no idea that the two task forces would be waiting for them at Midway. They were going to capture and occupy the island on June 1,1942. The following is Admiral Spruance's message to the task forces. The expected Japanese attacking force for the capture of Midway might be composed of all combatant types including train vessels. plus four or five carriers, he further stated: "great value to our country will come from the successful conclusion of the operations now commencing."

The following day rendezvous was made northeast of Midway with task force 17. Northampton with task force 16 operated ten miles southward of 17 two days later the Japanese armada was encountered to commence the battle of Midway.

Torpedo planes from all three carriers were first to find the enemy carriers. Only a few were able to launch torpedoes and only six returned to the carriers. But their sacrifice was not in vain. They had drawn the enemy fighters away from the dive bombers from the Enterprise, Hornet and Yorktown which were almost unopposed by enemy fighters in their attack on three enemy carriers, Sent to the bottom of the sea were Japanese carriers Akagi, Soroyu and Kaga. A fourth carrier the Hiryu was at large under escort of battleships, cruisers and destroyers. Planes from the Enterprise, Hornet and Yorktown left the enemy a mass of flames but 18 dive-bombers from Hiryu attacked Yorktown. Most were shot down but five broke through to score three bomb hits and two torpedo hits on Yorktown it had to be abandoned. While Northampton task force pursued the retiring Japanese, Yorktown was further damaged by two torpedoes from a Japanese submarine. At the time there were 180 men on board the Yorktown. The destroyer USS Hannan secured alongside the Yorktown took two torpedo hits and sank with many heavy explosions. Surviving men were rescued from the sea. Yorktown capsized and sank on the morning of June 7th. The previous day planes from the Hornet and Enterprise located two enemy groups, sinking the cruiser Mikuma damaging the cruiser Mogami and damaging other fleet units.

From all of this my opinion, as just a sailor, is, if Fletcher had operated with task force 16 there would have been a lot more firepower against the attack and that would not have happened in the way it did. Another story of the Midway battle was torpron eight. That was torpedo squadron 8 off the Enterprise. All planes were lost. Only one man survived and that was an ensign Gay. His plane crashed into the sea but he survived and floated around and watched much of the battle around him. He was finally picked up by a PBY flying boat and lived a long life. He was a captain when he died and was cremated. They took his ashes to Midway and in a PBY they flew over the latitude and longitude where the battle took place and cast his ashes in the sea. Thereby making all the men in torpron 8 together once again.

The action of 6 June 1942 wrote the finish to one of the most decisive battles of history that had far reaching and enduring results of the pacific war. The island of Midway was saved to become an important submarine base for operations into the western pacific. Like wise saved was Hawaii, the great bastion from which attacks were carried into the south pacific and Japan itself. The greatest importance was the crippling of the Japanese carrier striking force, a sever blow from which she never recovered. With the four large carriers and one cruiser at the bottom of the sea, went some 250 planes along with a large percentage of highly trained and battle experienced carrier pilots. This great victory at Midway spelled the doom of the Japanese empire. These were official words while all this was going on we in the radio room were very busy. There was no radio silence. We had speakers and could hear the pilots talking as they attacked. One of them said as he dropped a bomb that I guess went right down the stack of a ship said "I bet Yamamoto is wiping his a-- now" so there is humor in the face of danger. Our ship was busy picking up aircraft. Many planes came back short on gas and couldn't make the carriers so destroyer and cruiser were busy with that. Also when planes that could land the two carriers Hornet and Enterprise had to turn into the wind. That meant their screen had to turn too. Well the

Hornet made a right turn and the cruiser on her starboard side was in a collision course with the Northampton. All hell broke loose with ship horn whistles and what not. The Nora turned left and at as the two ships went stem to stern about six feet clearance it was a close shave. I never did figure out if it was the Salt Lake City or the Pensacola but it was one of them. I was standing by the lifeline when it happened and the speed of both cruisers at 30 knots meant a sixty-mile and hour crash had we hit. We never left the COM deck. They brought us sandwiches and were relieved to be relieved? All of us were up for 72 hours. Funny what you can do when you have to. Also in the evening and all the planes were still returning, all ships kept their lights on. It looked like a city in the middle of the ocean after all this happened and chasing the Japs we turned away as we were coming to close to land based enemy bombers. The task force headed north to Alaska. As there was an attack on Kiska and Attu islands. On the way we were met by the Saratoga that ferried planes to the Enterprise and Hornet to make up for the losses. When we got in Alaskan waters the fog was so thick you couldn't see a thing and the force turned around and went back to Pearl Harbor arriving on June 13th.

The ship went into overhaul in the Pearl Harbor Navy yard. It was then they lowered the forward stack. It had always had and extra piece on it. Was the only one of the treaty cruisers that had it. Seems the original skipper smelled sulfuric fumes from the stack and ordered the extension. She was henceforward known as the stack and a half cruiser. The Northampton was no longer in task force 16 and I don't know what she was in. On June 28th Arthur George Duggan radioman 2nd/c and I RM 3/c were transferred to new construction. When I wrote of the large numbers of men on the ships it was to give some men sea duty to man all the ships that were being built. Duggan and I filled that bill. We went to a Navy transport called the USS Procyon for transportation to Treasure Island San Francisco. While on it we had to work. Duggan and I and others were down in a hold chipping paint. The officer in charge wouldn't come down. I think he was afraid of torpedoes. During that work I broke the black enamel on my Budda ring. Bought it in Honolulu in 1940 for fifty dollars and then had a fifty dollar blue white diamond set in the belly of the Budda. I still have it. Almost pure red gold and silver. Has twelve elephants around the ring. A gold stairway leading to Budda. Was made in China and the china man that sold it to me said the elephants were good luck. I think he was right as it brought me though some tough times during the war.

After I left the Northampton she went to the South Pacific and earned four more battle stars. Her total was six stars.

1 star pacific raids Marshall -Gilbert raid

Wake Island raid

Marcus Island raid

1 star battle of Midway

1 star Buinäfaoso=tonolai Raid

1 star battle of Santa Cruz Islands

1 star Guadalcanal (third savo)

1 star battle of Tasafaronga (fourth savo)

We got to the states and were transferred to the receiving barracks on Treasure Island. A man made island that is connected to Yerba Buena Island.. Also known as Goat Island. When we checked in they said they had to many boots (new sailors) to check in and they gave all us sailors from the fleet a three-day pass. I was off to Palo Alto. While sitting in a nice lounge an older man noticed I was a radioman and said he was a ham radioman. Introduced me to his wife and they invited me to their house. I was shown his radio equipment. It was in a nice room all paneled with wood. His operating desk was huge with a telephone to dial frequencies. 20 meters 6o meters, 80 meters what ever he wanted. It was all automatic. The transmitter was behind the wall and he had what was called at that time a "California kilowatt" that was two thousand watts. That was what we had on the Northampton with two tbl-6's actually had about five transmitters but the tbl's were the high power. He could work the world. During the war they had some restrictions on the amature radio operators. His call letters were w6upv and a friend in Pasadena told me later the man was known through out amateur radio.

I got back to Frisco and checked into the army Navy YMCA on Embarcadero Street and I surprised to see my brother Gaylord checking in also. We got a room together. Gay had been transferred a couple days before Duggan and I. That night it was hard to sleep, as it was too quiet. I think it would have been better had we got a vacuum cleaner and run it. When you are used to all the motors and ventilator blowers on a ship the silence gets to you. I did have some sound but it was my ringing ears from 1940.

Well Gay and I went back to Treasure Island and tho he was in another barracks Duggan, who had gone his way for the three days, my brother and I went on a few liberties in San Francisco. We always ate at "Clifton's" a buffet in both L.A. and Frisco. Good place to eat. Each day we had to look at a bulletin board to see if we were going to be sent somewhere. Gay was missing he had been transferred. Then I was transferred to the Bremerton receiving station. I later learned that Duggan was transferred to a CVE a baby flat top. I took a train to Seattle and on arrival checked into the Army Navy "Y". The next morning I took the Black Ball ferry over to Bremerton, which is an island in Puget Sound.

When I got there and all this time I had my sea bag and hammock lashed together and over my shoulder. As I was going into the office who should be coming out but my brother Gay. After checking in he told me to apply for guard duty in the hospital as it was better than policing the ground with a stick with a nail in it. I got that duty. Meanwhile I always wanted flying. I had tried for it on the Nora and they came out with an alnav that put a height limit for rdogunners in an SOC. I had tried for naval aviation pilot and then they dropped that list and I applied again AP, aviation pilot. Left Pearl before I came up on that list. I went to the educations officer and told him I'd like to get in lighter than air duty, blimps.

He talked me into applying for air cadet, which sounded good to me. I was sent over to Seattle and the federal building. The gave me a series of tests. Fast swiveling in a chair. Lining up depth perception and other physical exams. Eyes were good but ears could be better. They said they were ok for the air cadet program but it could be improved by removing my tonsils. They cut the orders for my transfer to the naval hospital in Bremerton. It's just like getting transferred to another ship. Sea bag and hammock on my shoulder to walk about two blocks to the hospital. I was checked into the eyes ears and throat department. The next day I was standing by my bed as all the patients that could stand had to do. The Dr., a commander would ask each man how he was and etc. When he came to me he looked at the chart and turned to the lt.jg with him and he said do you want to try this?" that alone gave me a lot of confidence. It seems it would be the first tonsillectomy he ever attempted. The next day I was wheeled. Even if you can walk they wheel you around, to the little room where this operation would take place. About all there was was a chair. I sat in that and opened my mouth as wide as I could and he had a type of instrument with a loop of wire. As he turned a knob it slowly squeezed the tonsil out then the same on the other side. Well back to the ward and bed. The throat hurt a little bit but not all that bad. A couple days later after the morning inspections it was Friday and that means field day. I was ordered to clean the head. At last, I made captain? Captain of the head. I was moping the deck and had it all cleaned and it was time for the evening meal. I was sitting on the side of the bed with the food on a tray table. Just as I was taking a fork full of mashed potatoes a lot of blood covered me, the bed the tray and all. The corpsman on duty got the nurse, the nurse got a Dr. Most all the doctors had left the hospital for the weekend. The one with the duty I think was a foot doctor. He rushed in and with a cotton swab, put pressure on the bleeding and then said it was ok and left. A short time later as I was lying on the bed it looked like Vesuvius erupting. I lost more blood on me, and the bed. Now they give me a sputum bucket as it was pouring out of my mouth. The nurse again called the foot doctor and he seemed a bit mad at me like it was my fault. He could not stop it this time and they got hold of a Dr Adix (from Superior, Wisconsin who was a throat specialist). I was taken to the operating room. Miss French a Lt. nurse with a gold tooth but pretty as an angel. Held my hand assuring me I was going to be ok. The Dr had a couple of metal rods in my throat and was sewing down there. Then he would tie knot and slide it downs the little rods. This went on for sometime. It ended up being a major throat operation. They gave me adrenaline but no blood transfusion. And just a week before I went to the hospital I had donated a pint of blood to the Red Cross. They told me I had lost two quarts of blood that they had kept track of. I lost some in the beginning too. The body has only five quarts of blood so I lost a goodly amount. Now I couldn't pass for a human let alone the air cadet program in Pasco, Washington. When they were all through I was wheeled back to the ward on a gurney and put in a quiet room on the port side of the ward. All that night Miss French stayed with me putting small pieces of ice cube in my mouth and the cold water felt good I could have married her on the spot. I was beefing (cleaned the expression) about the JG that botched the operation, he took out more than just the tonsil. She kept reminding me that Dr Adix saved my life and I had to admit that. It took forever to get strength back. The other sailors said I looked like a dead man the night they brought me back. I could only be up for a short time in the solarium. Finally getting better there was a bos'n mate that had his jaw broken in a bar fight. His jaw was wired shut and all he could eat was liquid. He and I did a lot of jigsaw puzzles to pass the time. All the wards had eggnog in a little refrigerator and I drank a lot of that. When I could eat solid food in the mess hall in the hospital the food was 4,o. That means the best. You could order anything you wanted and they would make it in front of you. The Dr thought I could go to the movies in the hospital compound. I saw Claude Rains in "The Return of Mr. Jordan" then I wanted to go to the USO in Bremerton and was given permission by another doctor. I walked out the gate and it was about mile to town. I got there and felt so weak I just sat down and rested and then began the walk back to the hospital. When my doctor found out about it I thought someone was going to Alcatraz, he blew his top. There was no more liberty until he gave it to me. I spent the best part of two months recovering from that bad dream.

When I was transferred back to the receiving station I was back on guard duty. I had a mid watch on a young sailor and while I was outside the door I could hear the psychiatrist talking to him and trying to convince him that a grasshopper could have appendicitis. I kid you not. They should have put the Dr in the loony bin and let the sailor go. He wasn't about to agree to that. Another night I was guarding a sailor who had gone over the hill. Absent without leave. I was sitting in a chair right next to the bed with the duty belt on and a 45-service revolver on my side, when I was shaken awake. The first thing I saw was four gold stripes on the cuff of the officer. It was a captain. Lucky he was a reserve medical captain and all he said was "you better stay awake son" you know I could have been busted down to two years old for that.

While at the receiving station I applied for two weeks leave. They said I could only have a week, as the ship I was going to maybe be ready. It was April 1943 before it would be ready but they did not know that then. It was good to see my mother and father and the whole family. It was a good week. I went to the Nicolet Hotel with George Santrizos and at a performance I guess he had talked to the management and they put a spotlight on me and announced that I was had been in the Midway battle. A relative worked for the Minneapolis Star one of three papers in Mpls. I was interviewed on the front porch. I answered his questions as best I could but you wouldn't know it from what appeared in the paper if I can find it will appear in this book. Then back to Bremerton. In December I bought Seattle Post intelligence. It had a picture of the Northampton towing the Hornet in the battle of Santa Cruz, however the story they were telling about was the sinking of the Northampton. Guess you know I was worried about all my shipmates on the ship especially the radio gang. . It wasn't until I met Jason Nelson Robards in Chinatown in Frisco that I found out no radiomen were lost. Jason was in the flag on the ship. When you have an admiral aboard he has certain crewmembers that come under him so when Jason was picked up he was transferred to the USS Honolulu and back to the federal building at Fresco. He was about three sheets in the wind at the time. He always did drink too much but later in life he had a terrible accident in Malibu and from then on he was A.A. and never drank again.

I was transferred to Kirkland, Washington in January 1943. Again the lashed sea bag and hammock on my shoulder taking the ferry to Seattle then a bus on Madison Ave all the way to Lake Washington. they have a bridge now, and getting on a ferry for Kirkland. It was windy and water coming over the square bow of the ferry getting my stuff wet. On the other side I had to walk about four blocks to the American Legion Hall, the Navy appropriated it for barracks for the future crews of the seaplane tenders that were being built at the Lake Washington shipyards.

Lt. Comdr. Gardner the exec of the USS Chincoteague, which was the ship, I was assigned. Glomed on to me right in the beginning as I could type, I had to copy the ships regulations on stencil. It was a tedious job but I got it done, took a couple weeks. There were cots four high in the legion hall. Solid. One night while just musing in the sack (bunk) I heard Kenny Starret returning from liberty. A good shipmate from Boston. He was singing "you had plenty money back in 92, you" bang bang bong, he fell down the stairs to the landing "let other women", he fell again on the second set of stairs, and continued. "make a fool of you". He wasn't hurt at all. Kenny and I made a few liberties to the "Pink Elephant in Kirkland. Was sitting at a bar when a man came up to me. We talked awhile about the war and in the end he said," I have a model "A" sitting in a garage I'm not using why don't you take it and use it while your here." he gave me the keys and gasoline gas book and drove me to the place where it was stored. I started it up and it ran real well. He said when your thru with it just park it in front of the Pacific Electric office. Well I had it for a week when the Navy lowered the boom on me. I couldn't park it on Navy property, as I didn't have insurance. Was darn nice of the guy tho to lend it to me.

I went to a USO party in Kirkland and met a motherly woman that invited us to her house to make fudge. I had mentioned I played the piano accordion and lo and behold they had one. The night in question I had to call first and I got hold of a phone operator. Got talking to her and instead of making fudge I had a date with the operator. I went to the phone co., it was a small place and in the front I could see five operators working on the switchboards. I didn't know which one I had the date with. She had said she would be off work at a certain time and that was close so I just waited. Finally one stood up and came out. Luck was with me she was the prettiest of the five.

Another adventure?? Was a hot afternoon and Tommy Eads an rm1/c and I got stamps and bought a quart of "Four Roses" that whisky only came in quarts. Just the two of us walking around Kirkland drank our whole bottle of Four Roses. Needless to say we were quite inebriated. I went back to the barrack and the next day saw the doctor and he put me in bed for three days and talked to me about what could happen and an alcoholic and all that. I was far from that but I did listen and hard liquor and I parted the ways to this day doubt if I have had a bottle of it in all these years. Not counting what is in beer. But even that I see very little of now.

Finally the ship was ready and on the 12th of April 1943 the USS Chincoteague avp24 was commissioned. I attended the ceremonies. Now

USS Chincoteague, AVP24 as she looked at commissioning, April 12, 1943

all the crew had to select their lockers and bunks. It was by rate. The radio gang only had one first class so as senior 2/c I got second pick. I chose a high locker.

Close to the amidships bulkhead (wall). Also a bottom bunk in the same area. When all was ready we left the dock and headed to the locks between Lake Washington and Puget Sound. Once out in the sound we headed for the straits of Juan de Fuca. That is the way to the pacific. We were not going there yet but they had depth charge drills. Dropped off a couple ashcans (depth charges) and blew up a lot of water. I think they were not going fast enough because when the blew the ship almost became a surfboard and we rode the wave. Also killed a lot of fish. A whaleboat was lowered and they collected a lot of them with the idea of having a fish dinner. The ship's doctor put the kabosh on that and condemned the whole lot as the eyes were bulging out of the sockets. I don't think there was a thing wrong with the fish but he held the wheel. After some other drill we went back to Puget Sound to the Bremerton shipyard. You could tell there was some lack of seamanship as when we were coming into a dock it was a little too fast and we almost lost the whole bow. Actually they had to rebuild it a little. More work was done on the ship and I don't think we were there a week when we went to San Francisco. Out of the sound into the Pacific and down the coast. The waves made the ship roll quite a bit. We now were part of the fleet and copied NPM skeds, had a watch on 500 KCS the distress frequency and another Navy freq. The chief, and I use the term loosely, was sick and we never saw him in the radio shack. Philip Yee Lee a slight Chinese American was copying skeds with a pail, for certain reasons, right on the deck beside him. I've got to say I never got sea sick in my life and didn't on that trip. It lasted all the way top the Golden Gate. We went to Mare Island for just a couple of days and then out in the bay to calibrate the direction finder. I explained a bit about that before. It is done very precisely. Civilian experts do it. Then we were released to go to San Diego for final shakedown.

In Diego we took on a few more sailors. We tied up at North Island. Each day for about a week we went out to San Clemente Island for maneuvers and gun practice. When the crew knew somewhat what to do we left Diego for Pearl Harbor. When we were at Pearl we got a couple days liberty. In June 1943, I'm not sure of the date; we pulled away from the dock at Ford Island. A Navy band was playing "aloha nui" which means sad departing. They didn't know how right they were. The ship had a top speed of 19 knots. We had two engine rooms each had two huge Fairbanks Morse engines. They have pistons on top and bottom and run opposed. when the are running each compartment had a telephone booth much like was used in that day.

If they didn't have that they couldn't hear the bridge. Gunfire and engine room noise were the two biggest reasons for impairing hearing. On our way to the South Pacific there was a sub scare and the dropped a couple cans again. They most likely heard a whale on the sonar. Better safe than sorry. We arrived at Espirito Santo in the New Hebrides. The skipper, Captain Ira E. Hobbs, an aviator got in touch with our command which was Comfairwing 1 on the USS Tangier a large AVP. It had control of all the AVPs in the south pacific. We were ordered to go to Vanikoro Island in the Santa Cruz group. Not far from Guadalcanal. We took the place of the USS Mackinac another AVP. They were gone when we entered the reef and into Saboe Bay at Vanikoro. We were told it was good duty they had been there for nine months and everything was quiet.

This was on the 13th of May 1943. The next day I had shore leave, tho there was nothing to do. Just a few men natives. The women were on the other side of the island. Their hair was copper colored and rather good-looking natives. They wanted "T" shirts and would weave bracelets on your wrist with stripped palm leaves. Did not interest me. Now on the 14th things got a little more interesting. That night the electricians, they were in charge of movies, were showing "the moon and sixpence" with Herbert Marshall around the middle of the movie general quarters was sounded with a clanging bell. No bugles like the Nora Maru. On the topside (main deck" the whole bay was lit up with a kind of greenish flare. One lone Jap observation plane was taking pictures. The ship fired a few rounds of main battery the 5 inch 38's but no hits. At that time we didn't have the electronic shells that would go off if you were even close. At that time they had to set rings in the head of the projectile and when fired it would light the rings and you kind of had to guess at the altitude for it to explode. Things got better later with the magnetic shells. . As for the movie I never did get to see the end of it while the war was on but I did see it on TV many years later.

Then on the 15th at 1830(6:30 p.m.) radar picked up unidentified plane bearing 240 degrees. General quarters were sounded. Fire was not opened in order to conceal our position. On the morning of the 16th five Jap twin engine bombers picked up by radar circling the bay. Then sighted overhead we sounded general quarters. Jap bombers released bomb load from about 8000 feet bombs were observed to fall about 1500 feet from the ship. Bursting in the jungle.

The preceding information was from the official ships log. Now I can give what I saw. A couple of bombs went off right aft of the ship about a hundred yards. Shrapnel hit a couple places in on the of depth charges on racks on the stern. Another hit the gun sight for NR four 5" 38 turret smashing it. No great damage but was something. What happened next was the captain ordered the anchor slipped. It and all the chain went to the bottom and we went out the entrance in the reef and out to sea. You have a better chance of evading bombsights when moving and altering direction. When no more planes, hold the phone, I've got to go back a day. When the first planes missed up that was it for the day. Comfairwing one decided to return the favor to the Japs and sent twelve pby's from Espirito Santo to join with the twelve we serviced. And I'll explain that. An AVP is really a fueling station for aircraft. The crews and mechanics live aboard the ship. They ate first and bought most of the ice cream as they got flight skins (50%) of base pay plus the 20% we got for hazardous sea duty. That's life in the big city.

Now back to the war. They were armed with daisy cutter bombs. That is an aerial bomb with a six-foot prong. It is a personnel bomb. It detonates six feet from the surface spewing shrapnel in all directions. The target was a big Jap base on Naruu Island 600 miles north of Vanikoro. They took of in the afternoon and a in the night Mr. Crook the radio officer ordered me to send MO's on 500 kilo cycles. I did that.

It was around two o'clock in the morning I think. I must have keyed it for two hours. The Morse code for m is two dashes and o is three dashes. The idea was for the planes to take a bearing with their direction finders and give them a path back to Vanikoro, it worked too. They started landing while I was having breakfast and the last plane hit the water at eight o'clock plus or minus. At the same time we were bracketed with bombs. General quarters and back out to sea the only damage so far was Mcguier,TF sf3/c dropped a shell on his right hand and Finicum, R.J. s2/c powder case fell on hand, Richards, D.M. burned hands handling hot shells. I still don't know how that could happen as 5"38;s are a cold projectile with two silk bags of powder behind it. Comes up to the gun on a lift and automatically pushed into the breech, but then what do I know I was a radioman.

We zigged and zagged full steam and when that attack was over we reentered Palu Reef into Saboe Bay to continue fueling planes. For continuing flight back to Espirito Santo. Upon completion of that the two boats were to go to Peou Bay and await the return of the "chinc" at ten twenty maneuvering at different speeds on various courses and cleared Palu entrance into Saboe Bay. There were five-twin engine bomber in that group. In the official log they call them Vals, Sallies and Knells. I think they were our name for a Mitsubishi twin-engine bomber and that was "Bettys". At 11:10 sighted nine Jap bombers circling the bay. We opened fire with all four 5 38 guns fore and aft. Underway at various speeds to avoid bombs. 11:39 planes making third approach dropping bombs, no direct hits sustained.

Steaming as before on various courses and making preparations for entering Saboe Bay. We fueled the remaining PBY's with sufficient gas to return to Espirito Santo. We cleared the reef and back out to sea. Went to general quarters as unidentified planes were picked up on radar. There five bombers approaching from the NE. At 11:47 opened fire. Planes dropping bombs bracketing ship. No direct hits but sustaining splinter damage on boat, port side. 11:51 ceased firing. 11:59 five enemy bombers sighted in direction of the sun. Started firing.

Standing as before. Bombs bracketing the ship, one bomb piercing main deck and second deck exploding in the after engine room. All personnel (eight men) including Mr. Weaver (a wonderful officer) were killed. One fireman killed in forward messing compartment. Speed reduced to about ten knots. Steaming on starboard shaft only. 12:01 ceased firing. Began tracking. 12:15 one enemy plane approaching on port side. Commenced firing. 12:17 ceased firing. Developing engine trouble in forward engine room. Speed reduced to about five knots. 2:40 all ship's power failed. Commenced steering by manual control. 14:20 sighted three enemy bombers coming in at about 8,000 feet from starboard beam. 14:22 opened fire with all guns. Local control. On the run enemy bombers dropped a series of green flares while heading into the sun. 14:24 enemy bombers began circling and started another bombing run. Ship was bracketed by bombs.

At least one approximately 200 lb. Bomb fell along port side stopping forward engine. The splinters and concussion produced by this bomb resulted in considerable damage to personnel and ship. Number three five inch gun crew reports that one Jap plane broke formation and veered off trailing smoke during this attack and a second plane smoke trailing. At 1450 one enemy plane started a bombing run from port side, bombs fell about 200 yards off port. 1452 cease firing. After compartments completely flooded water coming in through numerous large splinter holes causing the ship to a heavy list to starboard. All available men, including gun crews organized into bucket brigades. Bucket brigades were placed in the main flooded compartments astern and amidships.

All handy billies (two cycle gas engine pumps) were put into service. As before continuous efforts being made to control flooding, ship listing 16 degrees to starboard. Water in forward engine room under control at a depth of three feet. All efforts being made to place forward engine in commission. 22:35 both the 100 kw and 200 were started. 23:05 forward main engine started. 23:30 underway at about 8 knots, steering course 163 degrees.

Now I have to take over as I saw it. There were hundreds of shrapnel holes in the stern on the starboard side. Sailors were in the water pounding wooden pegs in the holes. Not an easy job with sharks around.

In the radio shack when the power went out Mr. Crook the radio officer asked the chief to get the emergency radio out. He didn't know his name less the gear. He asked a first class and he never heard of it. I don't use names to protect the guilty. I was still sitting at the NPM sked position.

That was my g.q. station. He asked me and I said, "yes sir," remember on the Northampton we were drilled on that gear. Of all the men T.R. Gray trained it was likely I was the only one that ever had to use it. I got a couple of guys to go with me aft and bring the bags up to the radio shack. It had different ways to get power I used a three legged generator with hand cranks. A striker named Sage was on one side and Wilshon on the other. I set up the tranciever and loaded it up on the ships antenna. Then informed Mr. Crook I was ready. I called the USS Tangier, our command and made contact. Then some lame brain on the bridge and I knew who it was sent down a message by a yeoman to send. Crook made up the heading (address) and authentication and I sent it. "being bombed" then a second message "bombed again" then the third. "still being bombed by enemy bombers" the forth I took exception to. It read "deliberately being bombed by enemy bombers". I told Mr. Crook anyone seeing that would think we were hospital ship. These messages were forwarded to NPM in Pearl Harbor and sent to all ships and stations. My brother would see it. Believe me. This doesn't seem possible but it is all true. I finally got a decent msg to send. Our position. Due to this the USS Thornton came along side around midnight. On an earlier attack the fuel pumps on the stern were set afire. I have a picture of the chink burning off Vanikoro taken by French overseer and enlarged by a brother of the sailor killed in the forward mess hall. Kenny Starret, I mentioned him earlier was in radio two with Phillip Yee Lee. Wilbur Morgan and Lubbner. Kenny got curious and went out on the stern when the gasoline pumps were set afire. He was a human torch they told me and he ran and jumped over the lifeline into the water.

Chincoteague on fire from bombing, July 17, 1943. Off Vanikoro Island, Santa Cruz Group

Charlie Dog, Ransdell, John Shepherd and I visited him in the Quonset hospital in Santo. He was covered with bandages. I hope it was not true but I heard he died a week later. Meanwhile back at the ranch, the black gang is trying to get the engine in the forward engine room started. For the little while they had power they built up air pressure to turn over one engine. Lo and behold they got it running. Not quite like the log said.

It started out about eight knots and kept increasing until we almost did 19 knots that was as much as all four engines could do. What happened was the engine started sucking lube oil and ran away. It got so hot that part of it melted. They had to fill the engine room up with foam to stop the fire.

Meanwhile the best part of the crew abandoned ship to the Thornton which was now along side supplying help with submersibles and more handy billies. The skipper of the Thornton, an old four piper can from world war one converted into an avp. Had a battle lamp and instructed me to take the end of the submersible. We went down into the bowels of the ship to an officer's compartment. I was up to my waist in water. Something bumped me and the skipper put the light on it. It was the headless body of the man who was killed in the forward mess hall. When the bomb came thru to main deck it sliced right thru a water tight door between to two mess halls and exploded in the phone booth in the after engine room.

The blast thru the watertight door thru the air decapitating, Stroud, a sailor in a damage control party. They had placed him in this stateroom where I was wading around. I dropped the head of the submersible and the skipper and I ran back up the ladders (stairways) to the topside. Before that I was also involved in the bucket brigade.

My costly watch was ruined and I imagine a lot of wristwatches were ruined at that time. . Now back to the engine running away. The Thornton was not there yet so all the crew were either on the stern and the bow thinking about abandoning ship.

Meanwhile Captain Hobbs was on the stern shooting sharks. Nothing like a lot of blood in the water if you have to jump in. However the USS Thornton showed up. It is now the 18th of July. At 4:17 the Thornton passed over a line to tow at 6:43 the Thornton commenced towing. Speed five knots. At 7:40 the towline parted and Thornton made sound contact and dropped two depth charges. Towline was re-secured and at 10:03 cable took strain and again was towing.

They had to break towing as we were taking on water again more bucket brigades with the ship settling in the water. . The stern settled low with two feet of freeboard. List settling to 18 degrees to starboard. All hand again ordered to bailing with buckets.

Orders were given to lighten ship. All heavy gear was jettisoned over the side. We had six aerial torpedoes and the three on the starboard side were deep sixed. (to the bottom) at 13:30 a PBY landed along side bringing additional submersibles. Began transferring confidential and other valuable gear to the Thornton. At 17:30 flooding was under control. At 17:40 the USS Jenkins appeared off our starboard stern. At 17:41 sighted three enemy (sally type?) With four F4U's following them observed bombs being jettisoned into the water about 3 miles away the burning wreckage of three enemy planes struck the water at a distance of 7 miles. All of us on the topside were cheering like it was a touchdown at a foot ball game. At 18:30 the ship was on even keel the Jenkins circling the chink for anti submarine protection. At 1900 the USS Travers arrived for more anti sub protection.

What wasn't in the log was all of crew standing on the topside as these three Mitsubishi's flew along side at about 1200 feet. Before they got to us they had dropped a couple bombs on the Jenkins that landed aft of the ship. Then they flew on our starboard side and one of them flashed light at us like they were friendly. Lots of guts. That is when the Corsairs showed up. The Japs jettisoned their load and disappeared into a big white cloud. The three flaming planes fell to the sea. Japanese aircraft burned brilliantly. That was it for the night.

The next day was the 18th of July. At 09:00 we sighted the USS Sonoma a sea going tug coming to us. She was from Guadalcanal. On her way she found the sailors that were left at Vanikoro after fueling the PBY's, and they got some natives to help get the big gas tank in the boat out. Then they set out for Espirito Santos, believing the Chink had been sunk. They were transferred back on board.

From here to Santos was uneventful. The Sonoma towed us at five knots to safe harbor at Espirito Santo. When we got there they immediately put the ship in a floating dry-dock and drained the ship of water. They had a recovery team go into the after engine room for the bodies. They came out in sea bags. After that I was able to go down in the aft engine room.

It was uncanny. The bomb went off in the telephone booth but the phone was still on the hook. The engines were completely moved off the mounts. The control panel was half blown to bits but the other half all the instruments were still ok. A three-inch stanchion was bent but a 16-gauge sheet metal vent wasn't even bent. All very strange.

On the July 22nd this message was sent to comfairwing one,

We are holding burial services for Chincoteague dead tomorrow morning at 09:30 x if convenient to you would appreciate your visit before 0900 or after 1200, as I would like to attend the services.

That was from captain Hobbs. (message sent to Comfairwing One on

July 22, 1943 after coming into Espirito Santos in the New Hebrides Islands when a 250 lb bomb hit that part of the ship. She was dead in the water sixteen miles off Vanikoro of the Santa Cruz group.

Drury "Mac" McCall, VMF214, 22 yrs. Old. Of four planes he is the last one living. Two were shot down in 1942 and one died naturally.

While we were in the dry-dock they took off the screws (propellers) all the bombs out of the bomb stowage, there was enough to blow the ship to kingdom come. In fact the only places the bomb could have hit without looking like the atom bomb was the two-engine rooms and the peak tanks in the bow. Any other place would have gotten magazines, bomb stowage, or aviation fuel and of course our own diesel fuel. We lucked out. When she was patched up on the starboard side the dry-dock filled with water and we were floating like a cork. We were taken by tug to a dock where they loaded a big jungle generator from D.W. Onans and that would be our power for the trip to the states.

Most of the crew was put on a transport for the trip to the states. Just a skeleton crew was to be on it for the trip to Mare Island. In the forward mess hall they hung a huge water bag, for drinking water. It had a rubber taste. The cooks would only serve sandwiches but it was tolerable.

When we were ready the Sonoma again did the honors of towing us home. We bounced around quite a bit being so light. Twice on the trip she broke tow for sounding. Have no idea if it was subs or not. While on the trip, which took, 31 days, at six knots, we radio men, Charlie Ransdell, Phillip Yee Lee, John Shepherd and I had living quarters in the officer's staterooms. One day for lack of anything to do we began opening safes. Listening to the tumblers.

The first class (I know his name, but again to protect the guilty, found a 45 cal service revolver in one safe and then hid it under the bottom drawer of a file cabinet. I saw him do it and later I went back and put it in another safe and left a note "thou shalt not steal" in its place. I never knew if he found that or not.

I must also tell you that after I got the tby emergency gear on the air and completed all the messages. Lt. Stanley Crook told me your first class. I appreciated that.

We finally reached Mare Island and the Golden Gate never looked so good. The rest of the crew were in a barracks and we found that because we saved the ship all the crew would remain on the Chincoteague, we received a commendation for it.

Everyone got some leave and I got two weeks in Minneapolis. It was good to be home but there were extenuating circumstances. I was crying in the night. I would want to be alone but my dad and uncle followed me all over town.

When the bombing of the Chincoteague was happening no one kept his cool more than I. Nothing seemed to bother me. The other radiomen were on the deck praying and I was cussing. But I think the good Lord helped me keep that cool. Anyway after one week I left home I wanted to get back to the west coast and the Navy. I took a taxi alone to the Milwaukee station. As the train pulled out and ran under all the bridges on 29th street we came to Fourth Ave. where there were no bridges and in an open field on the corner was my mother waving a white handkerchief. She had no idea where I would be on the train, if I had been on the other side I wouldn't have seen her and I was sitting looking forward and if I had been the sailors opposite side I would not have seen her. As I type this tears are in an old 86-year man's eyes. I've always thought there was some more divine help.

Back at Mare Island I was again ok. Ransdell and I made a lot of liberties together. One night at "Sweets Ballroom" I was at the bar with a beer and Charlie comes running up to me and said he had two redheads and I should meet one of them. I left the beer on the bar and did meet a beautiful girl. We jitterbugged and when there was an intermission we went to one of the openings, they were arched with wrought iron bars.

There was a full moon and while looking up I said "it's only once in a man' s life that he can reach up into the sky and grasp the stars' I stole that from a Frederick March movie some years before. Little did I know that I was talking to my future wife. All during our rebuilding of the ship Mell and I danced like crazy.

There was one night I arrived in Oakland and Mell wasn't at the Stobings, the family she was living with since she had left St. Louis, Mo. I went to Sweets ballroom looking for her and was giving people a bad time. Sweets had a woman bouncer that could have played left guard for the Rams. She thru me out. But I had been thrown out of better places than this, I told her, t'was the dark side of "Sail Easy".

While the ship was being repaired and it was extensive. They removed all of the main deck over the two engine rooms. The second deck of the mess hall over the after engine room was blown up to about two feet from the overhead (ceiling) so it was completely removed so they could hoist out the damaged engines and everything in the engine room. The same for the forward engine room.

They rebuilt half the ship. While the shipyard took care of the Chincoteague I was sending code to the radio strikers to improve their skills. Then at 11 o'clock I would put on my tailor made blues and head for the beach. (Navy term for liberty) Oakland was my destination. I had a liberty card for both starboard and port so I had liberty every day. Mell and I would be at Sweets, Trader Vic's, Top of the Mark or Fisherman's wharf. We were on the go. A sailor at that time had to make use of time. One night I stopped and bought a giant panda. People looked a little askew at me on the bus I was riding in. Brought it to Mell and I named it Nicodemus.

Another time I came without eyelids or eyebrows. I had been to fire school at Mare Island. We fought oil fires; engine room fires, gasoline fires and I learned how to cut steel under water with an acetylene torch. Guess I looked kind of odd for a while. The time passed too fast and the ship was ready for sea. It was January 1944.

You know, during all that has happened to me to me on the Chincoteague I was 23 years old when the ship was bombed. After the bombing I think I was 53. All sailors and service men in combat I think feel that way.

We went out the Golden Gate and sadly think of those we left behind. To me it was Mell, then my family. The ship sailed for San Diego and another shakedown cruise. Have to make sure everything works. And off to Pearl Harbor. From Pearl Harbor we went to Kwajalein Atoll for the invasion of that Atoll. As mentioned earlier most of the battle ships that were sunk and damaged at Pearl Harbor were rebuilt. Now they came to good use. They stood off the atoll for a couple of weeks and pounded kKwajalein unmercifully.

After the atoll was secured I was able to go ashore. You wouldn't believe what we saw. Every Jap was dead and because this is the tropics they did not have uniforms on just a kind of diapers. The sun reeks havoc on any

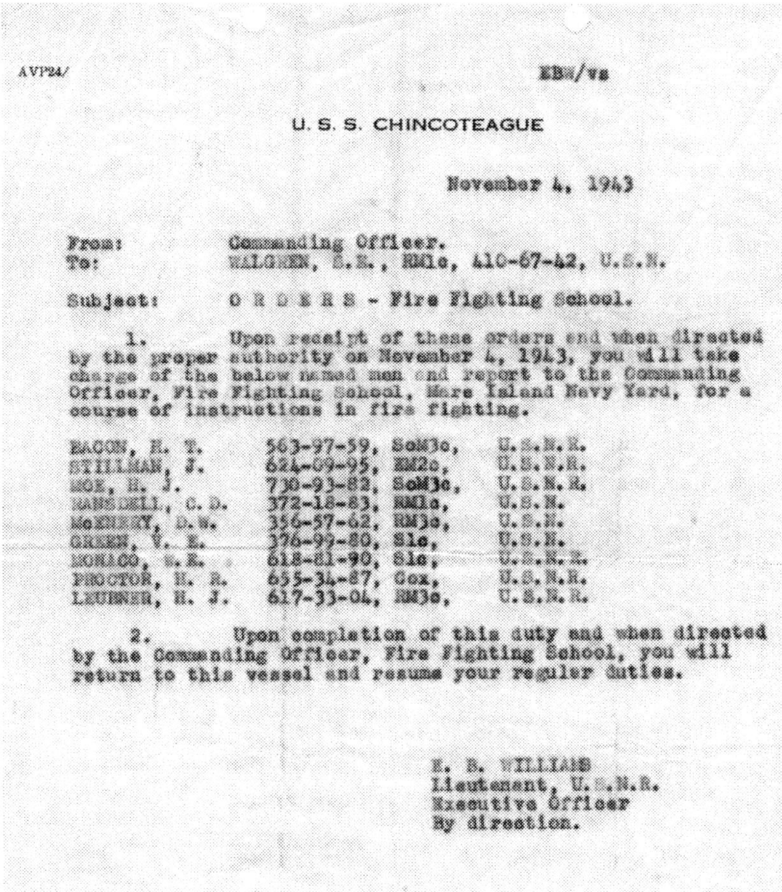

AVP24/ EBW/vs

U. S. S. CHINCOTEAGUE

November 4, 1943

From: Commanding Officer.
To: WALGREN, E.R., RM1c, 410-67-42, U.S.N.

Subject: O R D E R S - Fire Fighting School.

1. Upon receipt of these orders and when directed by the proper authority on November 4, 1943, you will take charge of the below named men and report to the Commanding Officer, Fire Fighting School, Mare Island Navy Yard, for a course of instructions in fire fighting.

BACON, H. T.	563-97-59,	SoM3c,	U.S.N.R.
STILLMAN, J.	624-09-95,	RM2c,	U.S.N.R.
MOE, H. J.	730-93-82,	SoM3c,	U.S.N.R.
HANSDELL, C. D.	372-18-83,	RM1c,	U.S.N.
McENERY, D.W.	356-57-62,	RM3c,	U.S.N.
GREEN, V. E.	376-99-80,	S1c,	U.S.N.
MONACO, W.R.	618-81-90,	S1c,	U.S.N.R.
PROCTOR, H. R.	655-34-87,	Cox,	U.S.N.R.
LEUBNER, H. J.	617-33-04,	RM3c,	U.S.N.R.

2. Upon completion of this duty and when directed by the Commanding Officer, Fire Fighting School, you will return to this vessel and resume your reguler duties.

E. B. WILLIAMS
Lieutenant, U.S.N.R.
Executive Officer
By direction.

living thing. And flies are the result. I couldn't hear the hum but those with good hearing could. All the atolls in the western pacific are again the rims of a long gone volcanos. So the atolls are shaped in a circle and not connected. The natives of Kwajalein were on the atolls that were not used by the Japanese so they were not leveled. They all survived.

From Kwajalien Atoll we went with the invasion force to Eniwetok Atoll that was treated the same as Kwajalein. Just the island, or island that the enemy used was decimated. Still the landing force again had a fight on their hands. I went ashore again and saw more of the same. Maggots and flies by the billions. Every time the motor launch went to the beach and returned you could see a cloud of flies over it. When it came to the gangway they transferred to the ship. The ship's doctor made some traps and killed so many flies the metal decks became slippery. Men had to hose them down frequently. While on the island I found a Japanese flat hat in fair shape and a battered suit case, empty, I put the flat hat on, the Jap flat hats had a couple ribbons hanging off the back, There was a road and about four Navy officers walking and I ran past them like crazy uttering an imitation of Japanese. They laughed like crazy. A bit of humor in hell.

All the crew was able to go ashore to look for souvenirs wasn't much to find. Some Jap money, yens and such but it was funny, not funny haha, what a lot of them brought back to the ship. One sailor brought a Jap helmet with part of the previous owners skull still in it. Many brought enemy hand grenades, still live and mortar shells. Guess they looked good in shining brass. The end result was the captain, now Rosy Resasco, ordered a locker inspection. All hands had to open their lockers and fall into quarters on the topside. They found more ordinance than we had in the magazines, not quite, but a lot. It was all donated to Davy Jones.

Eniwetok was like the others. Parry Island, one of the atolls was where all the natives were put and they all survived. All the atolls in the pacific are surrounded by live coral reefs. In some places they have not reached another reef thereby leaving an entrance for ships to enter. In another million years maybe they will close? In the harbor were two zero float type Japanese aircraft, Rosy wanted one of those. So the ship anchored close over the submerged plane and a diver was sent down to attach the cable. The crane operator began to lift slowly. It raised a bit of silt as it was coming up so we couldn't see a great deal. When it broke the surface all the cable had was the engine. Rather disappointing for the captain. The best part of the meatball was still on the bottom. Where we were it was only about twenty feet but in some places it could be a hundred.

One night the radar picked up a bandit (enemy plane) about three thousand yards approaching fast. General quarters was sounded and I'm up in the radio shack. They kept giving distances and it was thought to be a torpedo attack as the plane was close to the water. It was an anxious moment. As it got to 200 yards everyone was expecting a big bang. The plane flew directly over the ship. So close it left oil splatter on the stack. They fired 20 mm at it but it was over so fast there wasn't anytime to aim. I think the Japs were as surprised to pass over us as we were that they just flew over us. It was figured to be a reconnaissance flight. There was no moon so it was black black.

Another event at Eniwetok was again concerning the captain; I always thought that our being in the south pacific was a fishing cruise to Rosy. He liked to fish. One day a first class pharmacist mate was fishing with him. When they were through the captain's gig, I use the term loosely, came along side the gangway. The captain jumped over to the gangway and the pill peddler had all his fishing gear in hand. He jumped and missed and all of Rosy's fishing equipment went to Davy Jones. We anchored right there and he wanted one of the divers, we had two qualified, to go down and retrieve the gear. They wouldn't go down saying there were not any qualified handlers. I, having been in a divers suit in Mpls while in the sea scouts and dressed by a commercial diver and down twelve feet by a dock in Lake Calhoun, offered to dive for it. The divers put up a howl so the captain said no. We had two diving suits and two air compressors and I couldn't see any danger in it but that's life in the big city.

Another caper. The captain wanted transceiver portable telephones. They were rather bulky compared to the cell phones of today. M.K. Korf was a good guy and radio electrician warrant officer. Back in the states when a chief put me on report for being over leave, by less than an hour, because I was removed from a flight in Salt Lake City for a bag of mail, this was at Mare Island.

At the captain's mast the skippers asked Korf what kind of a man I was, Korf said, captain he is the best man in the radio division. The skipper then said he would issue a warning in my record and it would be expunged in six weeks. No problem. Back to Korf's caper. He took a fifth of liquor ashore and traded it to the army for two radio telephones. They weighed about five pounds apiece. Now when the skipper went ashore I was to call him every hour to see if he was ready to return to the ship. I knew I'd better not miss it on the hour.? I guess the trade worked so well Korf took another bottle ashore and sent for the motor launch. When it returned to the ship there was an olive drab colored jeep in it. They hoisted it aboard and it seemed like only half an hour that the jeep turned from olive color to Navy gray with U.S. Navy stenciled on it and serial numbers and all. It was reborn into the Navy. Well that takes care of Eniwetok.

From there we went to another atoll called Majuro in the Marshalls. All these islands were in the Marshalls the previous atolls we were at in February. Majuro was in March I don't recall anything interesting there at all. Still in March we went to Tarawa Atoll, this was well after the invasion of the island. We were not involved in that bloody invasion. But on the island we were able to see plenty of reinforced gun positions. Many were at least four feet of concrete and rebar but blown open. Tarawa is in the Gilbert Islands. We left there for Funi Futi Atoll where we took on all the spare gear for a flotilla of PT boats; we were to convoy them to Espirito Santo. They were camouflaged in black and white stripes erratically. Funi Futi is in the Tuvalu Islands. While leaving the lagoon we suddenly came top a grinding halt. It seem a buoy that should have been on the starboard side was on the port side. They were placed in the entrance of the atoll. We had run aground on live coral. Had it been dead coral the whole bottom of the ship would have been wiped out. Alas

alas. When a Navy ship runs aground it doesn't matter where the captain is he is responsible. The officer of the deck was the man on the bridge and also a first class quartermaster. The helmsman is given the course to take. He is in the clear. Oh woe is me, I'm sure Rosasco was saying. At low tide he was walking barefoot along the starboard bow and the water was just up to his ankles, I have a picture of the ship high and dry by the bow. Now is the fun part. It is an automatic court marshal for a captain to run aground but it has to be permanent. So the procedure to get it back in deep water began. First of all both our screws were in the water. They hooked up a destroyer to the stern and with the can full ahead and our engines full astern nothing moved. That was plan "A". Now the chief boats ordered all the crew to the bow. We were to run as fast as we could to the stern. Engines full astern the can full ahead and nothing moved. That was plan "B". The next thing was, all the crew on the stern. On the count of three we were all to jump in the air while the engines were full astern and the destroyer and now a tug were pulling forward full. Nothing moved. That was plan "C". Another try but adding firing of the forward 5 38;s simultaneously as we were jumping and the engines full astern and

Helmsman missed a buoy at Funi Futt Atoll close to Tarawa.
Took 3 days to get her clear. 1944

the can and tug full ahead and nothing moved. The firing of the gun forward is really a no no for the guns. You lose some recoil of the ship. That was plan "d" now things were getting serious. They brought out a flat barge. Every thing that was removable was put on the barge. Including the bombs in the bomb stowage, ammunition for the guns and the torpedoes. The whole crew was put on the barge also. They waited for high tide. This would be plan "E". With the tide high with the engines full astern. The destroyer and the tug pulling full ahead. Eureka the Chink slid off the reef and back in business. Now instead of a court marshal I think the skipper made points for getting the ship off in good shape. No damage. All hands had to help get every thing back on board the ship and we proceeded to Espirito Santos.

I forgot to mention when we left the states and got to Pearl Harbor. They transferred the chief for chronic sea sickness?? And Mr. Crook said to me you are now chief. Here I am, an apprentice seaman on the Nora Maru in 1940 to chief radioman and I'm 25 years old. In peace time a sailor would have to have at least twelve years in the Navy and go thru Bellevue, not the nut house, radio school in Washington D.C. to be a chief radioman. I was the great Kahuna; in Tahiti it is the Kahua. Not to be patting myself on the back but I felt good about it. There was no place to get a chief's uniform so I was in the chiefs quarters in dungarees, when a new chief comes in the chief's quarters life changes completely. We had a refrigerator with steaks in it and a nice range to prepare good stuff; I once made Norwegian lefsa there. Our bunks were so you could sit up in them and we were served by two mess cooks that were permanently assigned to the quarters. They brought the good food. Life was gude. The first meal I had to eat with my hands tied behind my back and they had a trough in front of me. I had to eat like a pig. All chiefs were put thru this initiation. I was in. It was funny to see all the chief's hats and my white hat lying amongst them .It didn't last for long however; I will relate getting my uniform in good time.

After dropping off the PT boats the command sent us to Guadalcanal in the Solomons. All action was over by that time but they said there were stray Japs hiding in the mountains and hills. I don't know what our business was there but we had Eddie Peabody a banjoist play on the fantail. It was with a USO show.

One evening before the movie on the stern, no worries about Jap planes by that time at Guadalcanal. The officers brought a couple nurses from the island for the movie. Meanwhile Benson's dog, I forget its name found a friend from Guadalcanal and proceeded to propagate the breed right in front of the movie screen. With that over the movie proceeded. Benson was the postmaster on the ship. I think he was a motor machinists mate. He had the dog for sometime. From Guadalcanal we went north to Tulagi. This is what became known as Iron Bottom Bay. It may be that we passed over the Northampton 2000 ft down on the bottom. At Tulagi we had liberty. Each man going to the beach could have two "chits" little cards that we could exchange for a can of beer. Morgan didn't drink and Phillip Lee didn't either so I had six cans of beer. I think McEnte was with too. We wandered up a road and came across a cave. It was full of huge centipedes at one time I think the Japs used the cave as a command post. I saw a tall tree with a platform towards the top. There were boards nailed to the tree as a ladder to get up there so I started up. I was quite aways up when as I climbed up there was one of these centipedes crawling down. I beat him to the bottom by three days I'm sure. We met another sailor from another ship that told us he knew where there was a native village about three miles into the island. Armed with the beer ammunition I was game for anything. We passed more of the centipedes in piles about six feet high and eight feet in diameter. Don't know what was under them to eat and I didn't ask to find out. We also saw land crabs. They crawl just like their counterparts and stand about a foot in the air under their bellies. They can move quite fast also. I also saw spiders bigger then I had ever seen. Tulagi is not a place I would build my house. As we climbed higher I thought, you know Frank Buck would have had rifles and native guides and supply bearers and here we are with cans of beer. When we got to the top of the mountain and I use the term mountain. I could use Mt. Everest. It seemed that high. There were two dugout canoes being built. I think they were almost done but no body was around. How they would ever get them down I don't know. They were about twenty feet long must have weighed a ton. Going on we started down a path? If you could call it that. It was really slipping and sliding all the way down. At the bottom there was the native village.

With bravado or stupidity we entered the village. We had to cross a river first. A big slippery log was the bridge. When we were more or less in the center of the huts. They were all grass covered, or whatever the stuff was, roofed. The sides were like lodge pole pine but these were no pine. Our fearless leader, or fool, I like the latter. Called out to the population. There was no answer. The place was deserted. I don't blame them with about six dummies coming into their village. We entered one of the huts and it was for sure someone was living??? There. So we had to start back to the ship. Across the log, and after learning that there were alligators in that river we navigated the log safely. Now another thing started to happen. It started raining cats and dogs. I was bitten three times?? But it did rain hard. You never saw it rain like it could in the south pacific. The path we came down was now a raging stream of water. As I was pulling my self up by a bush I suddenly saw the prettiest snake I had ever seen. Then it dawned on me I didn't like snakes. I didn't notice if the head was arrow shaped or not I just got our of there. We all saw that darn snake. When we finally got to the top and it was raining even harder, if that was possible, we passed the dugout canoes. And into the jungle. You know nothing looked like it did when we went in the other direction. Our fearless leader seemed stumped too. We all were tired but we had to push on and be sure we didn't miss the last boat to the ship. There were times I wondered if I would ever see the Chincoteague again. Push on. Push on. I thought of Mell. I thought of hitting the fearless leader. After ten hours (it seemed) we reached the boat landing. Oh joy, we made it and I was still breathing. So we made it back on board and reality set in. It was quite an adventure.

I typed letters to Mell most every night. I numbered the letters and she did too. When we got mail I got a big share. Mail was the moral builder of a sailor. I was glad I was a radioman as I had typewriters at my disposal. As chief I had no operator duties. I had to make out the duty list and take muster every morning to be sure we weren't missing anyone. Other than that every night I copied the news. For a time it was double duty as I would first copy it on paper then I had to retype it on stencil I can't think of the name of the machine that turned out the finished product. I did that every night. I got so good at it I copied the news; it was from KFS San Francisco at 35 words a minute, on a stencil. My best was three errors. Hey I thought of the name of the machine. It was a mimeograph. You put the stencil on a drum. The ink oozed thru the stencil as you turned the crank "voila" I had a newspaper.

I liked to add items of my own from time to time. One I especially liked was this. "a large air battle took place somewhere, several planes were shot down, and possibly others, if not more" right to the point. Another was "Angus McGregor the inventor of the pay toilet was found dead under the door of one of his pay toilets, he died of suffocation wedged under the door while trying to use it free".

From Tulagi we went to Green Island on the western tip of Bougainvill, in the Bismarck Archipelago. We were back in the firing line. This was taking place in May 1944. We tended PBY's Catalinas. PBM Mariners. And the four engined PB2Y'3. We saw no action there but there was action on Bougainvill. It was there that my good friend Nick Natchicas lost the use of both his legs. With a lot of therapy he finally could walk with braces. While on Green we would walk up a clear stream to a nice pool where we could swim. The water was pure and tasted good. It was jungle all around. While standing in the pool something was biting by toes. I looked and begorrah it was crayfish exactly like I was used to in Powderhorn Lake in Minnesota. I wondered how they got in that forsaken place. We also found out later that there were loose Japs hiding out there too as there were on Tulagi also. We didn't meet any thank God. At this time Rosasco wanted an aircraft receiver so he could listen to the Air Force planes. There was a junkyard; just about every American airfield had junked planes. Either crashed or something. I found a couple of fighters and got a radio out of it and then I had to get enough cable out of two planes to get from the radio shack thru the bulkheads into the captain's cabin. Sometimes I didn't know what I was doing but I did it. Back on the ship I had to splice the two cables together. The wires were color coded so I knew which ones to solder together. Another trick was to peel the shield back on both cables so I could stagger the splices. I did it and pulled the woven metal shield back together and carefully soldered it together. I popped some plugs out of the two bulkheads and threaded the cable thru and into the skippers cabin. I hooked it all up with a speaker but I had to have a special army type battery. I couldn't get it from Navy supply. So it was dead in the water for a time.

We left Green and went to the other end of Bougainvill to Treasury Island, not to be confused with Treasure Island in the bay of Frisco; Treasury was in the Shortland Islands, Bismarck Archipelago. I don't know what we did there so that's that. We went on to Tulagi again then on to Espirito Santo and Munda, New Georgia.

Now it is July 1944 and we are back at Munda and then Efate. Efate was in the movie "Mr. Roberts" with James Cagne, Jack Lemmon and Henry Fonda. It was a good movie. In it some sailors were looking thru a long glass, a powerful glass on the signal bridge. And looking at some nurses in the hospital there. Well I looked thru the longlass on the Chincoteague but I didn't see what they saw.

We were on our way to Auckland, New Zealand. When we got south of Efate we hit a huge storm. The waves were enormous. The chief's quarters were in the bow of the ship. Every time the bow would drop from a wave we were weightless in the air and then drop to the mattress. It was crazy. The storm finally subsided but there were a lot of sick sailors on the Chink. Never serve pork in a storm. When we got to New Zealand I was able to get my chief's uniform. I was given a requisition for the supply depot in Auckland. Chief Cullpepper went with me. I got all the clothes. Dress blues and khaki. Hat and overseas caps. All the goodies. None of it fit right but that would be taken care of. The supply storekeeper sent me to an old lady seamstress. It turn out that this lady did all the alterations for Admiral Byrd. She did all the alterations while we waited and when I put them on it was a perfect fit. She was good. There was no charge the Navy would pay her for it. We didn't have a lot of time to see Auckland. It was mostly a business trip. They loaded six aircraft engine in crates on the topside and we were underway first to Malakula then Guadalcanal where the engines were going to Henderson field. The ship made many islands with personnel and supplies. Esperito Santos, Eniwetok back and forth. Then to Pearl Harbor. That brings up an interesting event.

Somewhere along the line, an officer in CIC (central intelligence center). Which was located just above the radio room, wanted the direction finder removed from its table as he wanted it for a plotting table (i.e. place to put his coffee cup). When they ordered me to remove it I told them that I couldn't per bunavs (bureau of Navy) it would completely ruin the ability to take director finder bearings. Remember that civilian technicians calibrated it in Frisco Bay. Well the officer in question, (this is another name I know but will not use to protect the guilty) he went to the captain and the skipper called me in and said to take it out he would assume the responsibility. (Oh sure?). So I removed it. No small job. The receiver was easy but the azmith scale was another problem. It is a round wheel similar to a driver's wheel. The azmith is from zero to 360 degrees. When a signal is heard you rotate the wheel until the signal is loudest, then press a sense button and if the signal gets louder the direction is what you are reading.

If it gets softer it is 180 degrees in the other direction. That might give you some idea what the gear does. I disconnected the leads to the azmith and that enabled me to remove that part. Now I had two wires hanging down from the loop on the topside of the bridge. It was encased in spaghetti. And porcelain tubes about 3/8 inch. Up on the topside I had to remove the loop and then carefully pull up the wire leads. First making sure the tubes would not fall off. Then replace the loop. I put all the gear in our motor generator room behind the radio room. And this officer was happy. Now the fun stuff starts.

We returned to Pearl Harbor. I was told we had new orders to leave for Palau Island for search and rescue for bombers returning from Japan and that there was to be an admiral's inspection to see if all was in readiness for that operation. Aha?,. What do you think was the most important piece of equipment? Why sure it was the direction finder. The B29's returning from Japan that had to land in the ocean had rubber rafts with what was called a "Gibson Girl" from the ladies of the gay nineties. It was orange and shaped in an hourglass configuration. There was a crank on the top and the operator would hold it steady between his legs. He could send SOS distress signal or M.O.S for a direction finder to pick up. But we didn't have one installed. I didn't hear anything about the skipper taking the responsibility, I didn't hear a word from the officer that wanted the space, and all I heard was "reinstall it before the inspection." I took the receiver over to the electronic building in Pearl, that should have been a dead giveaway but maybe they were not as cognizant as I was about Bunav. It checked out okay so I put I back where it belonged. Then I went topside and removed the loop. Reconnected the leads, I didn't know which lead went where. I might have reversed them. Lowered the leads back down to the radar compartment, reinstalled the loop to the deck and went below. Hooked up the azmith wheel and reinstalled it like it was and told the captain that it was useless like it was but I don't think he cared as long as they would see it during the inspection. The admiral did go thru the ship and nothing was said. All the worrying duty was left to me. I'd never had a bit of material training in my life. What I knew came from manuals and thank god for them.

I have to go back to August again. The ship went to Saipan for a while and recall the episode of Benson's dog at Guadalcanal. Well the results were two puppies were born and named "Saipan and Tinian" I never did know what happened to the mother but I like to think Benson gave her to someone on the island. The two puppies were a star attraction to the whole crew. They were well taken care of and tho there were places things had to happen it was cleaned up. I don't remember where the mystery took place but it was well after a time when the puppies were missing. Now this is what the whole crew thought. There was one officer that didn't like the dogs. Again no names to protect the guilty, but we all figured we knew who the assassin was and he most likely threw the puppies over the side. It was a sad time on the Chicoteague. Those dogs were morale.

We left Pearl in October 1944 for Eniwetok, Bikini and Kossal Roads, the latter being a huge sea anchorage. The whole U.S. Navy could have anchored there. It is part of the Palau Islands, then on to Peleu Atoll in the Palau Group. On our way we picked up a rubber raft but no one was in it. They brought it aboard and I recovered a Gibson Girl from it. The thing was supposed to be waterproof but it was full of salt water. I took it apart and got some carbon tech the stuff you are not supposed to handle without rubber gloves, and with bare hands I washed out the guts of the Gibson Girl. I reassembled it and was very surprised that it worked. While at Kossal Roads an enemy sub launched a torpedo at high tide that enabled it to carry over the reef. It missed us, I don't think it was meant for us anyway, but got an oil tanker. Lots of fire and smoke. We left Kossal Roads for Pelelu and anchored off the island. It was an island that was very costly in life for the U.S. and later figured that it would have been unnecessary to have invaded it. Just bypass it like we did with a lot of enemy islands.

We had shore leave and could go swimming in the lagoon. It was great for finding cat's eyes that were in some to the snails. The cat's eyes made pretty rings. Also when the tide went out there were pools of some of the prettiest tropical fish. Was an interesting place. When we went to play ball the marines would have to sweep the area to be sure there were no Japs around. We had no problems.

It was here I decided to try and calibrate the direction finder. I didn't have a clue as to how to do it but like Sinatra, "I did it my way".

The ship was anchored by the bow and like a weather vane a ship faces the wind. On this day there wasn't much wind but enough so the ship did not stay steady. It would have been much better had we been anchored by the stern also. I gave the Gibson Girl to one of the radioman and had a whaleboat crew circle the ship about a half a mile from the ship. I had requested the boat go as slow as it could to give me time to take enough bearings. I was at the position and had a talker with sound power phones. We called them jx and jv sound power. Tho they had no ac power they worked great. The reason I had that is, as I took a bearing I wanted the quartermaster to give me a polaris reading. (north) I had a sine curve chart in front of me and as I took readings I would put a dot on the chart. When the boat had gone all around the ship I had a number of dots all over the chart and I then drew a perfect curve over the base line and under the base line. If all had been right it would have been through every dot but mine were above and below everything but it was the best I could do. Yet today I don't know how I was able to do some of the things I did without proper training. Common sense and divine help. I had to do it.

I took this masterpiece to the skipper and explained how it was not good but the best under the circumstances. He didn't give me any guff but I think in the back of his mind he knew now what a mistake it was to have taken it out in the first place.

Sail Easy Walgren, CRM, USS Chincoteague, October 1944

It so happened one night, Mr. Crook called me and told me they had a black cat down. That was a PBY that was painted all black and flew at night. I went up to the direction finder and began rotating the azmith and found the m.o.'s I took a bearing and I forget what it was but I'll say 245 degrees. Then I explained to Crook I didn't know if it was that or the reverse of the loop. He said they would send a destroyer the other direction and we would use my 245 degrees. This was all taking place about one a.m. I don't remember the correct time.

Hey I got to change the area. This took place at Kossal Roads. That is where I did the calibration. Anyhow we left the sea anchorage and proceeded on my course. It was leading us into water thought to be mined and close to the Jap held island of Babeltrop. It was figured there were maybe 100,00 Jap troops bypassed on it.

We were underway for the plane, if my bearing was right, when another black cat flew overhead. We gave him my bearing and shortly we heard from them they had flown right over the downed plane. Boy did I feel good part of my work paid off.

Now we are still going slow and wondering about mines. We got to the

PBY and took the crew aboard and hooked a towline to the plane. We slowly left the area and proceeded back to Kossal roads. As we were entering he opening in the reef, it was now daylight, the PBY sank.

So much for that. But I have to say I felt pride in myself for getting the direction finder as good as I did. A plane crew saved I have to say, I like to think that through my efforts during the bombing of the Chincoteague's eleven bombing runs and an estimated 180 bombs dropped at us at Vanikoro and the saving of the five men on the downed PBY in enemy waters I may have had a hand in saving all of our lves. I shouldn't pat my own back but it is the truth.

Chincoteague anchored off Suribachi at Iwo Jima.

All of the preceding events took place after our last trip to Pearl. It all covered the months of October 1944 to February 1945. At that time we left Kossal Roads for Guam. We anchored in the harbor on the west end of the island. I got permission to go to the other end of the island where there was an army supply depot and I figured I could get a battery there for the skipper's Air Force radio.

So I started bumming rides with jeeps 4x4's and anything with wheels. I went thru Agania the biggest town on Guam but it was just a bunch of blown up concrete. On down to the depot. As luck would have it I was able to get the battery and started the same process back to the ship. All alone at times on this God forsaken road until trucks came by. I had been told again that there were bad guys around. Howsoever I made it back safely and hooked it up to the radio and to my surprise it all worked. A thank you from the captain, not on your life.

At Guam we joined in a fleet bound for Iwo Jima. Our skipper had a choice; we could go to Iwo Jima or Okinawa. He chose Iwo. This island

Taken from the Chincoteague at Iwo Jima 1945

is considered one of the Japanese islands. In the latter part of Feb 1945 we went in with the invasion force. We anchored right close to hot rock real name Suribatchi. Our duty was to establish a sea drome for PBM's, mariner planes. They were for flying seriously injured marines and soldiers to hospitals in Guam and also mail what all men hoped for was letters from home. Right away we drew rifle fire from caves up on hot rock. I don't know why they ordered us to weigh anchor and move out of range and put a destroyer in our place and they blew the heck out of all the caves up near the top of the mountain, then we moved back in close. Where we were I could see all the action on the beach. Right below the mountain the island leveled off. There was a steep bank up to the top and all black sand. The marines were hit bad. I grieves me to relate the following. Just glad I wasn't a seaman. They had men, not only from our ship but others, out in whaleboats. They were to take one dog tag off a body and then sink it with pike poles. You have to understand there a lot of casualties and there was no way they could keep anything for a proper burial right on top of that hill was Yamamoto Airfield number one, past that was Yamamoto Field number two. They started getting a lot of equipment up the hill and onto level ground. Field nr. One was secured rather fast. There was cannon fire and flamethrowers all day. That night around one in the morning we were awoke by one of the biggest explosions I have ever heard. Getting to the top side we could see that the Japs had hit an ammo dump and sulfur bombs and all type of ordinance was blowing. Star shells filled the air all night long so the troops could see the enemy. You can't envision it unless you were there. Imagine the Marines fighting a suicidal enemy while you were aboard a clean ship sleeping in a clean bunk and eating hot meals. Makes you think. However we had gone through a bit of it at Vanikoro.

The next day they had advanced enough for a "cat" bulldozer to start making a road to the top of Suribachi. That cat operator was working under fire I know but he kept chugging and making a switchback road to the top. I've listened to some that said they had to climb to the top but they didn't mention it was on the road the dozer made. At any rate I think it was the third day that I watched with binoculars the men raising the first flag. It was a small flag but easily seen on a tall pipe pole. Not long after that they raised the second flag, much bigger and pole not as tall it seemed. It made us all feel good and I'm sure all the Marines and Army personnel on the island felt real good about it.

One afternoon we got word of bandits heading our way. Now there was a lot and I mean a lot of ships off Iwo. The order came to make smoke. Pots on the bow and stern were put to work and it did make a lot of smoke. There were kamikazi attacks but I don't know if anything was hit. All of it was unreal. To me it was like seeing a newsreel only it was real.

The P51 Mustang was a new plane in the pacific and they were at Iwo. I watched one plane making a strafing dive but he didn't pull out. He had to have been hit and he crashed. The same day a damaged B29 limped in. That was the reason for taking Iwo Jima. Mr. Billington, Mr. Crook, myself and the boat crew in a whaleboat took a trip along Iwo. Funny to take a boat trip and just a mile away were the Japs. They had so many tunnels on that volcanic island it must have been amazing. I think we were there for a couple of weeks plus or minus. The island may not have been completely secured but the handwriting as on the wall. We went to Saipan and then to the sea anchorage at Ulithi in the Yap Islands.

It was another huge sea anchorage. We spent March and April there we anchored and commenced usual sea duties. One day we saw a lone aircraft in the air, can you believe it. The darn thing crashed into an aircraft carrier. They figured it came from truk an enemy strong hold that was bypassed and they must have repaired one airplane for this Kamikaze attack. The Carrier Franklin and the Randolf came in and they were severely damaged at Okinawa. Flight deck all twisted and really in bad shape. I don't think they ever repaired them for service again. I don't know.

There was one atoll they called Mog Mog. It was the R&R Island. Many a day the chiefs took a case of beer and Culpepper brought filet steaks and butter. There was a huge cast iron frying pan about three feet by four feet. Culpepper would melt about three pounds of butter on it and then all the steaks and we had a feast fit for a king. Out there a million miles from nowhere. Water water and ships everywhere and we are enjoying ourselves. Looking back it was fun.

Many months before while in Honolulu I had bought a pastel crayon set. I liked to draw many evenings in the chief's quarters. I made many drawings and all of them were the female body. Most with apparel but some nude. Some were plagiarized. I drew them myself but used the playboy pictures to copy. Some I drew from memory. If I do say so I was pretty good. Still have some of the artwork.

Well there came a time when a great experience presented itself. The skipper, and I forgot write that way back in Pearl we got a new skipper named Smith. He was friends with the skipper of the USS Gar, a submarine in the harbor that was being used as a target for a hunter killer exercises out side the anchorage. They made a plan where five men off the sub could spend a day on the ship and five men from the Chincoteague could spend a day on a sub. Many of the crew got on that list. As the days went by my turn was still a little ways off. When it did come I was lucky as two days later we left for the states. We were taken by whaleboat over to the Gar and told we would be staying in the compartment according to our rate.

As I was a chief radioman I went to the radio compartment. It was very small. We were not to wander around the sub but stay there. I got to know one of the guys and he was an artist and a good one so I told him the next group of guys I would send the pastel case to him. He was happy, as all he was using was pencil and ink. We submerged first to a depth of 150 feet and de's (destroyer escorts would drop imaginary depth charges and the sub would blow compressed air out of the torpedo tubes and the bubble on the surface let the ships know how close they came. We went 250 and 350 feet down.

I found that submariners are angle happy. Especially if the sub dives at too steep an angle. When it surfaced it came up like a bubble and burst up and then settled in the water. Somewhat like driving over a hill real fast and your heart ends up in your mouth. I am glad I was able to make that dive in a sub. It enabled me to say years later that I sailed on the ocean, under the ocean and over the ocean when I was flying in the Korean War.

The next day I sent the are stuff to the guy on the Gar. They were the last group to go on her. The Gar, by the way had distinguished record. It had the number of tours to qualify for more safe duty. She sunk a lot of tonnage in her time at sea and they figure you get to a point when the law of averages is against you. I forget hour many tours were involved.

We made preparations for getting underway for the foreign country called "Amarika" ? We first went to Pearl Harbor. We spent enough time there for me to get in touch with a good buddy from home named Freddy Lehman. He was an "A" one mechanic and they put him in charge of keeping all the laundry machines on Ford Island running. He had his own show so to speak. Well he came with me to Honolulu to buy an engagement ring and wedding ring for Mell. I was directed to a jeweler located behind the Aloha Tower and the statue of King Kamehamaha. I picked out a diamond that I could afford, not exactly the "Hope" diamond but made of the same material. Hm. It was good to see Fred. He used to fix the body dents in the racecar.

We were underway in a week for the United States of America. Our destination was the Naval base in San Pedro. Calif. for overhaul.

I received leave immediately and flew up to Oakland. It was wonderful to hold Mell close again. We immediately made plans for our wedding. Mr. Crook was also on leave and lived in Berkeley where he had been an economic professor at the U of Calif. He was to be best man. Mell chose her friend Ida Lauer to be matron of honor and we found an evangelical church close to where Mell was living and made arrangements with Reverend Burr. We had to get blood tests, which we did and we were all set in three days to get married.

Crook and his wife Mina, Ida, Rev. Burrs wife, was witness and the beautiful bride in a light blue tailored coat and skirt with a classy white hat, the groom in his uniform, and Crook in his, it made a nice military wedding. The church could hold at least a thousand but there were only seven of us. The world was in attendance as far as I was concerned.

L to R: Ida Lauer, Mell, Sail Easy, Lt. Stanley Crook, July 3, 1945

It must have been a good marriage as Mell and I have been married for sixty years this coming July 3rd 2005.

Having been out to sea for so long I had a lot of money on the books so I was pretty flush. We made arrangements for our honeymoon and I bought tickets to St. Louis, Mo. On a Union Pacific Roomette. This was as classy as you could travel at the time. Our own little room with all the conveniences. Beautiful dining car. It was high living. In Salt Lake City they unhooked our car and now we were on the "Wabash Cannonball" we had time to walk around Salt Lake City for a little while and it was there I heard the song, "When Orchid Bloom in the Moonlight'' funny how songs help you to remember certain events.

We arrived in St. Louis and I met all of Mell's relatives. I had to pass inspection so to speak. I liked her Uncle Clifford and Aunt Cora immediately. They drove us to Carlyle, Illinois where her mother and father lived. About sixty miles east of St. Louis. I guess I passed inspection there too. They were all 4.0 people as far as I was concerned.

We went back to St. Louis and Mell had to buy lighter clothes as what she had was cool bay area apparel. Then we flew to Minneapolis to meet my family. It was just a little plane a Beechcraft two-engine job. Mell hates small airplanes. When we landed at Wold Chamberlain airport my whole family was let out of prison for the event? No they weren't they were all good Scandinavian stock. When we had gotten our luggage and I was pleasantly surprised to see one of the Maise twins from high school as a red cap there. We shook hands and hugged. They were two good friends, meanwhile back at the ranch; my brother passed himself off as my cousin.

I may have mentioned that we were all together in previous pages but all that came later. This was the first time he had seen Mell. Well, we all ended up at 3048 10th Ave. So. In the house I was born. We didn't have much time as I only had I think two weeks leave. But we made the most of it.

When it came time to leave the whole bunch was at the Milwaukee Station to see us off. My mother, bless her, handed me a bag of sandwiches to eat on the train. This time we did not travel in style. The coach I think was made in 1816 and the noise was clickity clak. We did have a pullman car tho. Top bunk. Boy did we enjoy the pork chop sandwiches my mother made. With pickle. We both thought we had never tasted anything so good.

We arrived in Los Angeles Union Station and took the P.E. (pacific electric) red car to Long Beach. Checked Naval housing and found it a lot to be desired so to a USO on Pacific Blvd to see about civilian homes.

We were given an address on Signal Hill on Cherry Street. I remembered the folks name for years but it must be tucked in brain cell I cannot open anymore. They were certainly nice people.

We went into Los Angeles and Hollywood. At a dance at the Palladium in Hollywood we had been there for a little while and between dances were in the foyer and I saw a chief in a gray uniform, we had different uniforms we could wear. Dress blues, tan, light gray and khaki. Anyway I hollered at this chief as I recognized him from the back, it was my brother Gaylord; neither of us knew the other was in the area. His minesweeper was in Long Beach too. Well we were together for dinner a few nights.

It was the first part of August 1945 when the U.S. dropped the atomic bomb on Hiroshima. That was on my father's birthday August 6th. Then within a week one on Nagasaki. That did it the war was over after five years. Mell and I were in downtown Los Angeles when this was announced and the people went crazy and I don't blame them. It was a good feeling. Things then started happening fast. For the Navy they came up with a point system. All you needed was twenty points to be discharged. There were points for time in the Navy, points for time out of the states. Points for sea duty and points for battles. Mine added up to over eighty points. I was high point man on the ship. My brother didn't

SAVE

WAR DEPARTMENT
OFFICE OF THE CHIEF OF STAFF
WASHINGTON 25, D. C.

25 July 1945

TO: General Carl Spaatz
Commanding General
United States Army Strategic Air Forces

1. The 509 Composite Group, 20th Air Force will deliver its first special bomb as soon as weather will permit visual bombing after about 3 August 1945 on one of the targets: Hiroshima, Kokura, Niigata and Nagasaki. To carry military and civilian scientific personnel from the War Department to observe and record the effects of the explosion of the bomb, additional aircraft will accompany the airplane carrying the bomb. The observing planes will stay several miles distant from the point of impact of the bomb.

2. Additional bombs will be delivered on the above targets as soon as made ready by the project staff. Further instructions will be issued concerning targets other than those listed above.

3. Dissemination of any and all information concerning the use of the weapon against Japan is reserved to the Secretary of War and the President of the United States. No communiques on the subject or releases of information will be ~~issued by Commanders~~ in the field without specific prior authority. Any news stories will be sent to the War Department for special clearance.

4. The foregoing directive is issued to you by direction and with the approval of the Secretary of War and of the Chief of Staff, USA. It is desired that you personally deliver one copy of this directive to General MacArthur and one copy to Admiral Nimitz for their information.

Thos T Handy
THOS. T. HANDY
General, G.S.C.
Acting Chief of Staff

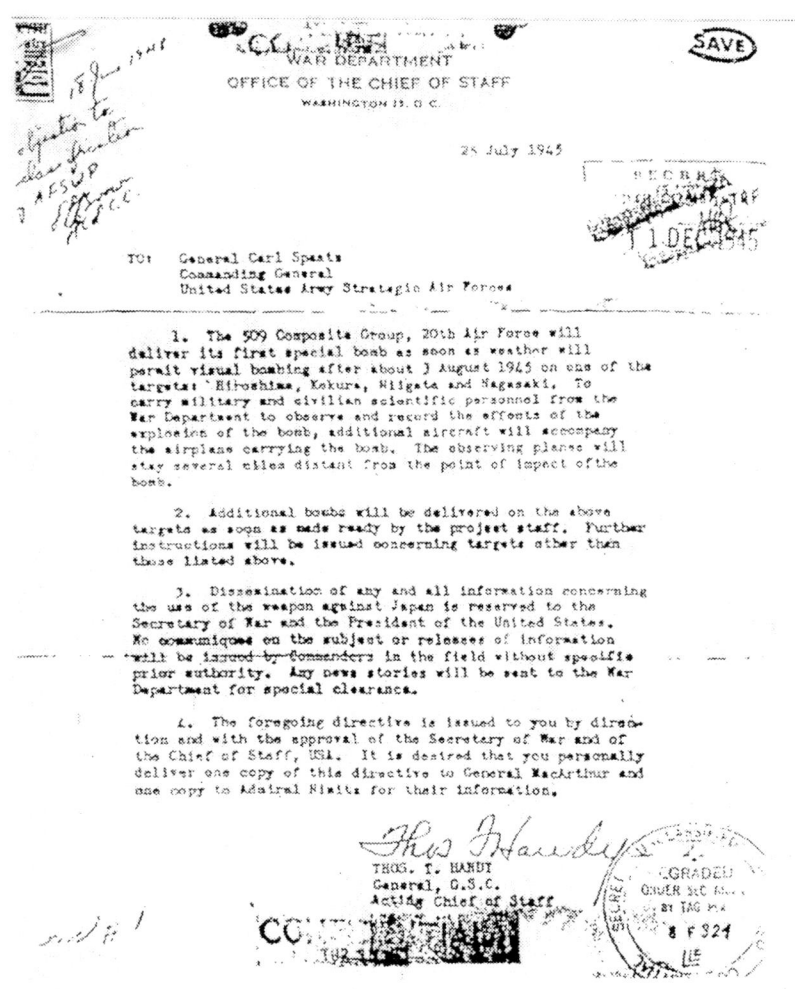

This is the Atomic Bomb message.

quite have twenty but they sent him to the Chicago Navy pier to get a half point I think it was and that is where he got his ruptured duck. The symbol of discharge. Captain Smith said he could keep me for sixty days as I was in communications. Yeoman and radiomen were vital to the discharging of personnel. Mell went back to Oakland and the Chincoteague went to San Diego. I sent for her again and she flew there. I was still disgusted at being held. I finally went to COM eleven. The admiral in charge, I always wanted to see the top man and I did. Told him my story and went back to the ship. Mell had already gone back to Oakland. A message from COM 11 came to the ship and it said "no man with points to be discharged would be taken away from the states. Ha ha I'd won. They offered me radio electrician to stay in the Navy that was a half of a commission. I wanted out. Brasswitz a yeoman first and I were told to get our things together for transfer to a discharge station in Diego. It was fast. I gave away a lot of things I would have liked to have kept but I couldn't handle it all. All my records in the chief's quarters I donated to them. Uniforms went to my buddies. Leo Neal Nash a chief gunners mate was a very close friend and I gave him a bunch of stuff. And Brasswitz and I walked down the gangway to North Island and the ferry to Diego without looking back. I have held that against him forever. Many men had the points but their enlistments were not over yet. When I left the Chincoteague it was only two hours later that she sailed for Tsingtao, China.

When I got to the building where other men being discharged were being sent to different camps closer to their homes. It was funny; there was the chief that had been on the Chincoteague that was transferred in Pearl Harbor. I always thought him to be a career sailor but here he was getting out. It was a very cool meeting. I don't think he cared for me and I cared less for him. We had had our differences. I just knew too much about Naval regulations for him to get the best of me. Thanks for my two years on the flagship USS Northampton. All of that is now behind me.

Benson and I flew to Oakland, I was supposed to be at Alameda Air Station but they made me get off in Frisco and I was put on a bus to Camp Shoemaker north of Oakland. Now Mell was waiting for me there. So I had Benson find her and tell her what happened. It didn't take long for us to go through the system and get our ruptured ducks. First they asked if there was anything wrong with us. I put no knowing that my hearing was bad and I had tinnitus, ringing ears. That was my big mistake. Anyhow I was discharged and had it in my nicotine stained fingers. I boarded a Navy bus for Oakland and finally had Mell in my arms again. Many Navy men don't know that when they are discharged you are legally still in the Navy for twenty-four hours. Then you are in the clear.

Chapter Five

Civilian Life

Mell was working at a photo co. called Bear Photo. And I was unemployed. I went to the Oakland police department and applied for motorcycle cop. I thank my lucky stars I did not get that job but I came close. My visit to a U.S. employment office was better. I had a little booklet from the Navy that explained what the duties and knowledge of a chief radioman was. The woman I talked to said it was the equivalent to two years of college and sent me to the Shell development plant in Emeryville a suburb of Oakland and I talked to a Mrs. Ainsworth the head of employment. The fact that I had taken chemistry in high school also helped. She hired me. It was a very interesting job and I took to it easily. My mechanical skills helped also. This was an experimental plant. Shell was, and I guess still is owned by the Netherlands. They had a lot of thick glasses there. What they developed in test tubes and retorts they made a pilot plant to refine materials from the waste products from gasoline and oil refineries. While I worked there they developed 100 motor oil. It was the first oil that stayed the same viscosity in below zero. That means it didn't thicken in cold weather. Years before with my motorcycle, it used nr 60 oil, I had to use a blowtorch to thin the oil so the kick-starter would work. I worked there for about nine months.

We learned soon that Mell was pregnant and the baby was due in July. We were exuberant. I had bought a 1942 Buick convertible, gosh it was neat. And I think it was in April or May we went to Yosemite Park. There was practically no one else there. We had the park to ourselves. I had a good plate camera with me and took pictures of Mell sitting on the tonneau of the Buick. With Yosemite Falls in back of her, another at Glacier Point and by the redwoods. Gee it was nice having the whole park to ourselves. That day is gone forever.

We bought baby things. And the wife of a friend at Shell loaned us the most beautiful bassinet that any baby ever had. In the meantime at work I was offered a chance to go to the U of Calif in Berkeley for chemical engineering. They would pay for my collage and make my work schedule work so I could go. At that time I got a letter from my father wanting me to return to Minneapolis and go into contracting building houses as a partner. I broached this to Mr. Wick who thought a lot of me and he said,"Sherman any time you can be your own boss is good and you should take it" well at the moment I could not as the baby was due soon. We went to the doctor and received some sad news. The doctor could not find a heartbeat. We knew we had some problems as Mell was rh negative and I was positive. Today that isn't a problem but in 1946 it was. You couldn't imagine to more sorrowful individuals then Mell and I. We got back to the apartment and saw all the baby things and I think we just sat there and cried. At around 7:15 pm Mell said her water broke. I got her in the car and raced for the hospital. She was admitted right away and I'm in the waiting room. Must have been around a little after eight a nurse came in and said I was the proud father of a baby girl. I didn't care which it was I asked, "does it have all it's buttons?" Thank God she did. They then said when they couldn't hear the heart beat it was because the hearts were beating in unison. I called Shell and Mr. Wick told me to take all the time I needed to take care of Mell and the baby. I was off two weeks and they paid me for the whole time. It didn't take a law or anything. The place was good to me. I took care of everything. I still have the graphs I made of many ounces of milk Carleen drank and every movement. It was like the Navy, concise. Still have those graphs.

I didn't leave Shell until September I think. Before that we had a big fire in the low side of chem two. It was where there were centrifuges for make epi clhoridren crystals very toxic. It was burning like fury and it was at night. A fire engine was stuck in a turn it couldn't make and couldn't back out they said. Well right outside the corrugated metal wall was about six fifty gallon drums of acetone. If that blew that would be all she wrote so three of us rolled them away from the fire. The fireman came in another entrance and soon had the fire out. Was scary to say the least.

I have to tell you about the baby. When I brought her home from the hospital, Mell had to stay about three days more. The wife of Thorgaard my friend from work helped me make formula and fix bottles etc. I was all-alone feeding Carleen a bottle but she wasn't getting any. I called the hospital maternity ward and they said take a red-hot needle and enlarge the hole in the nipple, I did that and tried again. I damn near drowned her. The hole was too big. So I tried again and it all worked out fine. I did all the laundry of diapers and the neighbors said I had the whitest wash in the neighborhood.

Now we are moving to the midwest. I think it was September, 1946. There wasn't much to pack we didn't have much. I drove Mell and the baby over the Oakland bay Frisco bridge to the airport and sent them to St. Louis. I then went back across the bridge and loaded what we had and gassed up and started driving to St. Louis. I had been up late the last night. Up early the next morning and it was afternoon before I was on the road. I went thru Vallejo and on my way to Salt Lake City. I drove all night and in the early light I don't know if I saw an illusion or what but a horse passed me going the other way. I was taking nodoz tablets. I reached Salt Lake and on my way to Kansas City which was my goal.

There was all kinds of road work going on and detours. Rough roads that worked against me. I was hearing noises when I stopped in Salina, Kansas. I got a room in a private house, as there were no rooms open at what motels there were. In those years there were not as many as there are today. They sent me to this private house. I parked the car and didn't even worry about it; again in those years most people were honest. The next day I took the car to a garage and they lowered the oil pan and said the crankshaft was grooved. That is real bad news. It was because a fifty cent small tube that went around the back of the engine from the crankcase and registered the oil pressure on the oil gauge on the dashboard had vibrated against the engine block and worn a small hole. I black topped a lot of road in back of me. But the pressure was still enough to tell me that I had pressure and all was well when it wasn't.

I reached St. Louis and the family was again together. My mother was visiting a cousin there. So I saw her too. Then I took the car to a Buick garage and they looked at it and said I'd be better buying a whole new blue flash engine then repairing all the parts that needed replacing. It would cost 5oo dollars. I only paid 1200 for the car. That was in opa days. Office of price administration. I had to borrow the money from my sister and brother in law in Minneapolis. Now I have a new car practically. I couldn't stay too long there and had to get to Mpls to earn money. Mell stayed with her aunt. My mother was with me for the trip north. In Mpls I lived with my sister Dorothy. Mell came home by train later and that was where we stayed. My father wasn't ready to do business so I got a job with a sheet metal outfit. Fred Holmberg was one of the most grouchy men I have ever met but I liked him just the same. I worked with an older man named Carl Norberg who also was a pilot and had an old Jenny that he flew by the seat of his pants. We got along real well.

Our first house, May, 1948.

When my father was ready, Fred wanted me to stay in sheet metal but I had to leave. My father had lost a lot of money in 1929 and he was not going to gamble. We built homes for private individuals for 10% cost plus or minus. We were locked in a small profit. The speculators were selling holes in the ground before the house was built. Remember there were millions of servicemen returning and needing housing. I had bought a lot for 600 dollars on 56th and 27th Ave. Right next to my sister Marjorie so we moved from Dor's to Mig's house, my dad and I built the house. He in the daytime and I at night. That was while I was still working in sheet metal. When it was done it was a pretty small 850 square foot house. And we moved into to it. I made a white picket fence around the backyard and we bought a Cocker Spaniel puppy and life was beautiful. Wasn't making a lot of money but it was still beautiful. One day as I was roofing our house Russ Lee my racing buddy drove up and hollered to me that the squadron he was in at the airport need a chief radioman. Here was my chance I thought, to fly. I did join the Navy again in 1947 I was in VP73 a patrol squadron. We had R4D's (Navy for dc3's) pv2's lodestars. PBY's and SNB's all I had to do was go to meetings one-week end a month. I went on a two-week cruise to Bemidji, Minnesota for drills and made enough money to buy new carpeting for our little living room. I enjoyed the squadron it was made up of a lot of friends from Central High School; Gordon Moe was the exec. Harold Blaackstad was a pilot. Burton Hovde also a pilot. We all graduated together. You might notice the preponderance of Norwegian names. That is Minnesota, uff dah. One Sunday we were to test fly an SNB Beech. A small two-engine plane. Blaackstad was the left side (main pilot) and I forget the right side co pilot. All Navy planes are gassed full when they land so to be ready for the next flight. There was de André the plane captain, Freddie Lehman who was also in the squadron and I. Five of us. I was just flying as a passenger to get my six hours a month for flight skins. We taxied to the start of the runway. And they poured the gas to it. We were rolling along for takeoff and I was looking at a new Boeing Stratocruiser at the airport terminal. All of a sudden I smelled smoke. An emergency horn sounded and I looked out to see the propellers banging concrete and we skidded for a long time to a stop. When it did stop we stepped out the door right onto the concrete. The plane was a total loss. What happened was. A switch on the instrument panel for the landing gear should have had a metal cover over it. That means the gear is locked and until the cover is removed so you can move the toggle switch for retracting the gear after you are airborne. The way it was when the plane started to lift a little the gear started to lift and then the weight of the airplane forced the motors to burn up and they said we looked like a rocket ship going down the runway. It was a more thrilling ride than anything at Disneyland. Navy air police took us immediately separately for questioning. Heck, I couldn't tell them anything. The next day I'm again flying with Blaackstad and a good pilot by the name of Chambers is flying right side. I'm in the tower in the radioman's position. We are coming in for a landing and I saw the fence of the airport below me when I looked out the windshield all I saw was blue sky, I should have seen runway. Just then Chambers grabbed the throat (the control name) and jerked Blaackstads hands off. We bounced in from quite high, Chambers hit the brakes we bounced again and he hit the brakes and were coming up to the other end of the runway and a big chain link fence Chambers turned the tail wheel the starboard wing almost dragged the ground and we came to a stop. Then and there I told Blaackstad I wouldn't fly with him again. In an aircrew if you don't have faith in your pilot you don't have to fly with him. My only crash in an airplane thank God. After much time they came up with 5o% pilot error and 50% mechanical failure. In my book there is no such thing. The cover should have been checked off the check off list before take off.

The skipper said we were going to have an inspection by Comnine. That would be the admiral in Glenview, Illinois; it would be held in one of the hangers. Eldon Leunow, a chief instrument man, and I decided not to wear any ribbons (signifying medals), as we had never had any presented to us officially. Well came the inspection. All the white hats were lined up in from of us. The inspection party with the admiral in front were walking by the white hats with a check of a hat here and a neckerchief adjustment there and then going by the ten chiefs. I noticed Eldon didn't live up to what we had agreed to so I was the only without ribbons. The admiral sailed by and then stopped about ten feet past me and all the rest of the entourage kind of bumped into each other. He came in front of me and said "you rate some ribbons don't you chief" and I replied "yes admiral but as yet I have not had any presented to me" he said "you can buy them over at the ship's store"". And I said "sir, I understand that medals are supposed to be awarded by the secretary of the Navy, or by an officer, per the secretary of the Navy and I don't believe a man should be able to buy glory" he had a chest full of them and he said, "your right, but get them" "yes sir" I replied. Well I was right. As they walked on Cmdr. Misner, the skipper said, "get a hair cut" this is for the lack of anything else to say.

Time went by. It was winter and around zero. I was in a PV2 warming up the engines. From the cockpit window I saw an officer and about six sailors in pea coats hupping along and coming to a halt off the port wingtip. The officer, by hand signals, motioned for me to depart the plane, which I did. I was called to attention and the officer pulled out a little case and opened it, took out a medal and pinned it on me and saluted me and I him. The officer was Gordon Moe my boyhood friend that I'd known all my life. The medal was a good conduct medal with my name on the back and 1943 denoting my first one. At last, I was awarded a medal the way it was supposed to be done. What is right is right.

Building was going right along and we were building a nice house just west of the city. It was interesting to work on. The only time I every laid a plank oak floor with walnut butterflies and pegs to cover the screw holes. Really was a piece of art or I should say, of Sherman. Bob Berdahl was putting up sidewall shingles on a scaffle on an end gable. When I heard a loud cuss word. I ran out to see him getting in a window finally out the door. His hammer was on the ground under where it all happened, Bob, without a word got in his car and went home. When I talked to him that evening he told me he had folded skin and meat off his finger. I don't blame him for throwing his hammer down and going home I would have done the same thing. In fact I've done it.

Chapter Six

Korean War

A few days later, it is now around the middle of June. The Korean "police action" by the United? Nations. Which means Uncle Sam. Is making the news. Bobby drives up got out of the car and hollered "your back in the Navy" they activated VP73 the squadron I was in. I was to report immediately. It was hard to leave my father at this time to finish the houses we had going but there was no way of getting out of the service. I didn't even try. One may be missed but can always be replaced I learned that a long time ago. Well, I had to report to the air station right away. We were in the auditorium and an intelligence officer spoke to us about what was happening. We signed "power of attorney" papers for our wives or parents what ever the case may be. I finally was able to go home and tell Mell, it broke her heart, that I had just three days to get things in order. We had just bought a new statesman Nash. Only had about three hundred miles on it. There we so many things to do. I was building a garage, most of it was finished but the garage door wasn't in yet. You know after world war two I just didn't think I would ever see another war but here it is. Such is life.

The day before our departure I had to stay at the Naval station to be ready early the next morning. They had ten r4d's to transport the squadron to Whidbey Island, Washington. When we were all loaded the planes one by one taxied to the strips and took off. We flew right over our house and I knew Mell was standing down there looking. Very sad. As we headed west we sat in bucket seats not like on commercial planes. Many of the men were very young and had never even flown before. The plane bounced up an down and sideways and there was a bit of sickness odors in the plane. That did not bother me but the engines seem to hum a song that was popular at the time. "Good bye Irene good bye" only the engines sang "good bye Carleen good bye" all the way west. We landed around noon in Rapid City, South Dakota for lunch. As we got out of the plane there were air police lined up from the planes to the mess hall. We were warned not to look at the aircraft on the base. They were B52's long-range bombers. Here we are the good guys and we can't look. We took off again and landed at Sand Point Naval Air Station in Seattle for dinner. Then on to Whidbey Island, Washington. It is right on Puget Sound.

World War two was just five years earlier so the base was in pretty good shape. The chiefs had their own barracks but it was nothing fancy. We were getting new aircraft. Not brand new but new to the squadron. Also they brought in a lot in regular Navy sailors so we were a fair sized bunch. The planes were P2V Neptunes loaded with electronic gear. Jamming radar and regular radar so we all had to go back to school. The radio aircrew members, of which I was one. Took many radar flight in a R4D. The pilots were ap's or enlisted men pilots. They were chiefs. I got to know in the chief's club on the base. We would fly up the 'Skagit Valley" between mountains. On the radar you could see all the mountain ridges and what was in front of you in glittering gold on the scope. When we would come in for a landing you could see the runway, all the hangers and with altitude rings on the scope you knew approximately how high you were. Flying over Seattle the buildings and streets were visible. Not like a picture but again glittering gold as the sweep went by. When landing we put it on quarter scan. The hand would look like a windshield wiper then. We were trained to land the plane just using radar. The pilot had a black shield in front of him. As we saw certain islands in the sound we would have him change course and again by another island and we could head him in straight for the airport. As we closed and watched the altitude rings we could tell him your 100 feet off the ground and he could take over by visual control. Believe it or not it worked.

We also trained in the automatic turret guns. Everyone had to know what the other did incase he was incapacitated. It took quite a time. The pilots wanted new earphones. They were in bad shape. They requisitioned to no avail. Old Walgren knowing a bit of Navy supply took one of the nonrated men and went to a barracks that had been used previously by radio personnel. I found a box with old earphones and took them to the supply room and handed them over. In the Navy if you turn one in you can draw one. Navy regulations. So I got all new phones and muffs for the pilots. Gained a little respect. We also needed an "apu" unit. That is a generator mounted on a jeep for starting aircraft engines. Again their requisitions did not work. I talked to a supply chief in the chief's club, he was in charge of all the mothballed equipment in Oak Harbor, the biggest little city on Whidbey. He told me to come over the next day and he would have one ready for me. I did and drove it back to ault field. More respect. It paid to listen when I was on the USS Northampton. The chiefs club was like all Navy chiefs.

There were many slot machines of different values. No dollar machines I don't thing they had them yet. It was from the money taken in that the club was able to be viable. We had it nice.

I was at the movies when they stopped the movie and inserted a message. It said chief radioman Walgren report to the execs office. I did and found that Mell and Carleen were in a cafe in Mount Vernon, Washington. She had taken driving lessons and with Carleen about four years old had driven west. The people in the cafe told her not to drive the road to Ault field. They called it suicide highway. It is all curves and crosses Deception Pass where the water is very fast depending if the tide is going out or coming in. Quite a sight. Anyhow I had to bum my way into Mount Vernon. When I found them it was quite the happy reunion. Mell told me how she started out and drove to Willmar, Minnesota and stopped to eat. Then both back in the car and things I guess didn't look right and when she got to Litchfield, Minn. She knew she was heading back to Mpls. Then things went better but for someone not used to mountain driving she had a time with, the Firth of the Forth, which is a pass in Idaho. Then she had to cross the Snoqualmie Pass in Washington and that is a high one. She did well and gets a gold star. Now we got wheels. The next thing was to get somewhere to live. It so happened that chief Hoy a, good friend, and his wife Lois she was a classy lady, the only one that, in the chief's club in Mpls I had drank beer out of her slipper only it was an opened toed slipper. I still did it. To go on, they were moving into a Quonset house in Naval housing so we rented the cabin on the sound about 18 miles from the base. It was a rock road and dusty but I drove it every morning home for lunch and back in the evening.

The lady that owned it had a big dog and Carleen was with it all the time. I worried a bit because she would go down by the water and look at all the jellyfish in the water. However she was a good kid. One day she brought something to show her mother. That was a real surprise, she had a black snake. I think it was a wood snake and non-poisoness. I would bring the other radioman home for dinner but they had to bring their own silverware. They were, Cotton, Gibbons, my partner in plane two, and Kucera. All 4.o guys. We decided to go to Mount Baker so off we went. By the time we got part way up and it was pitch dark. We suddenly had to stop. It seemed the road had disappeared and there were bulldozers trying to make a new one. Off to the side of the road all we could see were the tops of tall fir trees so it must have been quite a drop.

When they finished with a makeshift road we continued to the mount Baker Lodge. We had hot cocoa and then looked over the gift shop. Carleen liked a little bear that crawled so we got that for her. That bear lasted for many many years. Then Mell, Carleen in the front seat and the others in the back, we started down the mountain. Baker is a big one. Just a little below Rainier in height. When we reached lower elevations there was considerable fog so it was a little apprehensive driving but being a good driver we returned the guys to the base and we went to our cabin. Writing about Baker on one of our training flights. There were six radiomen at their own radar positions. Like a school room then the heart of the radar went out. That is the magnitron. A rather costly thing. Then the pilots would go hunting for places to go hunting. I had some of the darndest flights you can imagine. We flew over the top of Mount Baker and made a steep bank around the peak it almost looked like we left wingtip tracks in the snow. I am not kidding. That was a thousand dollar ride at Disneyland at least.

One morning when we left on a training flight I knew the pilot had had a bit to drink at the club the night before. We kind of fishtailed down the runway and into the wild blue yonder. Did our thing and when we landed you could have had a full coffee cup and not spilled a drop the landing was so smooth. He had good hands on the controls.

Mell, Carleen and I drove into Seattle to see John Shepherd, the radioman from the Chincoteague. We found his apartment and he asked if he could borrow a set of pictures I had bought back in 1945 that showed a lot of the islands, dead Japs. And etc. He said he wanted to make copies and then send them back. When Mell was home she sent those to him. I never saw them again. I never understood it because he was a darn good shipmate. On our way back to Ault Field I was back under water. Boy did it rain. Only place I ever saw it rain harder was in the south pacific.

We made another drive up to Vancouver, Canada. A very interesting town. Bought some bone ware china and I bought a nifty knife with a scissors. Then back to the base. It was then fall with winter in the forefront and Mell had to go back to our house in Minneapolis. She wanted me to drive her to Helena, Montana which I did. That skipped the two high passes and made it a little easier for her. In Helena I returned to Whidbey by bus. It was sad to leave them.

When she got back to Mpls. She rented our house to my racing buddy Russ Lee. You might remember he was the one that got me to join the squadron, as they needed a chief radioman. Well when we were activated Russ was transferred to a Fasron unit and he didn't go with us. Freddy Lehman got poisoned by the shot they gave him and he didn't go. I was the hero? To defend our country. To continue, Mell wanted to drive to St. Louis and stay with her Aunt Cora. There was one heck of a blizzard and Russ said no way he would drive her through the storm and he did. Then he took a bus back. One good guy now deceased.

I'm back flying; Mr. Hollingsworth is my pilot in plane 2 now I'm listening to code messages. In airplanes we did not have typewriters we hand printed the messages. I was having difficulty hearing the code at times. Also I had trouble setting frequencies up with the freq meter at the high kilocycles the signals. In vhf and uhf the signals are faint and I couldn't hear them due to the losing of some hearing just by altitude. "Houston, we have a problem" I went to the sick bay and reported this. They gave me a hearing test and said I was fifty percent deaf. That's a big help. But they were not going to do anything about it. I had to see another Navy doctor in Oak Harbor and they took action. They cut orders for me to be transferred to the Naval hospital in Bremerton, Washington immediately. So again I'm off. I spent all of December in the same quiet room I was in 1942 only this time there was no Miss French.

After about six hearing tests. Each one should be primarily the same. It is a graph showing the loss as opposed to 100 and where my ears were ringing the graph went all the way to the bottom this is done so one cannot fake their hearing. One could never push the button in the same place six times. So the end result was I would be immediately discharged. The doctor said there was no way to tell if my hearing would get worse or stay the same. For the most part I think he was right but as I write this I think it is worse. They said I was 40 percent loss on the left ear and 50 percent on the right. They discharged me around January 10th I think. It was funny, not haha, that, had they put me back on active duty, they would not have sent me back to the squadron as my rate was general duty chief which is senior to aviation chief but I wasn't an airdale so the billit I was going to was another AVP in Tsintao, China. Odd how things workout. But I was going home. I took an American Airline Constellation to Chicago and transferred to the Ozark Airline to St. Louis. Upon landing the family was together again and happiness reigned. While there we went to Carlyle to Mell's parents and I'm sitting in the living room and her dad across the room and he shouted real loud the famous words now on television for verizon "can you hear me now Sherman?" it was kind of funny, I wasn't that deaf but enough so I laughed at a lot of jokes tho I did not hear the punch line. You go thru life saying a lot of huh's. While in St. Louis I did a lot of carpenter work for her, Aunt Cora. She was the kind of person you really wanted to do things for. Her kitchen sink looked like 1902 so I tore out the whole thing and built a new cabinet, reset a new sink and new linoleum top. Would have used plastic but they didn't have it in small pieces. Then I found a big wasted space in the wall just to the left of the sink. I cut through that and found enough space for an insert cabinet. I built that and cased it like it had always been there. She sure appreciated the added shelf space for dishes. Uncle Clifford meanwhile had taken my half Wellington boots to the basement where he had a complete shoemaker shop. That was what he had always worked in, shoes was a big business in St. Louis. He resoled the boots and put on new heels. A first rate job too. Then it was time to return home to Minneapolis.

Chapter Seven

1954 Move to California

1990 Move to Illinois

2000 Move to Arizona

We left St. Louis and the weather was great but up in Iowa it started to snow. By the time I hit Hastings, Minnesota it was a blizzard and night. I took it easy and we got to 5552 27th Ave So. About nine in the evening. Colder than the Dickens. We got inside. Russ and his mother had left, as they knew we would be coming back. My sister Marjorie lived right next door so she came over. Then my brother in law Virgil came in and said the cops were writing a ticket on my car. I went out side. And they said I didn't have the new plates on for 1951. I explained that I had just been separated from the Navy and just arrived home and the new plates were inside the house on the TV. They just said they couldn't do anything about it as they had already written the ticket. Well a fine thing. The next day, in uniform, I went to the courthouse to see the mayor. I wasn't going to pay a fine. I did get to see mayor Poulson and he brought in his staff member and told him to take care of it and I was to go home and forget it. I did forget it until little later I got a call from the courthouse telling me there was a warrant for my arrest. A fast trip back down town and I did see the mayor again. Told him my story and he got another guy to take care of it and assured me this time it would be taken care of. I never got another call but a week later I read in the Minneapolis Journal that his assistant was fired. Always thought it was because of me that happened. Always go to the top if you want something done.

It didn't take long to get back to building houses. There was Bob Berdahl, Forrest Cornelius, Mr. Hanson and I. While I was gone. My dad came to the job being picked up by Forrest and so things went fairly good. There was just one owner that wasn't happy. I doubt if he was ever happy at anytime. He claimed my father had the carpenters space the roof boards, which wasn't so. The one by six or eight roof boards have moisture in them and when they dry they contract. If they are dry and get wet the expand causing roof shingle to rise I little in places I went up on the roof and pulled a few nails and renailed them down and he was happy. They would have gone down on their own had roof board had time to dry. Then a door didn't close right I fixed that and a few louvers in a vent were a little crooked and all this made him happy and he was glad I was back. The feelings were not mutual. He was a dingy.

Now there was a period of time life just goes on. We had some good neighbors Elmer Lotus and his wife. Elmer and Lotus, we called her by her last name had a lot of fun together. Elmer had finished putting in my garage door while I was on active duty. We were buddies. We went fishing a lot to Malmo on Lake Mille Lacs the guy that ran the fishing lodge was a farmer from Iowa that moved to Malmo. His wife was the ugliest woman I ever saw. I think she took ugly pills but she thought I was a movie star so I liked her. The fishing was for walleyes the best fresh water eating fish in the world. We got them up to six eight pounds. Elmer Dick, another friend, and I was at the helm we trolled a June bug spinner for walleye. I got a good one and Dick had one and Elmer was sleeping in the bow holding on to his fishing rod. I got the idea of pulling his line by hand and I put my fish on his hook and released it back into the water. When it was fully out I gave the line a tug and Elmer shot up all excited and began reeling in. All of a sudden the line went limp and he said it got away and he laid back down. I could have killed him. He lost my fish.

We were also hunting partners. I practically had my own hunting preserve for ducks and pheasants. My cousin Harold Felts farm in Kandiohi, Minnesota. Elmer and I are walking a fence line when I bird flew up. I shot and Elmer shot. I was at the side of the bird and Elmer shooting at the stern. Who killed cock robin no that was not it who got the bird. We pulled feathers right in the field to find the shot entered from the side. It was my bird. Another time Harold said he had to burn a big patch of reeds to keep down corn boarers, so he started the fire. Elmer and I laying in wait. The pheasants kept darting in and out and when the fire came to the end of the field.

It sounded like the battle of the bulge. We fired at anything. Harold said he would keep the roosters and we would have the hens. They were the only legal ones. We got our limit in no time. Bob Berdahl, Jonesie another neighbor another good guy and I can't remember his name but he was married to Nick Natchicas's sister "Vi" were hunting on my cousins farm. Jones had his uncle's hunting dog?? With him. His uncle also lived close to my cousin's farm and had loaned him his hunting???? Dog. We walked cornfields and the dog ahead of us about a block scaring up birds and we didn't get a shot at them. I could have shot the dog and eaten him. Meanwhile Bob and Nicks brother in law are playing war and shooting at each other. No really but like two little kids. Crawling on their bellies and such. It was a laugh but not hunting.

I've got to say. I had so many good friends I've got to pay them tribute right now. If friends were money I'd be a multi millionaire. There was Gordy Moe, Johnny Santrizos, Dave Berdahl, Robert Berdahl, Robert Orfield. Miney Orfield, Jim Hirchberg, Paul Bjork, Freddie Lehman,

James Holt, Clifford Anderson, and Russ Lee. All the preceding are now deceased. As Fred's wife said, "your the last of the Mohicans" so I guess I am "Uncus" he was the last. Mohican. I still have one neighborhood friend left that is Jimmy Knudson, he called me yesterday and we talked over old times that was on February 28, 2005. We are both 86 and will be 87 he on Sept 12th and I on the 21st of October. I thank God for knowing all of them.

In 1954 my brother in law Leo wanted to build a big motel on his property. My father drew up the plans and we started in the fall of 1951 I believe. My father was an architect, darn good carpenter, teacher and innovator. We made templates for the motel walls, as they were all the same and a template for rafters. We were way ahead of the game. Other builders didn't come up with this type of building until later. First with rafter trusses. I had to get power from a building almost a block away and one loses power in distance. Had to get heavier power cords. That done Forrest, Bob and I began construction. We turned out a lot of walls and trusses then began erection. Amazing how well it went. The motel was like a huge square. 325 ft in one direction and 298 feet in a right angle to it. We built a two-bedroom house for the manager. Right in the intersection. One winter day it was snowing like mad and Forrest was the only carpenter working with me that day. I was cutting rafters for the house part. We couldn't use templates for it, and I handed Forrest a rafter and I saw the tail of it disappear at the top plate. It was then I hollered at Forrest "let's go home".

In the spring we had a disagreement with my brother in law, there is an old saying "never do business with relatives" the first thing was, he didn't want the sign we had in front saying. "John M. Walgren and son builders" he said he was the builder. He was the owner. The other was payment. My father said he would do the plans and advise but would not take wages. I was getting fifty cents an hour more than the other carpenters for being the head honcho. The Kahuna so to speak. But he told me there should be some percentage of profit for the business. He gave me a plan to convey to my brother in law. We did not know just how much the finished motel would cost so the figures were not cut in stone. My dad thought $80,000.00 would be very close, and the carpenter labor would be around $7,500.00. The business would take 40% of the labor totaling $3000,00 or 4% of the gross %80,000.00 totaling $3,200.00 and in the end he could chose whichever was the lower. He didn't want to pay anything. He said we were trying to break him. My sister got in the act and my dad disowned her. We immediately pulled off the job. He had someone else finish it. He and I never did get together again. My father and he and my sister did but I had moved to California. Another contractor said he would have built it for ten percent. That was of the gross. What they were looking at was 40 percent like that was of the gross. Too bad after all it was proposed and one could have said I don't want either. And the beat goes on. It could have all been avoided one big misunderstanding.

Mell never liked the winters in Minnesota. We had three seasons, July, August and winter. They were long and to work in the cold weather left a lot to be desired. So the house sold for $11,300.00 and we paid off the G.I.loan and it didn't leave a lot. We said our goodbyes to all and I stopped at my sister's out by the motel but she wasn't home so I left a note. I was trying to mend fences with her. It was so funny, not haha because I had had such a high regard for my brother in law but it ended sadly. But my sister was still my sister. And we continued to California. In Mankato I stopped at a clothing store to see my cousin Howard Anderson, from the island years. It was good to see him not all that long later he died. When we reached Temple City where my sister Dorothy had moved my nephew Raymond had kept track of our coming on a map. Remember I was his sea pappy. We stayed with them until we rented a house in Arcadia, Calif. just three miles from Dor's house. The rental business I tried was a lost cause. After a few months the handwriting was on the wall and I had to get out of it. It so happened that Johnny Santrizos had the same type of store in Santa Barbara and was doing well. He bought my equipment. I was offered a partnership in a Shell gas station. I had worked at gas stations in the past. So I bought in. Mistake number two. I didn't mind the work but what I didn't know was my partner was a drunk and was running business away. I would get calls to get to the station many nights. Gas stations stayed open until ten in those days. I had to get out of that. It happened that he owned a house just four blocks from where I was renting and trying to buy. To get my money back he took that amount off the house and I bought it. We had a time getting some Okies out of it but finally succeeded. I counted 99 holes in the walls in the living room and dinette area. There was gum on the floor and the back yard was a disaster. While in the house we had rented we met some friends that were wonderful people. I improved the house I rented and the front looked great. I was watching a neighbor trying to cut some grass out of a flowerbed. The house was three houses from where Mell and I were. I went over and showed him how to remove sod. He was flabbergasted that a neighbor would come over and help. George Fuller and I became close friends and his wife Minnie and Mell got along great. But back to the house. I sanded the floors. Patched the walls got rid of a bunch of trash in the backyard, got a four by ten piece of lumber six feet long and put a lot of sixteen penny nails in it and pulled it like a donkey (clean language) and smoothed the whole yard. I should mention I went to the carpenters union and got everything straightened out there and now was back at something I really knew and enjoyed. Our house on Alster Ave. was one of the better-looking houses in the neighborhood when I was through with it.

When we left Minneapolis I had bought a 1953 Nash. Now I traded that in for a 1957 Oldsmobile. Good looking car. When it was new I drove over to my sister's house in Temple City as my mother and dad were leaving for Phoenix. Before we left for the station in Alhambra I did something on the spur of the moment. I had never kissed my father in my life. I was just getting into the car when I backed out went around the rear of the car to my father and kissed him full on the lips. I was proud of myself.

In 1957 Carleen was going to school so Mell had a chance to take a job. It worked out like gangbusters as she worked in a junior high school in the kitchen. When there were holidays and vacations both she and Carleen were off at the same time. It was the perfect job. Mell had a knack for the job and soon she was going up the ladder. She became the baker then the cook. She was good. One year while we were up in Oregon she got a call from a friend that worked with her that the manager job at the high school was open and she should apply. She did and I should have said before that she was the manager at the junior high when this came up. Mrs. Starr the director came over to the house and gave Mel the keys and said 'you are the senior manager. Not bad. She was a good one too. Worked for the school system for 32 years. Should have been food director but a new director was in by that time. Had it been Mrs. Starr Mell would have been elected governor of the state.

I was working for a good contractor named Homer J. Anderson & Son. We had as good a crew as any builder would want. Dale Hoover, Jack Albertson, and I could turnout more work and good work than any other three men I knew at the time. We built good houses at a time when other builders were building what I called dingbats. Homer was not too much on humor, I found that out when I found a 16-penny nail that was only about a half an inch long and pound it in the end of his hammer handle. When he saw that he turned blue in the face. I calmly? Walked over to him and took the hammer and removed the nail with my fingers. He kind of looked at me funny. We built houses all over the San Gabriel valley. I was laying a sub floor on a house all alone. It was Friday, payday, Homer drove up in his Jimmy and came over to the sub floor and handed me my check. I looked at it and said "Homer you made a mistake on my check" he said, "I never make mistakes" the man had given me a fifty cent raise. That was darn good at that time. Fifty cents over scale, but he appreciated good work and time in which it was done. I produced.

We had built a house just about three blocks from our house. It was on a Sunday and Homer was standing by it for anyone who may come to see it. I took a thermos of coffee and went down and sat with him for a bit. While we were talking he asked if I ever took a vacation. I told him I had never had one. He said every man should take a vacation. I took him at his word. Mell and I with Carleen rented a cabin up at Big Bear in the

San Gabriel mountains. The place belonged to Minnie Fuller's mother in law. Was a real quaint cabin. I could go down to the lake and fish for rainbow trout. But it still didn't fill the bill. I wrote to the Chambers of Commerce in Oregon and Washington. They sent me all kinds of brochures of resorts in their states. I picked out Diamond Lake resort in Oregon. The Fullers had moved up to Auburn, Calif as he had worked at Aerojet and they had moved to Sacramento and George and Minnie with the company.

In 1958 home building came to a screeching halt. Homer didn't want to but he had to lay us off. I went out to Azusa and applied at Aerojet. Space was going hot and that was their gig. I was the only journeyman carpenter in the shop. I had a lot of know how that others didn't have. I made cabinets and built things they could not do. Then the bubble busted and the space program also fell. As I was the last carpenter hired Mr. Larr the foreman of the shop told me you are the best man in the shop but you are the junior man in seniority and I was out the door. I didn't care but the whole company moved to Sacramento shortly after that. My self I went to work the next Monday with Jack Albertson. He got a contractor license and we built black walnut kitchens for people. They were beautiful. We also built a couple big homes. Jack was just about two years older than I but he treated me like I was his son. I swallowed a couple times and it was ok. Jack had a son that was blind at birth by oxygen and was also retarded. But that boy was something of a genius at the same time. In time he started playing a phonograph. He had hundreds of records. He would stack them offset and with his fingers touching the outside rims he could name the record or all the titles if it was an album. I would read a page of the little train that could. Any page and read maybe the first two lines. He would recite the whole book if you let him from where you stopped. I think if you read the constitution to him he could recite the whole thing. Jackie was a wonder. The only thing was he didn't understand what he was saying. Libby and Jack his parents lived completely for Jackie. I don't know where he is now as Jack died but if I was to call Libby if she is still in the same house and Jackie answered he would say hello Sherman. I haven't heard from them for about seven years.

Jack, his brother in law John Bonaparte, and I were building a house in Temple City. I was walking the ceiling joists 2 x 6's when one turned on me and I kind of cart wheeled down and hit my cheek on the top of another joist. It was a mess. A kid named Fred was just below me and he vomited at the sight of me. I crawled down a stepladder and Jack had to take me to a clinic on Las Tunis Blvd. We drove up to it and Jack was fumbling around for a Nickel for the parking meter. I'm bleeding to death and he's looking for a Nickel. I got out of the car. I'm sweating and dirty as all get out when we entered the clinic. There were all kinds of people sitting in chairs and I picked that time to faint out. Jack told me later they thought I had been in a fight. Well it was an industrial accident. After taking x rays they told me I had to go to the hospital so after all the paper work was done Jack drove back to the job site. I picked up all my tools and put them in the trunk of my car. Then I drove home with Jack following me. At home I took a shower and put on clean underwear because my mother always said to have clean undergarments if you had to go to a hospital. I also went across the street and told Clem Tomerlien what had happened and to tell Mell when she came home from the school where I would be. The queen of Angels hospital downtown LA. And that it wasn't anything to worry about. Jack and I drove back to the job and Fred Pitts was to drive me to the hospital. When we got there we were sitting along a wall and nothing is happening aside from my bleeding to death. When a flying nun, it was a Catholic hospital, came by and Fred talked to her. Things started to happen. She said they thought I was coming by ambulance. Well I'm put in a wheelchair and wheeled to an elevator and taken up to the twelfth floor. They gave me an "I see you gown" and in to bed. Now I can't get out or do anything I am now completely bedridden whether I like it or not. Then a doctor showed up and told me I had pretty well smashed my cheekbone. Also had cracked the skull from the eye to the nose. And I had double vision. There was not much they could do for me except rest and hope the bleeding would stop.

Another day Mell was driven to the hospital by Bob Shaw another great neighbor friend. The mother superior came in and asked the man in the next bed his name. He gave it to her and she said glad to know you Mr. Gonzalas and then to my side of the bed and asked my name. I told her Nicodemus Q. Ginglewatz and she said glad to know you Mr. Ginglewatz. Mell almost fell out of her chair and told the nun my real name. She took it good-naturedly. Another day Mell came and thought she would help the nurses by emptying the urinal. She came back all smiles but I knew something was on her mind. She left and said she had to see someone. Well she called the doctor and told him what bothered her and he assured her everything was all right. Then Mell and the nurse came in and the nurse said "Mr. Walgren have you been spitting in the urinal?'" and I said yes. Mell had told the doctor I was bleeding internally because she saw blood when she emptied the urinal. Life in the big city. After a couple of weeks I was discharged from the hospital. I spent about two months at home as every time I bent over it hurt like the Dickens. Finally I went back to work. The first thing I did was putting in baseboards. All leaning over work. I just suffered. In time it was over but. All the nerves in the left side of my face were short-circuited and I could scratch my lip and feel it by the eye. It is still that way but you get used to it.

My first cousin Leighton Coats came to see me and said he would pay me carpenter wages if I would work with him repairing jukeboxes, bowling machines and pinball machines. With my face still hurting I thought it would be a good thing. With my knowledge of electronic circuits from my Navy days it was a cinch. I did that for about a year and a half and I knew that was not the life for me and I got out of it. Back to what I know best. Carpentry.

I went to work for a young fellow that I had known from Homer J. Anderson days. He had framers take care of the building and I did all the finishing. Someone he knew asked him to loan me to them for a while and I was to meet a guy not far from my house and ride with him to work. His name was Jim Curry. He was twenty years younger than I. He drove like he was twelve he thought like he was 32 and he was actually 22. Never met a kid as good at building as him. We did a lot of good work together just he and I. We worked for two guys that called their company Traverse Construction Co. It was a case of two many chiefs and not enough indians. While with them we built a post and beam house right on the ocean. It was pretty neat. Then we did an addition on a big house where I got doused with hot tar and that evening Mell and Carleen and I drove to Las Vegas. I looked a sight. But our real challenges came on two hill houses in Pasadena. The front of the house would be level with the street but the back was a different story. We had to have casions drilled in the hillside about three feet in diameter with a six-foot bell at the bottom. They were at lest 25 feet deep. There was a building inspector that demanded we take out the loose rock in the bottom. There was no way it could be done without one of us going down there. Well I was too big and I was also the strong man on the job. So I lowered Jimmy down into the hole, as he went down more decomposed granite fell into the bottom. When he was there I lowered a pail, which he would fill, and I would pull up and knock more rocks in the bottom. When Nelson, the inspector thought it was good I pulled Jimmy back up by hand causing more rock to fall. I was so disgusted with that Norwegian inspector that I offered him a one-way ticket back to Norway. We always had trouble with the man. He really didn't know his job. Every inspector first has to have common sense. When we had the first floor done and putting up roof trusses Jimmy was on the steep side. We had to get the truss up and nail it to the plates. Well the wind blew Jimmy's cap off and he reached for it. Never do that. He fell and just luckily his heel caught on a let in brace and he was dangling about seventy feet off the ground. I took care of the truss and went over and got him back in the house we built five hill houses and right now in Feb, 2005 they had so much rain I wonder if they stayed up as many hillside homes fell down the hill. They have something like a hundred or more that are unsafe.

Meanwhile I rebuilt the kitchen in our house. All of it after work and weekends. New kitchen cabinets all in black walnut. With a light ceiling. It was a knock out. New electric range with drawer burners. It was class. Now Traverse Construction went south, broke, and Jimmy went with Bob Hansen's uncle, Tjomsland Contruction. They were big. There were five partners Dwane Tjomsland was the same age as I and he was the great white father. His two brothers and two other guys. They were good to work for. I couldn't get cleared to work in the Pasadena local so I had to wait until they had a building in my district. That came with a bank in Alhambra. I was hired and I told Dwane all I could promise him was a good days work. The only thing the same with class A building and class B building is you still use a hammer. The super was a fellow named Johnny Christopher he was a nephew to the great white father. But he knew his stuff. His two faults were walking around with his leather shoelaces trailing a foot behind him and drinking. He was a total drunk. Not on the job but he had dui's like it was a hobby. Jimmy and I kind of changed the way they worked. Seems we were more proficient then the other carpenters. Well it wasn't long before Jimmy was a super. John was also but they had more than one building going on at a time. Most of them were around fourteen floors. I hadn't worked heights but when you go up with building it is not so bad. The company had two gantry cranes. They lift material up and also buckets of cement. All the buildings we did were concrete in place so as a carpenter we built forms and stripped them off after the pours. It is really dangerous work. We built two twin towers in Hollywood on Wilshire Blvd. And behind a huge parking structure. There was one fatality it happened to be the union safetyman. His name was Owen Medlin. He came to work late and I watched him buying coffee off the catering truck and then came up on the deck we were working. It was about thirty feet down to the first floor. His job was to put wood ties like a railroad down on two steel beams about three feet apart. The ties were wet and a little slimy and as he walked one slipped on him and down he went. Just missed the prime contractors trailer office. It was bad. Jimmy wasn't the super on that job a nice guy named Bob Peterson rode with him to the hospital, but he died around seven that night. His wife got a bundle and Owens friend married her shortly aftewards. Life is nuts.

While working on the bank in Alhambra I was paired with a Latino named Auggie Trujillo. Darn nice guy. We were clamping columns and in no time I was fast at it. He kept calling me Partner and I went over to him and said my name is Sherman E. Walgren and he said ok Partner. We got along so well one day I cut my self on purpose and we put our wrists together and we became blood brothers. He Mexican Norwegian American and I Mexican Norwegian American. Our friendship lasted until he died two years ago. I knew him as Auggie and he named me "The Gray Fox" time went by and the company had apartment house fourteen floors in Vallejo the old Navy town. Jimmy was to be superintendent and I was assistant super. By that time the company had a big overhead crane that was shipped up there. It takes another crane to erect it. The company rented apartments for us and we had to hire men from the local union office. We had a timekeeper and a labor foreman with us. On Friday Jimmy and I rode into the Frisco airport and flew home for the weekend and on Sunday night we drove to the airport for the flight back to Frisco. We did this until we had seven floors up when I got a call from Mell that she had to have a serious operation. I told the bosses that working up in Vallejo was not worth it so I left a lot of my things there and took a plane home. Mell had a calcified middle lobe on her right lung. I took her to the hospital on the way she was still smoking a cigarette and I mentioned that to her and she put it out, a specialist was to do the surgery. They had to cut from the front to the back and open her up like a melon. It all went well and after a time in ICU and then a regular room she eventually could come home and take it easy. She was off work for I think it was three months and paid for all of it. The school dept was ok. When I came back for her I worked on a building locally in L.A. out of town work is just not worth it.

I'll write about good times at Diamond Lake. I think it was 1959 we first went up there. Our first year there we stayed in a cabin that had been built in 1921 by a movie company in Hollywood. Laying in bed at night you could see the stars thru open places that had no shingles. It was right on Two Bear Creek so there was a nice sound to sleep by. The stove was as old as the cabin and was propane. While George and I were fishing she was going to light the oven. She turned on the gas got a farmer match and it went out she got another and came to the range and the explosion knocked her backwards. When I came in she was crying and telling me to enjoy myself but she could not.

A couple days later she and Minnie were walking down by the lake and they saw some nice new cabins and walked through some fields with all kinds of humming birds. Mell is a bird person. She began to like the place. I had caught one good-sized fish and I was ready to come back also. This was the start of a lot of trips to Diamond Lake. It was situated between two snow-covered peaks Mount Bailey on the north and Mt. Thielson on the south. The lake was three miles across and six miles long. It was located fifteen miles north of Crater Lake. We came there so often we got to know the owners very well and their son and daughter. Everyone that worked there we came every summer for thirty-two years and stayed for two to three weeks. I spent so much money up there I bought three cabins and a dozen boats and motors. We watched the kids grow up and Steve go to Viet Nam and back. John Koch was one owner and Nell was his wife. There was Nellie the other partner and all the waitress's in the restaurant, all college kids for the summer and I pulled tricks on all of them for their tips. George came up with a trailer for a while and then it was just Mell and I Carleen and my granddaughter. I didn't tell about her I will have to do that.

In 1970 my daughter had a baby girl on April 16th. I raised a pink flag on my backyard flagpole so all the neighbors knew what happened. I did not tell about Carleen getting married either. To tell the truth if I wrote of everything in my life I'd be a 110 year old trying to finish it. So I have to leave a lot of things out. But she had a big wedding in our Saviors church, the same name as the church I was baptized in Mpls. A huge wedding party in our back yard and in the end I threw her baby bead bracelet at her and we sent them on their honeymoon to Diamond Lake. It was a marriage doomed to failure however and shortly after Laurel was born Carleen had to leave him that takes care of that. Laurel was about one year old when that happened and I have been her papa ever since. Mell is her "Dow" none of us know how that started.

Back to Diamond Lake. We had so many adventures there it is hard to bring them all to mind. Our second trip we of course rented cabin number 38, which was overlooking the lake and Mount Bailey. Nice grass yard. In the evening the sun set behind the mountain and life was beautiful. At that time we only had one dog and no Laurel. Steve Koch was just a boy, Linda Koch was around five. Besides George and I fishing and always doing well we would come in around nine thirty in the evening and clean the fish and go to dinner. The lodge then was original. There were French doors on the north side. At breakfast it was normal for chipmunks to come in and eat off the tables with you. Our first waitress was a redhead named Phyllis. Now 46 years later in 2005 she is still there. I never went out fishing until about five in the afternoon, as the evening was the best time. Always came in with a limit. When George stopped coming I went alone. There was one place on the north side there were a lot of reeds and at the end they stopped forming a point of weeds. I called it Sherman's Point. I even made a sign back at the lodge dock. I painted Sherman's point on it and a long stake went back to the point and drove it in the lake bottom. It lasted quite a while until the park rangers took it down. But it was there long enough so people began to refer to that part of the lake as Sherman's Point; I was hoping they would put it on the map of the lake. Wishful thinking. After a year of fishing alone I got Mell to come with and "voila" I had a fishing partner. The first few years I fished with flies only. I went to a fly tying class in Pasadena and learned how to tie flies. I had a black fly I called the Diamond Lake black fly. It was a good one. But as the years passed and more and more people were fishing and they started chumming and depleting the fish I had to turn to a number five Eagle hook and worms. Steve Koch showed me a place at the west end of the lake called Silent Creek. You had to be in the right place. I would come in slow not over thirty feet from the shore looking at the bottom for and old log. When right over it I would throw out the bow anchor and then one off the stern (back) so the boat would stay put. I had boat nr 45 a scow nose but it was a perfect fishing boat. I cast the hook straight off the side about fifty sixty feet. The bed. The flow of the creek over time formed a channel that ran out that way and then turned into the lake proper. If you can understand that I was in the lake but fishing in a channel in the lake. Confusing isn't it? Well trout like cold water and they just lazily swim against the current in the coldest water. I caught many a trout from 17 inches to 24 inches in that spot. One year Mell and I were there and when I had the boat set I baited the hook and cast it out then gave her the rod and proceeded to bait mine. Bang, she had a fish. She reeled it in and I netted a nice rainbow trout. Baited her hook, cast it out and was baiting my hook and Mell had another fish. I netted that and fixed it for her and that went on until she had caught ten fish that was our limit for the day. I didn't even have a chance to fish and we had to quit. People used to follow me to find out where I was catching all the fish. Early morning and evening the best times. One man found out my place.

When I would find him there I would just go somewhere else. He didn't know just where to fish but it would still ruin it for me. I always had enough fish to have a big fish fry every summer when we were in Arcadia. God I loved fishing.

There was plenty else to do there/ both Carleen and Laurel went horseback riding. First owner of the Diamond Lake corrals was a nice cowboy named Dusty. And then to young brothers and lastly Wayne Watson. The last of the real cowboys. He built a rodeo arena all his corrals, tack room and everything out of pine and fir from the forest. Gates had no iron hinges they were wood forks and such. Just a little fellow but big in western stature. Now he is thinking of retiring and he deserves too. Laurel learned her love of horses there. Every summer the people of the resort and Mell and I had a big party. Sometimes in the woods and a big fire. Hot dogs, hamburgers etc. Another place was Steve and Peggy's place. Food, steaks and desserts. It would end bashing Mell or me with a pie in the face. I tried to get Jack Mattos, Linda's husband in the face and he ducked and the pie ended up in Carleen's face all in all it was fun. I will have to write more about Diamond Lake but will go back in years to other things that happened in my life.

Back to buildings. I had a hand in building many commercial buildings, hospitals and parking garages. In 1974 we were building a huge parking garage in El Segundo. Right across from the Los Angeles International Airport. It would be eleven stories high and fourteen tennis courts on the roof. The eleventh floor would be office. Parking space for three thousand cars. Jimmy Curry was the super and I had charge of raising the forms. We had two twenty two hundred Peco overhead cranes. The largest cranes there are. One for part "A" and one for part "B" actually one building but erected as two. When one side was ready for a pour (cement) the other was being readied. In may 1974 we had all the footings in the first floor slab and ready to pour the second floor in part "A" it would be the next morning but we had to work overtime to get the forms up for part "B" I followed all the rules of safety by having shores under everything I had crews doing. There were some beams that we needed the crane to set and I was helping lower these sixty feet long beams into place, when done they form a hundred and twenty feet of beam. Auggie's brother Sammy. We called him Little Beaver. Was on the column opposite me and I was in the middle. I asked a black foreman, who's job this was and we were helping, if it was ready to receive the beam. He said yes. So jumped in the beam and signaled young Randy Avers, one of the partner's sons, to lower the beam. As it was lowered to where I could get a hand on it and help guide it into place it caught the end of the beam I was in. The beam weight about six hundred pounds and crash I was on my way down to the first floor about fifteen feet. There was no shore under the four by four that held up the beam I was in. Had there been a shore under there you could have put a pickup truck on it and it would not have broke. I was booby trapped, not on purpose but by someone that thought speed was more important than safety. The beam stayed up on the column in back of me. It was on a slant. My right leg for some reason was in the air and all my weight was on my left foot and most of it the heel. There was pandemonium. I was carried out of the building and I had a carpenter take my boot off so it wouldn't have to be cut off. Willy Risper the safetyman was just returning from bringing another carpenter back from the hospital for something minor. As he came running I hollered, no mouth to mouth, in humor. Willy is black. A real good friend. He took me to the El Segundo hospital and they x-rayed my foot. Told me it was not good. They sent for an ambulance and I was transported to the Arcadia Methodist Hospital that would become my home away from home. Jimmy drove my car home and told Mell, meanwhile back in the ambulance I had opted to ride with the driver. Big mistake. It hurt like blazes and I would have liked to have been laying down. At the hospital Dr. Burchinger, an orthopedic and a highly rated one, talked to me and said "we are going to be friends for a long time" and we were. At first they thought it should heal the way it was. There are to many bones in the ankle. To try and straighten. The heel bone was cracked in two places and felt like a knife was in them. There were bones sticking out of the skin, these were cut off and with bone marrow out of my left hip were stuffed in a 3/4-inch hole he had drilled in my ankle. After sewing up that I got a big cast on the leg. I was in the hospital quite a time and then they taught me how to use crutches and I went home. After many X-rays Dr. Burchinger told me I healed too fast and the operation didn't fuse so I had to go back to my home away from home and go though the procedure again. They drilled out the hole and then took bone from my right hip and cut it in strips about a quarter of an inch and stuffed them in. Again a cast and time in the hospital and finally home. This time it worked but over a lot of time. I spent 27 months on crutches. Not consecutively but between operations. Had five surgeries. The last straightening two toe joints that had gone hammer toed, all four except the big toe did that but the two biggest would have given me the most trouble. All this time I am on workman's compensation.

I asked the doctor if I could go fishing up at Diamond Lake and he gave me the ok. He was a great fisherman also. Well Mell and I and Laurel packed up and headed north. I'm on crutches and a cast. But with help I was able to get in and out of the boat so all was well. Mell and I left the dock and headed for Sherman's Point. We went by Rocky Point and there were at least fifty boats there chumming?? Man I hated all the boats in one place I always trolled. I heard a man calling for help and off to the left there was a man clinging to the bottom of his boat. None of the fifty boats gave any concern. I changed course and got to the man and pulled him up into the boat by his belt. I asked if anyone else had been in the boat. I was ready to dive in twenty feet of water with my cast had there been someone. But he was fishing alone. He had a daughter and son in law screaming all this time but they didn't help. They were in a boat not too far away. What happened was, he had caught a trout that was all there was in the lake. He got so excited he stood up and his boat was a round-bottomed aluminum boat the most unsafe of any boat and it capsized on him. Then Mell and I went fishing. The next day I'm standing in front of the huge fireplace in the lodge resting on my crutches and he spied me and came over to thank me for saving? His life. He was surprised to see me with a cast and crutches. Another year I was with a cane and we had one of our big parties in the forest. I threw my cane in the fire and Wayne rescued it. Fun fun fun.

Eventually I had a leg brace and no more operations. So I got around pretty decent. But. I was still in a cast when we had one of our big fish fries in the back yard. I had borrowed all the neighbors braisers to fry the trout. We had about eighty people and all the tables and chairs came from the high school. They helped me set them up and take them down. They all thought a lot of Mell and liked to help. At the fry I announced Mell and I were going to Tahiti. Jimmy Curry on is own took up a collection from the guests to help our trip. It was good he had because we were going on a shoestring. This all came up one afternoon when Mell and I were watching the "Hal Linker Travel Show" on TV. They were in Tahiti at the Bali Hai on Raiataa. Havla, his wife from Iceland, said in strong Scandinavian accent, "and ve stayed in da bungalow all de way on the right" Mell said I'd like to stay in the bungalow all the way to the right also. Wheels started turning in my head. I went to a travel agency in Arcadia and without her knowledge set up the whole thing making sure we would be in that particular bungalow. Never did tell her other than we were going to Tahiti.

We flew on Air New Zealand a wonderful airline. For the only time in my life I was boarded before the rest of the passengers. Getting up the stairs on crutches. They didn't have a ramp at the airport. Why? I don't know. We arrived in Tahiti and were taken to the Holiday Inn hotel. A very beautiful hotel right on the ocean overlooking the "sea of the moon" with Moorea across the water. Very striking. But I couldn't understand the name. It seemed when people would ask where you stayed and you say the Holiday Inn. Oh yes! I stayed there in Fresno. Didn't have the right sound. I wrote a letter after returning home about it and they changed the name to "the Beachcomber" it happened that they were celebrating "Bastille" (sp?) Day and had a great show for the guests. Tahitian dancers and drums. Really something to see. There was also a French Navy party one night and a 15-year-old Tahitian girl arranged for us to attend. The only two Americans there. She was getting us wine bottles off the other tables even tho I don't like wine but she really took care of us. It was the start of a never-ending relationship. After we left Tahiti we went to Riataa. And what do you think? Mell got to stay in the bungalow all the way to the right. It was over water and in the floor of the "fare" or bungalow was a glass floor and you could watch all the fish under the fare. Big angelfish and hundreds of different kinds. Tahiti of course is under the equator so you can see the Southern Cross, which was a first for Mell. This was all at the Bali Hai. They had firewalkers there. It's hard to believe but they walk thru burning embers with a Kahua (chief) and a Thai branch in his hand and about ten Tahitians follow him. One of the waitress's we knew from the restaurant was one of them. The next morning I walked across the rocks and felt the heat thru my boots.

Next we went to the island of Bora Bora. Mitchiner (sp?) The author said it was the most beautiful island in the world. And I concur. We had another bungalow over water with a glass floor not the whole floor but about three feet by six feet. There was another surprise for us. At night a flood light lights up the water. Standing on the back porch we saw giant Manta Rays. Wings about twelve feet or more come up from the deep and make a loop. They were eating plankton drawn by the light. It you didn't drink you would start and if you did drink you would stop. What a sight. Kind of scary but they are not harmful to humans. Then we went back to the holiday inn. We met the same waitress and her name was Yolande. Her last was Taae. In Tahiti when they sign their name the last is first. She wanted us to meet her parents and arranged for us

have lunch at their fare. When we got there all her sisters and brothers were gawking at us. It seems it is a step up the ladder to have American's visit them. Miriama, her mother, prepared the food and Teroo, her father stood by. They all stood by. Just Mell and I were eating. Miriama was injured in an accident years before so she limped badly. They had a dog with a bad leg and a rooster with a bad leg so I fit right in. We ate but we didn't know what it all was. I know I had breadfruit and I didn't like that but they had banana "poi" that was good. Not like Hawaii where poi tastes like wallpaper paste. It was another adventure to have visited them. They all play a uke and guitars and they sang Tahitian music. They were great.

I forgot to mention that before we went to Raiataa we went to Moorea and also over water bungalows. Another Bali Hai. In fact the first one the three American partners started. The first Tahitian they hired was a young girl named Bernadette. We got to know her well also. It is on the island of Moorea that the mountain called that name is located. In the last scene in the movie "Hawaii" it is featured. The Tahitian don't like that name as it has a Tahitian name. Tahiti and all the islands are part of French Polynesia composed of Tahiti, Tahitiä itte, Moorea, Raiataa, Moorea, Tahaa, Huahinie and Bora Bora. There are more but these are the main islands. We have been to all of them. Like I said. A lasting relationship. We went to Tahiti five times. After the second time we stayed at the Taae's fare. They adopted us as "Papa Rua" and "Momma Rua" that is grandfather and grandmother. The parents visited us in Arcadia and later in Illinois and Arizona but that comes later.

The last trip we made to Tahiti we also went to the other islands. On Bora Bora Bernadette came to see us at our over water bungalow and excitingly said, "I'm working with a famous American actor," I asked who it was and she said Jason Nelson Robards. I wrote "Nora Maru" on a piece of paper and gave it to her and told her to give this note to him. By this time it was a few years since we had first met her and she was about five feet high and five feet around. Her hair was at least four feet long. Imagine her on a two-wheeled motor scooter. They call them two wheeled Mercedes. Her hair flying out behind she went back to where Jason was. In a very short time she was back and said, "he wants to see you" I knew it, as Jason was a fellow radioman with me on the cruiser Northampton. I rode double with her with her hair in my face and to the other side of the island where the movie company was shooting "Hurricane" when I met Jason and we were both happy to see each other. He introduced me to Laurel Bacall's son Sam however he was not married to her at that time. His wife Lois had been there with him but the kids got sick and she went back to the states. They were married until his death. Then Bernadette took me back to the hotel Bora Bora as Jason said he would come over to visit. When he came we had a good chat on our deck and later had dinner at the hotel. Told me about his accident in Malibu and all the reconstruction of his jaw and that now he was "AA" Jason was a darn nice guy and I was glad to call him shipmate and friend. The next day he came and took us to the movie lot. We sat in director chairs while they filmed the picture. They had two great big aircraft engines with the propellers backwards and blowing water from jets making it seem like a hurricane. Max Van Sydo, a Swede, was trying to get in a building thru the wind. I could have been in the picture if we had been a couple weeks earlier. They needed Caucasians to take Naval officer roles. We met Mia Farro and Van Sydo and the director etc. I told Van Sydo a Norwegian saying; I don't think he took kindly to it. It was "ten thousand Swedes ran thru the weeds chased by one Norwegian". Seemed kind of cool after that. It was all interesting.

Jason promised to visit us in the states. We were going to have another fish fry and I invited him. I had to talk to his "agent" it was a go. However he had slipped off the wagon I guess as he and another guy were arrested at three in the morning in Hollywood out side Jon Hall's house. They were making quite a disturbance. Jon was the actor in the first Hurricane. Jason's agent bailed him out and he went directly back home to Connecticut. Never saw him again but I always called him when I saw him in a movie and told him how good he was. He won a couple of Oscars and made a lot of good movies. Jason wanted me to see his doctor, a doctor Kerlan, who was the doctor of the Los Angeles Dodgers. He was a noted orthopedic. Jason thought he could help me with my injured foot, however there was nothing more that could be done for it. If there was anything Dr. Burchinger would have done it.

I got off the track there about my injury. After we got back from our first trip to Tahiti the company wanted me back for my expertise. What they really wanted was to get me off workman's comp. But I did go back. I took care of checks on payday. I had a gas-powered four-wheeler to get around with. One day I heard loud call for help. Looking up I saw Riley Johnson hanging by his hands on the parapet of the top floor. The staging for the ceiling of the eleventh floor was on wheels. The parking structure was slanted to the center for draining. When he was on the perimeter of the form prying the form loose from the concrete it suddenly broke loose. When that happened the whole staging began to roll to the center of the building. Riley grabbed the parapet that formed the edge of the roof. It snapped off the two by four rails and there he was hanging. I've got a loud voice and was hollering for someone on the roof to look over. A laborer finally looked down and I hollered for him to grab Riley. Luckily they got to him before he would have to let go. Must have been very frightening to him. They did get him up over the parapet. Now I know why they wanted me back on the job. It wasn't them but a higher up so I would be there to help Riley Johnson. That is my belief. I was on the job until it was finished. Then they started to lay off carpenters and I was told to go on unemployment. It came close to being a disaster for me. I couldn't do that, as I couldn't any longer work as a carpenter. I went to a union lawyer in Pomona, Calif. I told him my problem and he contacted the headquarters of the union representing carpenters and found that in one week it would have been too late to file a case. Too close for comfort. It was an industrial accident that didn't have to happen. It took about a year to litigate. Numerous depositions to be held. The attorney for me said that in Dwane Tjomsland's deposition he said I was the best man on the job. I felt that was quite a complement. In the end I was awarded a sum of money. No fortune. They took out the cost of all the depositions. The doctor cost and the attorney got 33 1/3 of the rest. I ended up with very little but better than nothing. It was enough for me to have my house remodeled and Mell and I had it very well. It paid off to have it done as I recouped a great deal when we sold. The accident happened when I was 55 years old; they put me on Social Security disability. I could not earn any money other than what I drew and if I did it would be deducted dollar for dollar. When I was 65 they transferred me to regular Social Security and it was the same as I had gotten but now I could earn something like $3000 some a year. I played the game honestly never earned a penny until then.

I had no idea how to earn more money until a job of school attendant came up at the high school where Mell was manager of the cafeteria. The students at first thought I was an undercover cop. There were four campus attendants two of them completely useless. After a bit the students called me John Wayne and the Duke. At one time the senior class was voting for class president and I was nominated. I got along good with the good students but the few bad apples gave me some trouble. It was my job to stop them smoking, skipping class, leaving the grounds with out passes and lastly narcotics. I did my job and one of the teachers said at their meeting that they never had a campus attendant like Mr. Walgren.

It had its drawbacks however. One morning I went out to find flat tires on both our cars. They were knifed. Another morning I found the car door open and kids had sprayed carbonated wine into the ceiling of my 1971 Lincoln Mark Three. Also took the gas cap so I had no way of knowing if they had put sugar in there. In the front seat one of them had urinated on the front floor. A neighbor girl gave me a clue by describing a car she had seen. I had motion light on the driveway so that helped. Detective Walgren walked up and down the student parking lot and along Campus Drive and I did find a car that fit the description. I turned my evidence over to the Arcadia police dept. And they picked up the suspects. One confessed and we had them all. They had to compensate me for the damage but there wasn't any apology from the students or their parents. We live in a brand new world.

Another caper was knocking my mailbox off. We had rural type mail delivery. Once didn't seem like any big deal so I put it back. Then it happened again. I sat up one night and saw a red convertible with chrome

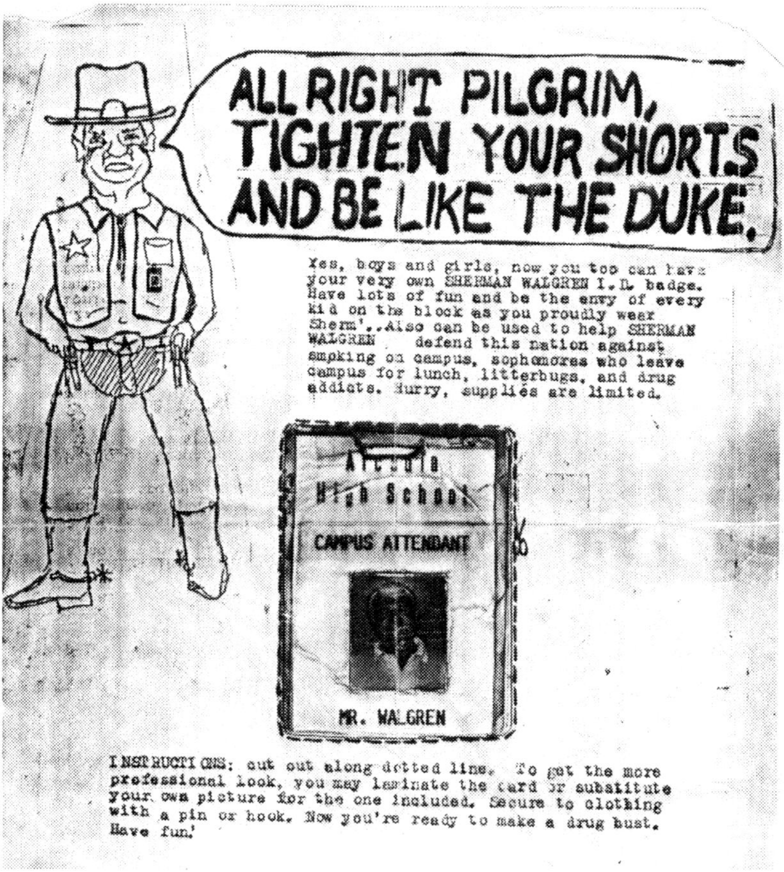

rings on the wheels pull up and a kid jumped out with a baseball bat and hit the mailbox and sent it flying. That gave me an idea. I made a mailbox out of cardboard. When I was through it looked exactly like a real one. I mounted that on the post and that night I waited. All this seemed to happen on Friday nights. I had called the police to be ready if I called. Sure enough here they come. They stopped and the kid with the bat sent the box flying. It must have surprised him how easy it went. I alerted the police and they were there in a minute. It was one cop and an explorer student from the school, nice kid, and we're talking about it when I saw the car coming back to the scene of the crime. It was too late for them and when they saw the patrol car they sped passed and the cop and the student ran for their patrol car and took off like crazy and fast turn at the end of the block and they caught them. Baseball bat and all. Another caper was some kids threw a lot of good paper all over my front yard and the street. Someone had to have access to reams of good paper. I cleaned it up. I caught those kids too. The school wanted to discipline them for all these things. Had it been the police they would have had records. After the paper thing the police said he wished they had had the city clean it up with city help and street cleaners and charged the parents. That would have been a good way to handle that. Other things happened but no real damage involved. Rule #1 don't live in the same town as the school. I was put in charge of the student parking lot. The kids are supposed to pay a fee each semester to park there. Many kids would sneak in and park. I tagged all the cars that didn't have stickers.

Then I called the police and they would write tickets on them. After a while it mounted to about $1500 worth of tickets. Guess you know I wasn't winning any popularity contests. I had a little house with windows all around so I could see what was going on. One noon I noticed a student getting into the trunk of a car. They were going off the campus for lunch. The kid in the trunk did not have a pass. I stopped them at the gate and had them open the trunk. And off to the office with the student. Well all these things added up to real trouble one weekend. In the dead of night the kids came into the parking lot and I don't know what they used but they blew up the parking office. They also had painted nice things like "kill John Wayne" to this day I don't know why I stayed but I did. The teachers went on strike.... what a world we live in..... The students gathered around them and started a mini riot. There were about fifty of them on the library lawn and smoking. The principle said to go in that crowd and take them to the office. Oh sure! Well I did and it was a lucky thing I got out of there alive. But I did get two students ID cards. Then I noticed some students ruining the sprinkler heads and I got on my mobile radio and reported that and was told it wasn't important enough. I had had it. I went to the assistant principle's office, my boss, put the radio on a desk and said give it to some other joker. As I went out the front door I said to the principle "I know that campus attendant is the bottom of the barrel but Mr. Walgren is important to me" and with that I quit.

The police department came to me and asked if I would be interested in being a crossing guard. I was and took the job. I was up in the high rent district. When I was eleven years old I was a crossing guard on 34th and Chicago Ave. A Sam Brown belt and a sign. Now I am about 68 years old and doing the same thing. Don't laugh. It paid better than the school. I had to be there in the morning until all the kids were in school. Again at noon for an hour and the when school let out. The pay believe it or not amounted to about $11.00 and hour. A good job for half a cripple.

Back to Diamond Lake and shenanigans. One year we had just arrived and I put on a costume I used in the Shrine. It was an Arab costume. I had a fake beard and moustache and went up to the desk in the lodge. John Koch the owner was there. I demanded rooms for my harem and gave him a bad time. John was mad as hops and I didn't know until later that he didn't like those people. Well he laughed when I took off my coffia and beard. Another we arrive to find the cabin full of balloons. Linda had wanted to put a horse in it but they vetoed that. There was a potty right in the middle of the living room of the cabin. This was all in retaliation for the tricks I played on the waitresses in the restaurant. In those days a dollar was a dollar and it was a good tip for a sixteen seventeen-year-old girl. I would glue a fine monofilament fishing line to a dollar with a weight over the edge of the table. Put it under the sugar jar. When we left and she lifted the sugar the dollar would disappear. I also did the same thing to a dollar only I held the end of the monofilament. When I gave her the tip and walked away it would fly out of her hand. For Linda I froze a dollar in an ice tray and left that on the table. And made them get on chairs and get it out of the tiles in the ceiling. But, the best one was on Julie, a young waitress from Medford, Ore. I casually glued a bunch of coins to a table napkin. I put loose money on a second one. It looked just like the glued one. When we got up to leave, I had clued John at the desk to what was going on and he could see very plainly in a mirror. We got up to leave and Julie came to the table to clean it and picked up the napkin with the glued money. She laughed and picked up the other one and money fell all over the floor. She took it all good-naturedly. Actually there was about $2.50 there so it was a good tip. They fought back. One year I ordered a hot beef sandwich. They fixed it up in the kitchen. Sewed all the bread together with monofilament. I gave them a gold star for that. Peggy our favorite waitress of all time, she could play the piano like Paderuski. She made me a chocolate sundae out of whipped butter and all the trimmings on the top. Well it was all great.

Because of all the chumming going on I sent a note to the owner and said I was going to drain the lake out North Creek and turn the lake into a cornfield. I would blow up the boathouse and pay my bill with aluminum cans. Mell and I were eating in the restaurant when there was a loud explosion. We went down to the dock and a security office grabbed me and put handcuffs on me. With my hands behind my back he took me down the path to cabin 38 and there on the front lawn were about two hundred empty cans.

We were up in the Diamond room many nights. It came to pass when Linda had a tiger hat and Peggy made a swimming suit out of it. They wanted me to model it but I would not. At that time I was in fair shape. Well when we were back in Arcadia I did put it on and Mell took a front view picture. It wasn't too racy but it was like Charles Atlas. I had two large, about two feet by four feet; pictures made and sent them to Peggy and Linda. Said they could throw darts at it. The next summer when we arrived at Diamond Lake. There on a stone monument at the head of the drive into the lodge is my picture mounted on plywood with a sign saying "appearing nightly in the Diamond room. As if that was not enough when I went into the lodge to register there on the end of the desk surrounded by Christmas lights was the other picture. One woman came up and said she recognized me. They won the leather-covered spoon for that. Peggy married Steve and now they run the place. Linda and Jack, my fishing buddy, we once caught the same trout at the same time, takes care of the snowmobiles in the winter. I'm not sure what Linda does but I know she is busy at it. John died two years ago and had been blind for about three years. Nell his wife died many years ago. She could play the organ with one hand better than I with two. She had a stroke but still played for the guests. I also played the old songs there. Just this last summer after a Chincoteague reunion in Portland Jack drove up and brought us to the lake. And Peggy and I played together. She on the piano and I on the Hammond organ played Jim Reeves hit "He'll Have to Go". When we left Steve and Peggy's beautiful home in Roseberg, Peggy said we were a legend at the resort. Sure played a big part in Mells', Carleen's, Laurel's and my life. The place was full of ghosts for me. All the people that had worked there and those that had passed on. They were as good a people as one can meet in a lifetime. About three years ago after a reunion in Portland a busload of shipmates took a tour to Astoria, Tillamook, Crater Lake and then to Diamond Lake. They had a big sign over the Diamond room entrance "Welcome USS Northampton" we had a buffet in the Diamond room and then in the big dining room for a five star dinner. They had a cake with a picture of the Northampton on the top that Mell and I had to cut. Peggy and Steve went all out for us. After the dinner Peggy played the piano and Steve and I sang with her. Gosh it was fun. John was there and smiling. We were close to being the same age. He died shortly after that visit. The shipmates that went on that tour considered it the best we had ever had.

I have jumped around in years as when something hits my brain I type it. In 1979 I became a Master Mason. I always wanted to join it but seemed I never had the time when I was working. But I memorized what I had to and am glad to be a Mason. I took the long course and became a 32nd degree mason. Then I went on and became a Shriner. I am proud to be in Masonry and the Shrine. I belonged to Al Mailaika Temple in Los Angeles. The day I received my fez I joined the Arabic band. There were about thirty men, drummers, bass drum, symbols and I played and oriental reed horn. Darned if I can think of the name of it. We were good; won first place in many a parade.

Now it is a day later and I remember the name of the horn. It was a "musette" the sound is kind of screechee, if that is a word. It is similar to horns used by Indian fakers playing in front of a basket of cobras. We went to all the Imperials around the states including Toronto, Canada and Mexico City. Mell and I got to travel a lot with the shrine. In Atlanta there were 1100 shriners from California participating in the parade on Peach Tree Blvd. Some of the parades were five miles long. In Toronto, Canada after the parade we went thru department stores and onto a subway car and playing all the time. Brad Canfield was the director and leader and a good one. Sad to say that the band does not exist anymore. Young people are not joining fraternal organizations like they used to. Too much TV, affluent cars and attractions. I myself am very proud of my affiliation, as I've helped disabled children. The one I am most pleased about was a baby in Breeze, Ill. That was born with a problem and one week later they had to amputate one leg. I signed as a shriner for the child to be taken care of until he is eighteen years old by the shriner's hospital in St. Louis Mo. At no cost to the parents. All prosthesis and whatever will be taken care of. Makes me feel great to have had a part of it.

I have to correct a birth year for my father. I wrote he was born in 1884, it was 1883 Aug 6th. My mother was born July 11, 1884. While Mell and I lived in Arcadia I never missed a "mother's day" that I didn't fly to be with her. She lived in Phoenix with my sister Mig. For her 100th birthday I wrote to Willard on the Today show and he announced it. I also wrote to the following. The mayor of Minneapolis as that was where she was born. The governor of Minnesota, Richard Nixon as I didn't care for the tooth fairy. She received a written congratulation from him, King Olaf of Norway and she got a nice card from him. The king of Sweden also. The queen of England's lady in waiting sent a card with the royal seal but explained the queen only wishes British citizens happy birthday. Lastly I wrote to the Vatican, even tho most if not all Norwegians are Lutheran, and the Pope's secretary sent a nice card and a picture of the Pope. She was overwhelmed with it all. We were all there for her 100th birthday. She died eleven days before her 102nd birthday. The greatest "mom' that ever lived. When she was 83 I took her on a helicopter ride over Long Beach and the Queen Mary. She loved it. Referred to it as a fishbowl. I wasn't a pilot we were passengers in a sight seeing trip.

All work by Sherman, grass, bowls & Japanese lanterns.

You know I lay in bed thinking of things to write and then when I am typing I 'm not sure if I am repeating things or not?

We moved from 5552 27th Ave South Minneapolis in 1954 to Arcadia, California. We rented a house for a while at 414 Las Flores Ave and then bought a house from a partner in a Shell station and I think I mentioned that. Was at 315 Alster Avenue. It was like a park in the back yard. I was good with cement and made Japanese lanterns, I carved a tiki out of a big palm tree that got too close to the power lines. In one week I made three big bowls and constructed a waterfall. The only thing I bought was the water pump. I made all the rest. I had colored spots on it at night. It was a work of art. Not art but of Sherman. At one time I had it in black light t'was something to see. I also made a stained glass window that is still in the house whoever owns it now. I designed the flower and did all the cutting and soldering. I will say I was quite the artisan. Made many things. I always felt if I couldn't make it I couldn't have it.

Stained glass window by Sherman Walgren. Designed, cut and installed in Arcadia, CA.

Mell, me, Don Powell, Sal Arbucci, and nephew Raymond.

Mainly this book is for my daughter my granddaughter and my great grandsons, plus all my nieces and nephews. But I think there are a lot of interesting things to everyone.

My cars included a 1942 Buick convertible, 1933 Dodge sedan, 1947 Oldsmobile, 1948 Buick Super, 1950 Nash Statesman, 1953 Nash, 1957 Oldsmobile, 1956 Chevrolet station wagon, 1962 Oldsmobile Starfire, 1971 Lincoln Mark Three, 1986 Lincoln Mark Seven. 1990 Lincoln Town Car, and our present car a 1998 Lincoln Mark Eight. Going back to the ancient times my father had a 1922 Hupmobile, 1924 Hupmobile 1926 Hupmobile, 1928 Hupp a Ford model "A" for one week, it wasn't big enough, and got a 1931 Hupp and in 1939 a 1939 Packard sedan. That takes care of cars. For motorcycles I had first the 1930 Henderson 45 cc. Then the 1937 Indian Chief 74 cc. A 1930 Harley in the Navy. A 1948 Indian Chief. Then no more two wheels for Sherman.

It would take too much time to write about all our neighbors but two of them stand out. They were Sal Abucchi and

Gloria and Bob Shaw and his wife Pat. I had too many friends to mention in California and glad to have known them. Sad to say most of have passed on. In 1990 we decided to move as the whole town was changing. I quit my job with the police dept. And Mell and I started packing. It was my idea to move to Illinois where Mell was born and most of her family lived. We took our three dogs and I think I'll bring in all our dogs of the past, first there was Taffy a full blood cocker spaniel, then Tammy the same breed, then Sugar the same. Babbette a mix, Cherie full blood silver poodle, Sussie a Lasaoppso, Tinkerbell, an orphan left by a neighbor, then Boy a lost full blooded white poodle, then Cherie Two another silver poodle, then Timothy an apricot full poodle, then Charlie an apricot poodle and we have him at present. One of very few dogs that has a driver's license? Had it made at Walgreen's drug store. My license cost ten dollars. Charlie's cost twenty nine dollars. It gets a lot of smiles and that is the name of the game.

Now back to the moving. I shipped the 71 Lincoln and drove all of us to Illinois. There was a fair sized house in Boulder, Ill. Owned by a multi millionaire. It had been on the market for two years. Well I offered an amount that was refused then upped it by ten grand and he took it. The house was 201 feet long. A two-story apartment on one end. Space for five cars, and in ground pool. Right on the biggest lake in Illinois, a great room living room, four bedrooms, a pool room, six bathrooms, four furnaces. Four air conditioners two acres of lawn. A ten-foot satellite and 31 trees. And I'm a retired carpenter. The place was surrounded all but the lakeside with a wrought iron fence and beautiful gates. Well I put up a forty-foot flagpole and had camp Sherman once again. There was 6500 square feet under roof.

The only Norwegian in the group, 1995

With the move I acquired a whole bunch of Mell's relatives. Her sister Shirley was more like a sister to me and I always called her that. I also told her if she had let me pick a brother in law I couldn't have found a better one. I always called him "bro".

We had some of the best parties. Thanksgivings. Christmas's one could have. We drove to Minnesota and introduced them to my family that was still there and then up to 3rd crow Wing Lake where the Berdahls lived. We had a ball. In the nine years we lived in Illinois I roasted three pigs and had 50 60 people. Just like we used to do in Arcadia. I joined Ainaad Shrine in East St. Louis, Ill, and the motor patrol that met in Centralia, Ill. I also bought a bagpipe, as I always like the sound. I met some Scotch people that taught me to play it and was the only Norwegian piper in the Celtic band. The pig roasts came about when Mell was talking to the wife of a farmer, a shriner that had a huge farm, grain, cattle and pigs. She said they would provide the pig if we would roast it. Mell said ok and then left it up to me. Well, I found an old playground swing set in the woods, got it home and used the two "a" frames for the ends. Cut them off short. There was a big half of a fifty-gallon barrel with a half welded on it so it was about five feet long. I found a piece of pipe and had round rods welded on it. Had a guy weld a sprocket from a bicycle on one end. A good buddy named Robert Carpenter gave me a motorized auger that fed coal into a furnace years ago all I used was the transmission part and welded another sprocket on that. It rotated one revolution per minute. Bought a new bicycle chain and hooked up the "Rube Goldberg" contraption and it worked great. When I roasted the first pig however I found that as the back, the heavy part, came over the top it would drop a little. Not good. With the second pig I had a counter balance on the spit and that solved that. With the third pig I announced to the crowd if they ever had thought of the last time they did something. Like when you roller-skated as a kid did you know that was the last time you would do that. When you left high school and went out the door did you know that was the last time. There are many last times. The one to worry about is the last breath. However I announced to the gathering that I knew that, that was the last pig I would ever roast. It was a wonderful nine years we spent there until Mell got a phone call that Shirley had a heart attack and passed on. It was a blow. I admired the woman nothing seemed the same. The place got harder to take care of and the upkeep and one day after cutting the two acres of grass I came in the house and told Mell it was time to go. I asked her where she wanted to move to and she said Tucson, Arizona and I said ok. Seeing as how I had picked Illinois it was her turn to pick. It was hard to leave as we had done so much there. We celebrated out fiftieth wedding anniversary there. The shipmate that had introduced me to Mell at Sweet's ballroom came, I told the people that we had had a lot of good liberties together and had almost died together in the bombing of the Chincoteague. I played the bagpipes. Sang with the western band we had and Mell danced on the tables. We also were married again by a superior court judge from Edwardsville, ill. We had met him when Mell's niece Becky got married on our deck overlooking Lake Carlyle. Even the Tahitians, Miriama, Teroo and a granddaughter and grandson visited us there. But it was time top go. It was lots harder to pack so we had Atlas Van Lines do all of it and we had what we couldn't take sold at auction. It was sold for pennies but then we cold not take it to the house we bought in Tucson. The winters lasted too long and we had a lot of bugs in the summer. So off we went.

On the drive to Tucson with Cherie, Guy the white poodle and Charlie we had to stay in motels that would let us have them in the room. Not all that hard to find them. When we got to Albuquerque I was going to go south to Las Cruces and west on Interstate Ten to Tucson. I got to thinking. I knew that my sister Mig was not well and something told me we should go thru Phoenix before going on to Tucson. It was lucky we did. When arriving at my sister's house my two nieces Carol and Candy, all her life I called her "Pogey Bait" as that is what we called Candy in the Navy. Told us that Mig was in a bad way. I entered the bedroom and her dog was right next to her protecting. I held her hand for three hours and we talked of our childhood and a lot of happy memories and she hoped to get better so she could come to our new house in Tucson. We had to leave as our furniture was coming the next morning. When we got there and slept on the floor. We plugged in the phone as the real-estate lady had taken care of that. The phone rang and Carol, my niece said Mig had passed away. The last words she had uttered were to me and she lapsed into silence. Again a Divine voice told me to go thru Phoenix. He works in mysterious ways.

We got all settled and I joined the local Shrine Temple "Sabbar" and joined the unit "Legion of Honor" our duty was to carry the colors for the meetings and parades. We parade in Tombstone. Wilcox, Arizona City,

Front row: Honwald, Olson, Prosser, Bronn
Back: Sail Easy, Hladk, Fritzler, Kaster, Richards, Duggan & Sanders

and many other towns around the state. My daughter Carleen moved here also and the granddaughter had married the rancher in Colorado that ended sadly. So much is different then it used to be. When I got married I made the statement that I will marry only once.

We still went to all the Northampton reunions. Ever since I had one for radiomen around 1978 I been going to the Nora Maru reunions. I don't know which one it was when I met a blind ex sailor from the second Northampton that we had taken in with us. He has more humor than sighted people. He lost his eyesight from DDT spraying in Guantanamo, Cuba. His first wife left him because of it but now he has an angel that takes care of him. She gets a gold star. Her name is Alice. I have to mention them, as Fred Brutko has been bugging for years to write this book. I kept telling him I was close but it never happened. Now it has materialized.

I was president of the reunion association when it was held in 1993 in Norfolk, Va. At that time a shipmate named Glenn Randolph wanted stories of shipmate and pictures for a book that his wife Frankie and he would make. He explained that was a type of business they were in. He visited me in Illinois and I gave him pictures and information. The final book is a good one. There were only so many made for the shipmates that ordered them and one for the Library of Congress and one to the Naval Academy in Annapolis. It is a "Tome" as time went by here in Tucson a man in California wanted to do a website on Jason Nelson Robards. He got my name from the chairman of the association. It all sounded ok to me and one thing led to another.

He asked about my computer and said it was too old and he had about six of them and would send me one. But first he wanted mine to see if he could update it. I thought I had found Santa Claus. As it was I found the Devil. He trashed my computer and I lost my address book and favorites. Gone forever. He sent a nice computer but it was to advanced for me and I didn't want it. I sent it back and got the one I have now but not before I had spent eighty bucks for a new hard drive and 350 for a new monitor. For some reason he wouldn't talk to me any more. He did make a good web site honoring Jason and I had sent him twelve pictures of Mell and I with Jason on Bora Bora and also the one hundred dollar book that he promised to return to me. I lost all of it. I should have known. The old adage "beware of Greeks bearing gifts" he was half Greek by decent. I was sick over it. He would not answer telephones or letters. I lost a lot of sleep over the book, as I am all Navy. This all took place three years ago. I even had a lawyer try to scare him into returning the book but he paid no attention. Out of the blue I got an "e" mail and he was going to send the book this week and would call and tell me why I hadn't got it. Neither one came true. I had to accept the fact that it was gone and there was no way to ever get another.

In the meantime I got an e-mail from a shipmate on the other Northampton that a person was trying to get in touch with someone from the USS Northampton (CA26) that was my ship. I contacted the person and by e-mail I found that he had an uncle, that he never knew, that was killed on the Northampton. I was not on her when she went down but I have a lot of information of what happened. I told him I would put together lot of material about the ship both peacetime and war. The young sailor killed was born on Dec. 1, 1923 and died on Dec.1, 1942; he had just been nineteen for a few moments.

I gathered up a lot of memorabilia and went to Office Max and had it all printed. Made quite a package. I sent it all to Texas where this gentleman lived. He was so appreciative that I got an e-mail asking if his wife could make a picture in cloth and would I send him a picture. It was an offer I could not refuse and told him so. His wife has made many fantastic pictures of Indians, animals, servicemen etc. She is a genius. They wanted the picture when I was 23 and another as I am now, and at that time I was 85. The 19 by 24 quilt was out of this world. They didn't want to just send it to me and they were unable to come to Oro Valley to present it so Phillip Bucklew contacted the mayor and set it up to be presented at the Town Hall in November, 2004.

I got a call from a Mr. Kovitz that on Nov.3rd they would like me to come to city hall for a presentation. It was the day after the presidential election. Mell, Carleen and I arrived about seven o'clock. Some of my neighbors came and my nephew Raymond McNulty came down from Phoenix with his wife Carol and daughter Diana. There were quiet a few people in attendance I wore my chief uniform for the occasion. They had newspaper reporters and photographers in attendance. Then they showed the web site by the Bucklews on a huge movie screen. Just one movie that was really moving. Then the mayor addressed me and proclaimed Nov 3rd "Sherman E. Walgren Day" and gave me a proclamation

Office of the Mayor

Ore Valley, Arizona

Proclamation

Where as, Veterans Day gives every citizen the opportunity to honor the service of all past members of our armed forces; and

Where as, president Eisenhower called on all citizens to observe the day by paying appropriate homage to the veterans of all wars who have contributed so much to the preservation of this nation and through the rededication to the task of promoting an enduring peace; and

Where as, Mr. Sherman Walgren of Oro Valley did honorably serve his country in the U.S. Navy during world war 11; and

Where as, Mr. Walgren was inspired to write the poem "Sailing Home"

During his service aboard the USS Northampton; and

Where as. Mr. Walgren has been designated the "poet laureate" of the USS Northampton reunion association; and

Where as, Mr. Walgren provided significant assistance to Mr. And Mrs. Philip Bucklew of Boonsville, Texas as they researched the family history of Mr. Bucklews's uncle, Philip Dean Parsons, who was lost aboard the USS Northampton.

Now therefore, I Paul H. Loomis, mayor of the town of Oro Valley, Arizona do hereby proclaim November 3, 2004 as Sherman E. Walgren Day in Oro Valley; and

Be it further resolved that the Oro Valley town council wishes to express it's gratitude to Mr. Walgren for his service and for his inspiring poem as we recognize and honor all past members of the armed forces on Veteran's day, 2004.

Singed Paul H. Loomis

You can understand how honored I felt over this. Then the mayor presented the "quilt" to me and they asked that I recite the poem, which I was proud to do. This was all done over the world wide Internet. I thanked the mayor and the council and talked directly to the Bucklews and told them how moved I was and that Mell and I would have to visit them in Texas.

To my readers, if any, you can see all the wonderful things Margaret Bucklew has made. Just get on the internet and the address is http://www.chiseledincloth.com when your in the web site look for anything that says USS Northampton navigation and click on it. There are several links to be seen.

Just this February Mell and I went to Texas to meet these wonderful people that have done so much for his uncle and for me. For his uncle's memory and for me in my later life. I can't possibly thank them enough. We flew to Texas and they met us at the airport. It was like we had known them all our life. They drove us about eighty miles to their ranch. "Vaca Vista" they have twenty eight acres and five cows. Was a great three and a half days.

They took us to a big rodeo in Fort Worth. About half way through the lights went out and two spotlights were shown on Mell and I. The announcer told of my service in the Navy and that Mell and I had been married fifty-nine years, all this was on two large screens on either end of the arena and then a big heart enveloped her and they and I requested I kiss her. That was easy, I still enjoy kissing my wife. The audience cheered and clapped and I never ever expected such a wonderful greeting. The 'Trail boss" as I now call him and "M" for Margaret went all out to make us have a wonderful time and we did.

I also did recited the "two bell ceremony for the men lost on the ship. They feel I have a voice of resonance. Also another poem by Edgar Guest on "My Father's Name" and all too soon it was time to go home. On returning to Oro Valley it gave me the will to start this book. I've threatened to do it for a long time. As I near the end, but not of my life, I'm not planning on going anywhere soon other than my Chincoteague reunion in June and the Northampton reunion in October.

I hate to stop. It has been a trip through my life even tho there is so much I couldn't include. One may have had as exciting a life as mine but no one had a more exciting life. I keep on thinking this and that should have been included but you have to stop somewhere.

I want to take this opportunity to thank my wife Armella for such a wonderful trip through life. For Carleen my daughter, my granddaughter Laurel for calling me "Papa all these years. I truly was the only father she ever had. And also for my great grandsons "Justin" and "Tristin".

While in Fort Worth I bought them both huge belt buckles. So for now I thank God for sparing me on July 17, 1943 as without the help of the Lord the whole crew would have gone up like the atomic bomb. I thank my mother and father for my existence and all the friends that I have had and those I still have. I'm a happy man so long folks..............

The end.

Chapter Eight

Documents and Pictures

Action Reports:

~~CONFIDENTIAL~~

ACTION REPORT

USS CHINCOTEAGUE AVP 24

SERIAL 049 28 JULY 1943

ANTI-AIRCRAFT ACTION FROM JULY 14-17, 1943, REPORT ON.

[COVERS AIR ATTACKS ON VESSEL IN HARBOR AT SABOE BAY, VANIKORO ISLAND, SOLOMONS. SUSTAINED CONSIDERABLE DAMAGE.]

~~SECRET~~ DECLASSIFIED

ACTION REPORT

ORIGINAL

USS CHINCOTEAGUE AVP 24

SERIAL 048 25 JULY 1943

NARRATIVE OF ACTION AND SUBSEQUENT EVENTS FROM 14 TO 21 JULY.

[AIR ATTACK OFF ENTRANCE TO SABOE BAY PALAU PASSAGE, AND 15 MILES SOUTHWEST OF VANIKORO ISLAND, SANTA CRUZ GROUP, 16-17 JULY 1943.]

52531

OFFICE OF NAVAL RECORDS AND LIBRARY

CONFIDENTIAL

WAR DAMAGE REPORT

USS CHINCOTEAGUE AVP 24

SERIAL 054 28 JULY 1943

WAR DAMAGE TO U.S.S. CHINCOTEAGUE.

[SUSTAINED ON JULY 16, AND 17, 1943, OFF ENTRANCE TO SABOE BAY, PALLU PASSAGE, SANTA CRUZ GROUP.]

52531

OFFICE OF NAVAL RECORDS AND LIBRARY

CONFIDENTIAL

ACTION REPORT

USS CHINCOTEAGUE AVP 24

SERIAL 050 28 JULY 1943

ANTI-AIRCRAFT ACTION FROM JULY 14-17, 1943.

[REPEATED AIR ATTACKS ON VESSEL IN HARBOR AT SABOE BAY, VANIKORO ISLAND, SOLOMON ISLANDS, DURING WHICH THIS VESSEL SUSTAINED CONSIDERABLE DAMAGE.]

Ser.No.(048)

DECLASSIFIED CONFIDENTIAL

U. S. S. CHINCOTEAGUE

July 29, 1943.

From: Commanding Officer.
To: Commander South Pacific Force.

Via: Commander Fleet Air Wing ONE.
Commander Fleet Air, South Pacific
Commander Aircraft, South Pacific Force.

Subject: Narrative of Action and Subsequent Events from 14 to 21 July.

1. On July 6, 1943, the CHINCOTEAGUE reporting as relief for U.S.S. MACKINAC dropped anchor in Saboe Bay, Vanikoro Island for the purpose of carrying out seaplane tending operations. This work proceeded without incident to the afternoon of July 14th. On that day at about 1230 a plane, believed to be on a photographic mission was sighted at an altitude of approximately fifteen thousand feet. Fire was opened immediately, but with undetermined results. The ship stood out to sea and remained outside for about an hour, returning to base upon losing contact with the plane.

2. Normal routine continued through the rest of that day and during all of the next until 1847 in the evening when a Jap twin engined bomber was picked up by radar. That plane believed to be a Sally type after circling about for some minutes dropped two brilliant white flares about two thousand yards off the port quarter from an altitude of approximately fifteen hundred feet. These flares landed near the entrance to Saboe Bay. During this incident fire was not opened in order that full advantage might be taken of the darkness and our position kept hidden. Contact was lost shortly after the flares were dropped, the ship then returned to normal.

3. On the morning of the sixteenth at 0717, five Jap twin engined bombers were picked up by radar circling the bay and then sighted overhead. They released their bomb loads from an altitude of approximately eight thousand feet. The sticks fell about fifteen hundred yards from the ship, bursting in the jungle east of Saboe Bay head. Only the one run was made, the planes continuing on out of contact. A few hours later, at 1110, another formation was sighted overhead making a dummy run on the ship. Again these were thought to be the Sally type and this time there were nine of them flying in a close V of V's. On this run they passed on the starboard side heading out to sea. After circling about they came in from the sea, passing this time on the portside.

-1-

DECLASSIFIED - DOD DIR. 5200.9 of 27 SEP 58
BY ______ DATE ______

U. S. S. CHINCOTEAGUE

DECLASSIFIED

July 25, 1943.

Subject: Narrative of Action and Subsequent Events from 14 to 21 July.

- -

4. The ship got underway immediately by slipping the starboard anchor, and at the same time opened fire. No bombs were dropped, the planes disappearing eastward. Five minutes later at 1136 they came in again. This was the bombing run. They dropped sticks of three bombs each in a pattern, which, with our maneuvering, placed two sticks on our port quarter and one directly astern. No direct hits were sustained, the closest bomb falling about fifty yards from the stern resulting in some minor splinter damage about the fantail and to the trainers sight of number four 5"/38 gun. The ship continued on out to sea and when contact was lost returned at 1300 in order to receive VP 71 which was about to land for rest and fueling prior to proceeding on a bombing mission.

5. During this and all subsequent actions the guns were fired by local control. The ship carried no director and without one any anti-aircraft fire is not of great value.

6. During the night there was no activity. Early the next morning the planes of VP 71 began arriving from their overnight bombing mission. Radar had picked their IFF identification up as they came in. The last plane was landing at 0725 when the first stick of bombs from five twin engined enemy bombers bracketed the ship across the forecastle. They came in from the Northwest at about eight thousand feet, apparently having followed our planes all the way in. The ship got underway at 0726 heading out of the bay. Immediately thereafter the planes came in from the Southeast on their second run. The stick of bombs that was dropped fell about fifty yards astern. The planes circled off preparatory to making a third run. At 0738, just as the ship was emerging from the mouth of the bay, the bombs struck. The nearest burst about fifty feet from the ship on the starboard side at frame 105. Gasoline lines were ruptured and ignited as were pyrotechnics in the No. 1 M.W.B. (also numerous splinter holes were made in the ship's side). Fire parties proceeded to scene, gasoline system was blocked off between the rupture and the system below decks, and the fires were extinguished by the use of fog nozzles. Fires also started in living compartments C-201, C-203 and were extinguished by the fixed fog sprinkler system.

7. During this time the ship was moving at flank speed. This speed was not reduced when at 0757 the ship cleared the passage through the reefs. It should be noted here that until these reefs were cleared only evasive action other than recourse to speed was impracticable.

-2-

DECLASSIFIED CONFIDENTIAL.   U. S. S. CHINCOTEAGUE

July 25, 1943.

Subject: Narrative of Action and Subsequent Events from 14 to 21 July.

- -

8. At 0805 a new attack developed, four planes coming in from the starboard quarter. On this attack all bombs fell clear. This was made possible because having reached open sea evasive action could be taken by using flank speed and full rudder. When all contact was lost, and since it was necessary to return in order to dispatch VP 71 planes for Santos, the ship returned to port at 0853.

9. Having received orders to return to Santos, we dispatched all patrol planes with the exception of three that needed fueling. At 1020 we weighed anchor and stood off the entrance leaving bowser boats to fuel the remaining planes. It was intended to return to Saboe Bay at 1500 to pick up bowser boats and personnel. By 1120 the ship had cleared the reefs and was standing out to sea. Twenty five minutes later a new attack came on. Five Sallys overhead released sticks which bracketed the ship. We were maneuvering to the extreme degree again which helped to prevent any direct hits although some splinter damage was sustained. A few minutes later, having circled about into the sun they came in again. The stick of bombs again bracketed the ship. This time we received a direct hit by what is believed to be a one hundred k.g. delayed action bomb which pierced three decks, the super, main and second, before exploding in the after engine room. All after engineering personnel including the Chief Engineer were killed, as well as a fireman in the forward messing compartment. Number four gun went out of commission at the same time due to water damage.

10. The ship was now steaming at reduced speed on the forward engines using the starboard shaft. Furthermore power was lost on steering gear and hand steering was used during subsequent actions. At 1420 another attack developed. Three bombers came in on a run at eight thousand feet. On their first approach they streamed out a series of green flares while heading into the sun. Having circled about they started the bombing run. The ship opened fire with all guns. Again the ship was bracketed by bombs. At least one five hundred pound bomb falling along the port side stopped the forward engine room. The splinters and concussion produced by this stick resulted in considerable damage to personnel, the ship, and boats, one of which caught on fire. The remaining guns in commission from then on had to be manually operated.

(6)

-3-

U. S. S. CHINCOTEAGUE

July 25, 1943.

Subject: Narrative of Action and Subsequent Events from 14 to 21 July.

- -

11. Number three five inch reported one Jap plane broke formation during this attack and veered off trailing smoke. This was the only observed result of our firing. But this was later verified by a P.B.Y. that was in the vicinity.

12. As the ship lay dead in the water a final attack occurred at 1450. It was made by a single plane whose bombs fell two hundred yards abeam. This marked the end of the attacks, although at the time more were expected.

13. With the after engine room flooded, with some after compartments partly flooded, and water coming in through splinter holes the ship developed a heavy list to starboard. All available men including crews from the guns were immediately thrown in the fight to save the ship. Nothing could be done with the after engine room, but bucket brigades were placed in the flooded compartments at the stern and amidships. Handy billy pumps were likewise pressed into service.

14. The bucket brigades went into action at 1500 working without cease in the effort to bail the ship out. That night the struggle appeared to be hopeless, until power for submersible pumps could be obtained. Despite all efforts the water continued to gain.

15. It was discovered that in the forward engine room the water could be controlled at a depth of a few feet and efforts were undertaken to place the engines in commission. The first to respond were the generators, both the one hundred k.w. and the two hundred k.w. were started. At 2300 the main engines were turned over. After one unsuccessful attempt the next one caught hold and the ship got underway at 2350. After sailing for about an hour we were picked up by the THORNTON. That vessel sent a boat over with additional handy billy pumps which were immediately thrown into service.

16. With the THORNTON as escort we sailed for close on to two more hours. On two occasions in this period electrical fires were started and extinguished with CO2 in the forward engine room. At 0245 fire again broke out in this room.

(7)

July 25, 1943.

Subject: Narrative of Action and Subsequent Events from 14 to 21 July.

- -

On the inboard engine the scavaging belt was seen to be filling with lubricating oil as well as diesel. It was immediately decided to secure the engine. However with the excess amount of oil present on the belt the engine continued to run. There was then no means of control left; in a few seconds the engine began to overspeed, and in a few minutes to destroy itself. It was necessary to remove the crew, while the room was secured in an effort to smother the fire. At the same time foam generators were set up, the THORNTON came alongside, hoses were connected to her fire mains, and foam poured into the compartment.

17. The fire was fought with fog nozzles and foam until about 0545 the morning of the 18th when the last of the foam was used up. The fire appeared to be localized but still smoldering. The forward engine room was then battened down and all intakes covered by blankets and mattresses. All hands moved topside with the exception of the bucket brigades, which continued to function in other areas. At this time certain non essential men were transferred to the THORNTON which then pulled away in order to take us in tow.

18. At 0740 tow line was broken because of a submarine contact. The THORNTON proceeded to attack dropping two depth charges, returning when contact was lost. Tow was resumed at 0929 and continued until 1217 at which time the tow was cast off with the ship listing badly to starboard. Bucket brigades continued work but the flooding could not be checked. The stern was now settling low with less than two feet of free board remaining. As the degree of list was varying between twelve and eighteen degrees order was given to lighten ship, at which time torpedoes, heavy machinery, winches, and other heavy gear were jettisoned on the starboard side. This lightening of the ship plus the use of additional pumps flown in by P.B.Y., and the fight of the bucket brigades, enabled us to check the flooding and eventually to right the ship.

19. During this effort, at 1304, the THORNTON again came along the starboard side to furnish power for submersible pumps, and to receive our confidential and other valuable gear. She remained alongside until the next morning refusing to cast off that same evening when an air attack developed at 1743 just as the JENKINS hove in sight.

DECLASSIFIED CONFIDENTIAL

U. S. S. CHINCOTEAGUE

July 25, 1943.

Subject: Narrative of Action and Subsequent Events from 14 to 21 July.

- -

Three Jap bombers made one pass at the JENKINS, but before reaching us jettisoned the rest of their bombs as they sought to flee from four of our fighters. All three were seen shot down in flames which provided a great boost to morale.

20. That night the ship lay dead in the water with the JENKINS and TREVOR, which had arrived at 1820, acting as anti-submarine screen. Pumping and bucket brigades continued without stop.

21. At 1021 the morning of the 19th, the THORNTON was forced to cast off. Heavier seas arising resulted in a pounding together of the two ships, producing leaks into the THORNTON fireroom. The flooding was now under control and the fire died out in the forward engine room. The tug SONOMA came alongside at 1113 with more pumping equipment. She also had in tow a CHINCOTEAGUE motor launch containing sixteen men. These men left behind at Vanikoro, had fueled and despatched the three remaining planes, and had then decided to head for Espirito Santos in the open launch. The tug picked them up while underway to us. We were taken in tow by the SONOMA at 1220. From then until we arrived in port at 0825 the morning of the 21st nothing of consequence took place.

I. E. HOBBS.

File: FP1/A16-3/(2)
Serial No. 0249

UNITED STATES PACIFIC FLEET
U. S. Naval Air Force
FLEET AIR WING ONE

Ms

OF

DECLASSIFIED
[CONFIDENTIAL]

FIRST ENDORSEMENT to
USS CHINCOTEAGUE conf.
ltr. AVP24/A9 (048)
of July 25, 1943.

From: Commander Fleet Air Wing ONE.
To : Commander South Pacific Force.

Via : (1) Commander Fleet Air, South Pacific.
(2) Commander Aircraft, South Pacific Force.

Subject: Narrative of Action and Subsequent Events from 14 to 21 July.

1. Forwarded.

2. Attention is invited to the obvious need of a director to control antiaircraft gun fire when directed at a high formation of enemy aircraft.

3. By separate correspondence, recommendations have been submitted for recognition of outstanding conduct shown by the Commanding Officers of the U.S.S. CHINCOTEAGUE and U.S.S. THORNTON.

H. S. KENDALL.

0374

UNITED STATES PACIFIC FLEET

FLEET AIR COMMAND, SOUTH PACIFIC

CONFIDENTIAL

12 AUG 1943

SECOND ENDORSEMENT to
CO, USS CHINCOTEAGUE
conf. ltr. AVP24/A9,
ser. 048 of 25 July 1943.

From: Commander Fleet Air, South Pacific.
To : Commander South Pacific Force.

Via : Commander Aircraft, South Pacific Force.

Subject: Narrative of Action and Subsequent Events from 14 to 21 July.

1. Forwarded.

A. C. OLNEY,
Chief of Staff.

A16-3

UNITED STATES PACIFIC FLEET
AIRCRAFT SOUTH PACIFIC FORCE

Serial ______

C-O-N-F-I-D-E-N-T-I-A-L

4 SEP 1943

THIRD ENDORSEMENT to
CO, USS CHINCOTEAGUE
Conf. ltr. AVP24/A9
Ser. 048 of 25 July
1943.

From: Commander Aircraft, South Pacific Force.
To : Commander South Pacific Force.

Subject: Narrative of Action and Subsequent Events from 14 to 21 July.

1. Forwarded.

2. The foregoing action report indicates that the heavy batteries of the CHINCOTEAGUE were inadequate to protect the ship from high level bombing attack. These 5"/38 calibre guns were ineffectual due to lack of director control. Serious doubt exists as to the advisability of the present installation of non director controlled anti-aircraft protection on this class tender. Under the present system of control it is considered that the batteries are wasted and it is strongly recommended that an efficient director system be installed.

3. It is pointed out that emergency diesel driven auxiliary power unitslocated forward and aft clear of the engineering spaces would have survived the bombing attacks experienced by this ship and would have been of inestimable value as a source of power for emergency pumps.

4. It is of interest to note that electric submersible pumps were flown from Espiritu Santo to the distressed ship in a PBY-5 airplane. The airplane landed at sea and effected the transfer of the pumps to the escort vessel secured alongside the CHINCOTEAGUE. The escort vessel furnished the electric power for pumping. It is considered entirely feasible, with proper suspension bands, to transfer by air submersible pumps weighing up to 1000 pounds on the bomb racks.

A16-3

UNITED STATES PACIFIC FLEET
AIRCRAFT SOUTH PACIFIC FORCE

Serial [illegible]

C-O-N-F-I-D-E-N-T-I-A-L

THIRD ENDORSEMENT to
CO, USS CHINCOTEAGUE
Conf. ltr. AVP24/A9
ser. 048 of 25 July
1943.

Subject: Narrative of Action and subsequent events from
14 to 21 July. (cont'd.)

- -

5. Commander Aircraft, South Pacific Force cannot close without expressing his admiration for a splendid piece of seamanship and a superb fight against heavy odds in which all hands exemplified the best traditions of the Naval Service.

AUBREY W. FITCH

Copy to:
ComFairSouth.
ComFairWing One.
CO, USS CHINCOTEAGUE.

A16-3/(90)
Serial 001915

SOUTH PACIFIC FORCE
OF THE UNITED STATES PACIFIC FLEET
HEADQUARTERS OF THE COMMANDER

S-E-C-R-E-T

FOURTH ENDORSEMENT on
CO. USS CHINCOTEAGUE
Conf. ltr. AVP24/A9
Ser. 048 of 25 July 1943.

23 SEP 1943

From: The Commander South Pacific.
To : The Commander in Chief, U. S. Pacific Fleet.

Subject: Narrative of Action and Subsequent Events from
14 to 21 July.

1. Forwarded, heartily concurring in paragraph 5 of the third endorsement.

2. Commander South Pacific strongly recommends the immediate installation of an efficient director system for the control of the 5"/38 battery on this class of vessels.

3. Classification of this correspondence has been changed to secret.

T. F. SHAFROTH
Deputy Commander
South Pacific

Copy to:
Comairsopac
Comfair South
Comfairwing ONE
CO CHINCOTEAGUE

Dispatches:

[TH]E FOLLOWING DESPATCH FROM CINCPAC TO COMTASKFORCE EIGHT
[I]S QUOTED FOR INFORMATION:

CINCPAC TAKES PLEASURE IN PASSING FOLLOWING RECEIVED FROM OPNAV QUOTE CONVEY TO VICE ADMIRAL HALSEY AND TO ALL OFFICERS AND MEN OF FORCES EIGHT AND SEVENTEEN MY QUOTE WELL DONE UNQUOTE FOR THEIR EXCELLENT WORK X YOU STRUCK THE ENEMY A TELLING BLOW WHICH GIVES PROMISE OF MORE HARD BLOWS TO FOLLOW X YOUR DEEDS WERE MOST WELCOME TO THE COUNTRY AS CONCRETE EVIDENCE THAT OUT NAVY CAN AND WILL STRIKE HARD AND OFTEN FULL STOP PLEASE CONVEY TO FORCES UNQUOTE.

THE NORTHAMPTON WAS ONE OF THE SHIPS IN TASKFORCE EIGHT..... OUT OBJECTIVE WAS THE ISLAND OF WOTJE IN THE MARSHALL ISLANDS. CAME INTO THE ISLAND AT 0730 IN THE MORNING AND SHELLED FOR ONE HOUR AND A HALF. THE ISLAND WAS A BURNING MESS AFTER WE LEFT. ALL THEAT MORNING WAS SMOOTH SAILING AND CLEAR. THAT AFTERNOON THEIR PLANES FOUND US AND ATTACKED THE ENTERPRISE ONE PLANE RAMMING THE FLIGHT DECK AND DESTROYING TWO PLANES. NONE OF THE SHIPS WERE HIT BY BOMBS. OF THE SIX PLANES ALL BUT ONE WAS DESTROYE[D] A TORPEDO PLANE ALSO ESCAPED. AFTER THAT IT SOON TURNED TO FOUL WEATHER AND WE WERE ABLE TO ELUDE ANY FURTHER CHASE. THE NEXT DAY WAS ALSO COUDY AND VISIBILTY ALMOST NIL. EVERYONE WAS VERY GLAD TO SEE THE RAIN. WE KNOW THAT THEIR PLANES WERE STILL SEARCHING BUT THEY COULD NOT SEE US. THANK GOD FOR THAT. THE WHOLE ATTACK WAS HIGHLY SUCCESSFUL.........................
THE CHESTER WAS NOT WITH US FOR A WHILE. SHE WAS HIT BY ONE BOMB AND EIGHT MEN WERE KILLED. SHE DOWNED FOUR ENEMY PLANES IN HER ENCOUNTER. TWO DAY LATER SHE CAUGHT UP WITH US. THE WHOLE HARBOR CHEERED AS THE SHIPS ENTERED PEARL AFTER FOUR WEEKS AT SEA.

USS. Northampton—1-14-41—15M.

DISPATCH

Admiral 00 | Flag Sec. 66 | Staff Duty Off. 14 | Flag Lieut. 15 | Radio 19 | Aviator 95

Z DIVC5 191935 C85 C86 GR 174 BT

COMMANDER CRUISER DIVISION FIVE, THE SENIOR SHELLBACK PRESENT HAS REPORTED TO HIS IMPERIAL HIGHNESS NEPTUNUS REX, MOST HIGH AND EXALTING RULER OF THE SEVEN SEAS THAT HE IS APPROACHING THE HEADQUARTERS OF THE ROYAL DOMAIN WITH THE NORTHAMPTON AND SALTLAKECITY, BOTH SHIPS LOADED TO THE GUARDS WITH POLLYWOGS AND TADPOLES WHO HUMBLY SEEK ADMISSION INTO THE LOYAL ORDER OF SHELLBACKS X
THERE HAS JUST BEEN RECEIVED BY SEAWEED COMMUNICATIONS IN KELP CODE INFORMATION THAT DAVY JONES PEOLPO AND THE ROYAL SCRIBE ARE BEING DESPATCHED BY HIS GRACIOUS MAJESTY NEPTUNUS REX VIA SEA HORSE SQUADRONS TO BOARD EACH VESSEL ON SUNDAY AT 1500 TO SERVE NOTICE ON ALL POLLYWOGS TO BE PREPARED TO APPEAR BEFORE THE ROYAL COURT ON MONDAY AT 0930, READY TO FORSWEAR THEIR UNCERTAIN STANDING AS AMATEUR SAILORS AND IF DULY PENITENT AND FOUND WORTHY TO BE INITIATED INTO THE LOYAL ORDER OF SHELLBACKS X AND FURTHER HIS ROYAL HIGHNESS NEPTUNUS REX HAS GRANTED THESE TWO HEAVY CRUISERS THAT HE HAS NOT SEEN FOR SO LONG A PERIOD, PERMISSION TO REMAIN UNDERWAY WHILE BEING BOARDED BY DAVY JONES, THIS BEING AN EXTRAORDINARY COURTESY AS THE LAW OF THE SEA REQUIRES ALL SHIPS TO STOP ON THIS OCCASION.

VISUAL TO SALTLAKECITY MSGR TO NOR.

From	Action	Info.
COMCRUDIV 5	NORTHAMPTON SALTLAKECITY	022 TE 0738 LZT.
Date 19 JULY 41 GCT.		

Cupt.	Exec.	Comm.	Nav.	Gun.	Eng.	1st Lt.	Supply	Avis.	Rdo.	OOD	Head Dept.	Signal	Marine	Med.	Ath.	Dental	M.O.
10	11	20	60	90	70	50	40	95	19				66	75			

Admiral 00 | Flag Sec. 05 | Staff Duty Off. 14 | Flag Lieut. 15 | Radio 19 | Aviator 95

M-E-S-S-E-N-G-E-R-G-R-A-M

2Ø2Ø53

REQUEST YOU INFORM THOSE CONCERNED THAT THE VENGEANCE OF NEPTUNIS REX IS SWIFT AND TERRIBLE X WARN POLLYWOGS WHO ARE APPROACHING THE DREADFUL MYSTERIES IN ORDER THAT THEIR MINDS SOULS AND BODIES MAY BE STEELED TO THE ORDEAL THAT AWAITS THEM.

NOTE:- PASS TO NORTHAMPTON AND SALTLAKECITY FOR ACTION. JAGERSFONTEIN FOR INFORMATION

ORIG: FLAG SEC.
VISUAL ROUTINE.
WU S&F

From	Action	Info.
NAVAIDE TO NEPTUNUS REX	COMTASKFORCE 19	#3Ø C Ø954 LZT.
Date: 20 JULY '41 GCT.		

Capt. 10 | Exec. 11 | Comm. 20 | Nav. 60 | Gun. 90 | Eng. 70 | 1st Lt. 50 | Supply 40 | Avia. 95 | Rdo. 19 | OOD | Head Dept. | Signal | Marine 86 | Med. 75 | Ath. | Dental | M.O.

Admiral 00 | Flag Sec. 05 | Staff Duty Off. 14 | Flag Lieut. 15 | Radio 19 | Aviator 95

(C85 V DIVC5) Z DIVC5 211938 C85 C86 GR 2Ø BT

TAKE PRECAUTIONS TO INSURE THAT NO PERSONNEL ARE HURT DURING CEREMONIES AND IN CONNECTION WITH ANY NON SWIMMERS IN THE TANKS

(V-7)

C85 1945
SEM DIOL

From	Action	Info.
COMCRUDIV FIVE	NORTHAMPTON SALTLAKECITY	# 12 JF Ø845 LZT.
Date: 21 JULY '41GCT.		

Capt. 10 | Exec. 11 | Comm. 20 | Nav. 60 | Gun. 90 | Eng. 70 | 1st Lt. 50 | Supply 40 | Avia. 95 | Rdo. 19 | OOD | Head Dept. | Signal | Marine 86 | Med. 75 | Ath. | Dental | M.O.

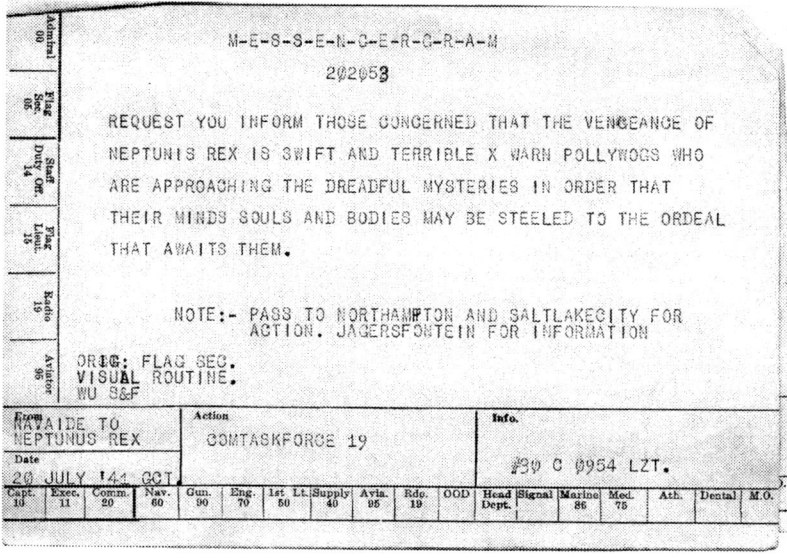

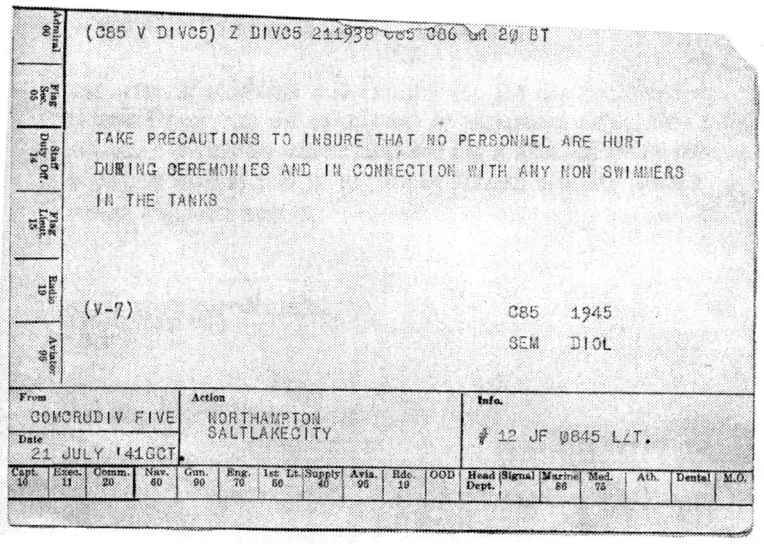

Z DIVC5 220055 C85 C86 GR 48 BT

THE DIVISION COMMANDER CONGRATULATES ALL THE NEW SHELLBACKS AND WELCOMES THEM INTO THE LOYAL ORDER OF SHELLBACKS OF THE DEEP X THE OLDER SHELLBACKS WORKED HARD AND DID A FINE JOB OF INITIATION X NEPTUNE REPORTS THAT HE IS GREATLY PLEASED WITH ALL HANDS X FUTURE POLLYWOGS BEWARE.

ORIG: STAFF DUTY OFFICER.
VISUAL ROUTINE.
WUS&F

From: COMCRUDIV 5
Date: 22 JULY 41 GCT.
Action: NORTHAMPTON, SALTLAKECITY
Info.: #1 CA 1356 LZT.

DISPATCH

C85 V DIVC5) 220333 GR 23 BT

NORTHAMPTON REPORTS THAT AT THE INITIATION CEREMONIES TODAY 39 OFFICERS AND 895 ENLISTED MEN X A TOTAL OF 934 X WERE MADE SHELLBACKS.

TOD
C85 0339
SEM TUFTS.

V-3
ORIG: FLAG LT.
WUS&F

From: COMCRUDIV 5
Date: 22 JULY41 GCT.
Action: SALTLAKECITY.
Info.: NORTHAMPTON
#5 CA 1645 LZT.

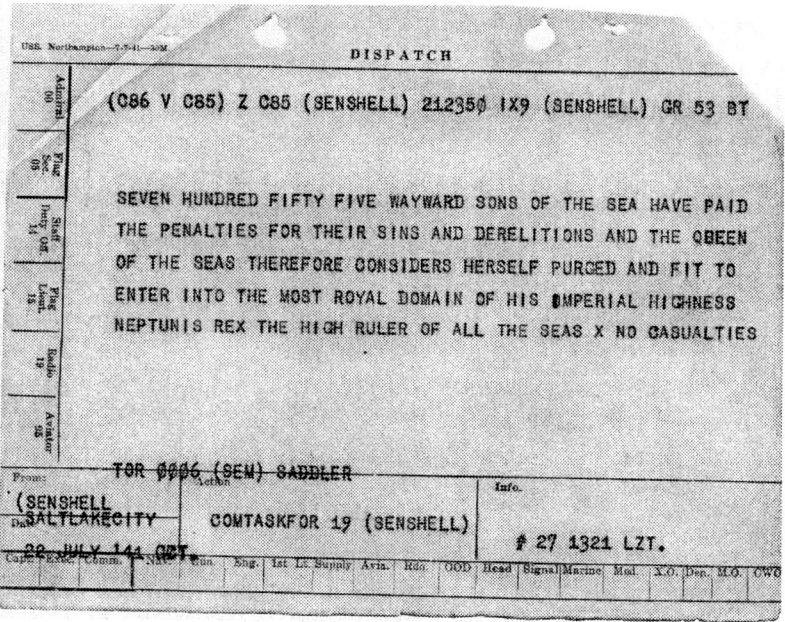

USS Northampton—7-5-41—30M

DISPATCH

(C86 V C85) Z C85 (SENSHELL) 212350 IX9 (SENSHELL) GR 53 BT

SEVEN HUNDRED FIFTY FIVE WAYWARD SONS OF THE SEA HAVE PAID THE PENALTIES FOR THEIR SINS AND DERELITIONS AND THE QBEEN OF THE SEAS THEREFORE CONSIDERS HERSELF PURGED AND FIT TO ENTER INTO THE MOST ROYAL DOMAIN OF HIS IMPERIAL HIGHNESS NEPTUNIS REX THE HIGH RULER OF ALL THE SEAS X NO CASUALTIES

TOR 0006 (SEM) SADDLER

From:	Action	Info.
(SENSHELL SALTLAKECITY	COMTASKFOR 19 (SENSHELL)	# 27 1321 LZT.
Date 20 JULY 1941 GCT.		

Admiral 06 · Flag Sec. 08 · Staff Duty Off. 14 · Flag Lieut. 15 · Radio 19 · Aviator 25

Capt. · Exec. · Comm. · Nav. · Gun. · Eng. · 1st Lt. · Supply · Avia. · Rdo. · OOD · Head · Signal · Marine · Med. · X.O. · Dep. · M.O. · CWO

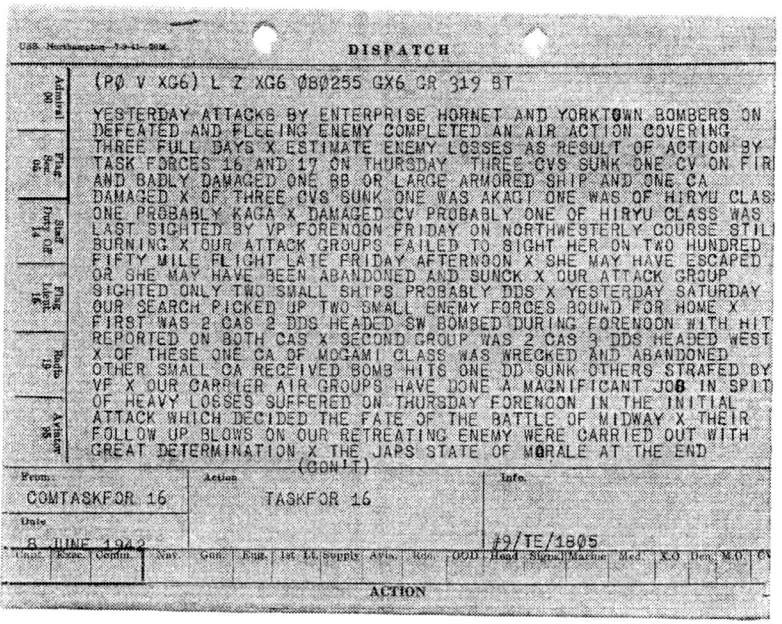

USS. Northampton—7-9-41—[illegible]

DISPATCH

(PØ V XG6) L Z XG6 ØBØ255 GX6 GR 319 BT

YESTERDAY ATTACKS BY ENTERPRISE HORNET AND YORKTOWN BOMBERS ON DEFEATED AND FLEEING ENEMY COMPLETED AN AIR ACTION COVERING THREE FULL DAYS X ESTIMATE ENEMY LOSSES AS RESULT OF ACTION BY TASK FORCES 16 AND 17 ON THURSDAY THREE CVS SUNK ONE CV ON FIR[E] AND BADLY DAMAGED ONE BB OR LARGE ARMORED SHIP AND ONE CA DAMAGED X OF THREE CVS SUNK ONE WAS AKAGI ONE WAS OF HIRYU CLAS[S] ONE PROBABLY KAGA X DAMAGED CV PROBABLY ONE OF HIRYU CLASS WAS LAST SIGHTED BY VP FORENOON FRIDAY ON NORTHWESTERLY COURSE STIL[L] BURNING X OUR ATTACK GROUPS FAILED TO SIGHT HER ON TWO HUNDRED FIFTY MILE FLIGHT LATE FRIDAY AFTERNOON X SHE MAY HAVE ESCAPED OR SHE MAY HAVE BEEN ABANDONED AND SUNCK X OUR ATTACK GROUP SIGHTED ONLY TWO SMALL SHIPS PROBABLY DDS X YESTERDAY SATURDAY OUR SEARCH PICKED UP TWO SMALL ENEMY FORCES BOUND FOR HOME X FIRST WAS 2 CAS 2 DDS HEADED SW BOMBED DURING FORENOON WITH HIT[S] REPORTED ON BOTH CAS X SECOND GROUP WAS 2 CAS 3 DDS HEADED WEST X OF THESE ONE CA OF MOGAMI CLASS WAS WRECKED AND ABANDONED OTHER SMALL CA RECEIVED BOMB HITS ONE DD SUNK OTHERS STRAFED BY VF X OUR CARRIER AIR GROUPS HAVE DONE A MAGNIFICANT JOB IN SPIT[E] OF HEAVY LOSSES SUFFERED ON THURSDAY FORENOON IN THE INITIAL ATTACK WHICH DECIDED THE FATE OF THE BATTLE OF MIDWAY X THEIR FOLLOW UP BLOWS ON OUR RETREATING ENEMY WERE CARRIED OUT WITH GREAT DETERMINATION X THE JAPS STATE OF MORALE AT THE END

(CON'T)

From:	Action	Info.
COMTASKFOR 16	TASKFOR 16	
Date: 8 JUNE 1942		#9/TE/1805

Capt. | Exec. | Comm. | Nav. | Gun. | Eng. | 1st Lt. | Supply | Avia. | Rdo. | OOD | Head | Signal | Marine | Med. | X.O. | Den. | M.O. | C[V]

ACTION

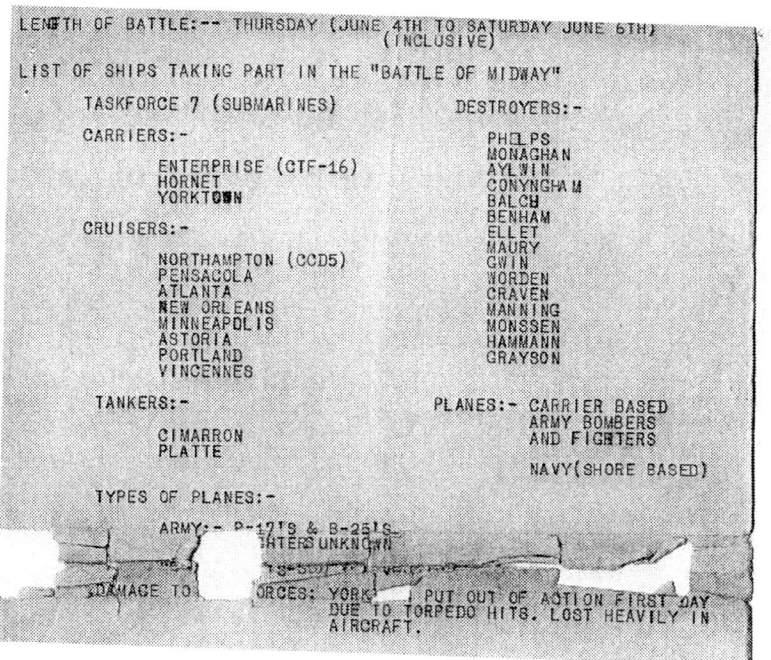

LENGTH OF BATTLE:-- THURSDAY (JUNE 4TH TO SATURDAY JUNE 6TH)
(INCLUSIVE)

LIST OF SHIPS TAKING PART IN THE "BATTLE OF MIDWAY"

TASKFORCE 7 (SUBMARINES)

CARRIERS:-

ENTERPRISE (CTF-16)
HORNET
YORKTOWN

CRUISERS:-

NORTHAMPTON (CCD5)
PENSACOLA
ATLANTA
NEW ORLEANS
MINNEAPOLIS
ASTORIA
PORTLAND
VINCENNES

DESTROYERS:-

PHELPS
MONAGHAN
AYLWIN
CONYNGHAM
BALCH
BENHAM
ELLET
MAURY
GWIN
WORDEN
CRAVEN
MANNING
MONSSEN
HAMMANN
GRAYSON

TANKERS:-

CIMARRON
PLATTE

PLANES:- CARRIER BASED
ARMY BOMBERS
AND FIGHTERS

NAVY(SHORE BASED)

TYPES OF PLANES:-

ARMY:- B-17'S & B-25'S
[illegible]GHTERS UNKNOWN
[illegible]

DAMAGE TO [illegible]ORCES: YORK[illegible] PUT OUT OF ACTION FIRST DAY
DUE TO TORPEDO HITS. LOST HEAVILY IN
AIRCRAFT.

USS Chincoteague Bomb Damage Reports:

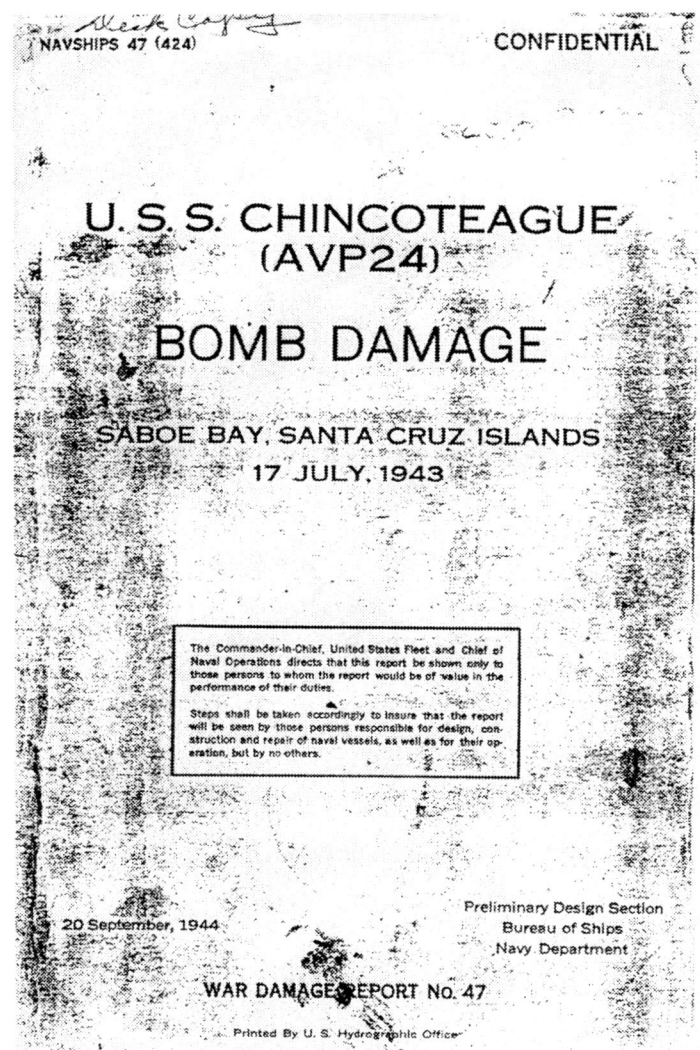

Aleck Copy

NAVSHIPS 47 (424)

CONFIDENTIAL

U. S. S. CHINCOTEAGUE (AVP24)

BOMB DAMAGE

SABOE BAY, SANTA CRUZ ISLANDS
17 JULY, 1943

The Commander-in-Chief, United States Fleet and Chief of Naval Operations directs that this report be shown only to those persons to whom the report would be of value in the performance of their duties.

Steps shall be taken accordingly to insure that the report will be seen by those persons responsible for design, construction and repair of naval vessels, as well as for their operation, but by no others.

20 September, 1944

Preliminary Design Section
Bureau of Ships
Navy Department

WAR DAMAGE REPORT No. 47

Printed By U. S. Hydrographic Office

U. S. S. CHINCOTEAGUE (AVP24)

Bomb Damage

Saboe Bay, Santa Cruz Islands
17 July, 1943

Class..........Seaplane Tender Small (AVP10)	Length (W.L.)................300 Ft. 0 In.
Launched........April 15, 1942	Beam (W.L.)..................41 Ft. 1 In.
Displacement........1,695 Tons	Draft (Before Damage) Forward..... 12 Ft. 0 In. Aft......14 Ft. 7 In.

Reference:

(a) C.O. CHINCOTEAGUE ltr. AVP24/A9/(048) of 25 July 1943, (Action Report).
(b) C.O. CHINCOTEAGUE ltr. AVP24/A9/(054) of 28 July 1943, (War Damage Report).
(c) Comdt. NYMI ltr. AVP24/L11-1(351-621876) of 30 November 1943.
(d) C.O. CHINCOTEAGUE ltr. AVP24/A9(01) of 13 January 1944.
(e) C.O. CHINCOTEAGUE ltr. AVP24/S93 of 11 Feb. 1944.
(f) Comdt. NYMI ltr. AVP24/L11-1(351-621904) of 20 March 1944. (War Damage Report).
(g) Comservpac.ltr. Aux/S41/(70-6) (1276) of 17 Aug. 1944.
(h) C.O. CHINCOTEAGUE ltr. AVP24/S41(0111) of 18 Nov. 1944.

CONTENTS

LIST OF PHOTOGRAPHS

SECTION I - SUMMARY

1. CHINCOTEAGUE underwent [redacted] The attacking groups varied from a single plane to a formation of nine bombers. Flooding which resulted from the damage was extensive. CHINCOTEAGUE's survival is attributable both to the aggressive manner in which her personnel took action to remove the damage water and to her adequate stability characteristics.

2. At 0738, on 17 July, two bombs missed the ship and landed in the water about 50 feet from the starboard side, detonating a short distance below the surface. Numerous fragments pierced the shell, some below the waterline. Several fires were ignited, including a gasoline fire, but these were effectively extinguished. Flooding through the fragment holes below the waterline reduced the GM of the vessel from about 3.2 feet to about 1.6 feet. In spite of this reduction in GM, the stability characteristics were still satisfactory for keeping the vessel upright in case of some additional damage or flooding. Efforts to plug fragment holes a short distance above the waterline were unsuccessful, and these holes caused considerable additional flooding after a later attack. Plugs inserted from the outside worked loose from some of the holes and fell out, while the ship was underway, and a mat, improvised from canvas, proved unsuitable as a watertight covering. Undoubtedly, efforts of personnel were taxed to the limit by the necessity of fueling planes, manning the anti-aircraft battery, and at the same time, endeavoring to meet all damage control requirements.

3. At 1150, some four hours later, a small general purpose bomb* with a short delay in the fuze struck and penetrated the superstructure, main and second decks and detonated in the after engine room. The hull was not ruptured, but the engine room was flooded through a broken 8-inch sea suction line supplying cooling water to the main propulsion diesel engine. As the draft increased, water entered the ship through the fragment holes above the second deck, which had not been plugged effectively. Large free surface areas were created on the second deck. CHINCOTEAGUE soon became unstable with a negative GM of about (-)0.4 feet and lolled to starboard at an angle variously reported as 12 to 18 degrees. The vessel proceeded at half speed, using the forward engines.

4. At 1420, another bomb landed in the water about 15 feet from the port side, detonating underwater. This did not rupture the hull, but the shell was indented in way of the forward engine room. The forward main engines stopped due to shock, leaving the vessel dead in the

---

* The identification of this bomb will be discussed in paragraph 25.

water. After repairs had been made by the engine room force, the vessel got underway again at 2350.

5. At 0245, on 18 July, the inboard one of the two main propulsion diesels in the forward engine room overheated, and in an attempt to secure the engine, control was lost and the engine ran away, driving the crew from the engine room and starting a serious fire. The fire was confined to the engine room and gradually burned itself out.

6. The unusual nature of the casualty highlights the necessity for keeping heavy duty diesel prime movers under load, and thus under control when operational difficulties are encountered. This is especially true after battle damage. The racing engine forced the abandoning of the engine room. The fire which the engine caused was thus permitted to gain such headway that it was brought under control only with difficulty.

7. The condition of negative stability was the result of free surface caused by:

(a) Free water remaining from the first attack.

(b) Water on the second deck which entered after the direct hit through holes ineffectively plugged after the first attack.

(c) Flooding incident to the direct hit.

This combined flooding created a stability condition closely paralleling that of ERIE*. Jettisoning of weights from the low side was instituted in an effort to correct the list, indicating that the negative stability condition was not recognized. Fortunately, the unwatering process corrected the dangerous condition of negative stability before an upsetting moment could occur from the injudicious removal of weights. Eventually, the list was removed, and the ship was then towed to Espiritu Santo where temporary repairs were made.

8. The many and varied aspects of war damage which arose in this case, strained the damage control organization to the utmost. It is an excellent example of the contingencies for which a damage control organization must be trained.

SECTION II - NARRATIVE

(All Photos and Plates).

9. This report is based on the information contained in the references. The photographs were furnished by the Commanding Officer and

* BuShips War Damage Report Number 31.

the Navy Yard, Mare Island. The plates were prepared by the Bureau of Ships from plans submitted by the Navy Yard, Mare Island.

10. On 6 July, 1943, CHINCOTEAGUE anchored in Saboe Bay, Vanikoro Island, for the purpose of carrying out seaplane tending operations. The work proceeded without incident until 14 July. On the fourteenth and fifteenth of July, several contacts were made with enemy planes. These planes, however, did not attack CHINCOTEAGUE.

11. On the morning of the sixteenth at 0717, five Japanese bombers made a bombing run, releasing at 8,000 feet, and then retired. The bombs landed in the jungle about 1500 yards away. At 1110, another formation of nine bombers was sighted. These planes made several practice runs on the vessel, during which CHINCOTEAGUE got underway by slipping the starboard anchor cable. At 1136, the planes made a bombing run which resulted in misses astern and on the port quarter. The nearest bomb, falling about 50 yards from the stern, caused minor fragment damage to the fantail, and the trainer's sight of No. 4, 5-inch/38 gun. CHINCOTEAGUE continued out to sea and after contact was lost, returned at 1300 to proceed with fueling of a patrol bomber group which was scheduled to carry out a night bombing mission.

12. There was no activity during the night. Early the next morning, the bomber group returned from its mission and landed. As the last plane was landed at 0725, CHINCOTEAGUE was bracketed by a stick of bombs from five enemy twin-engined bombers which apparently had followed the patrol bombers. The ship got underway immediately and started out of the bay. A second attack was made by the same group of bombers shortly after the ship was underway. The bombs fell about 50 yards astern. No damage was received from either of the first two attacks. At 0738, as the ship was emerging from the mouth of the bay, a third attack developed. Two bombs landed in the water about 50 feet off the starboard side, detonating a short distance below the surface opposite frames 54 and 105. Numerous fragments pierced the shell, some below the waterline.

13. Fragments from the bomb opposite frame 105 (No. 1 on Plate 1) penetrated the starboard shell strakes above and below the waterline, damaging the interior structure and starting fires in bedding in C-201L and C-202L. These fires were extinguished by means of the fixed fog sprinkler system. Hot fragments also ruptured gasoline lines at the fueling station on the main deck at frame 110 and ignited the gasoline. Damage control parties isolated the damaged portion of the gasoline system and extinguished the fire, by the use of fog nozzles. The gasoline tanks were not punctured, the 1/2-inch HTS doubler plates in way of these tanks being sufficient to prevent penetration of the shell. Minor flooding was reported in C-201L and C-202L. It is probable that this flooding was entirely due to firefighting, as the second deck at this time was about 2-1/2 feet above the existing waterline, and no appreciable list was reported. Some of the fragment holes in these compartments were plugged from the outside, and an external mat improvised from canvas was used in an attempt to cover other holes. However, while the ship was underway,

plugs worked loose and fell out, while air gaps along the edges of the mat nullified its value. It will be brought out later how this failure to make the hull watertight above the second deck permitted the formation of large areas of free surface which would have been avoided had the holes been plugged effectively at this time.

14. Cofferdam C-6V flooded to the waterline through fragment holes. All compartments in the refrigerator space on the platform deck between bulkheads 113 and 121, except the meat room, flooded to a depth of 4 feet through fragment holes in the shell below the second deck. This flooding was eliminated by opening manholes in the platform deck and allowing the water to enter stuffing box compartments C-414E and C-413E from which it was pumped overboard by the ship's drainage system. Aviation lubricating oil pump room C-415E flooded to the overhead through open watertight access hatch 3-117-1 on the platform deck. Fragment holes below the second deck were plugged.

15. As a result of the bomb (No. 2 on Plate I) detonating opposite frame 54 starboard, numerous fragments dented and pierced the shell of the vessel. Little interior damage was noted. The column of water caused by the bomb detonation deluged the topsides and buckled the 1/4-inch STS splinter protection bulwark on the main deck in way of the torpedo stowage. Hot fragments ignited the starboard motor whaleboat. The fire was extinguished quickly. Water entered all starboard compartments between bulkheads 44 and 65 on the platform deck through fragment holes in the shell. The armory (A-310-1A) flooded to a depth of 2 feet 6 inches. Water traveled athwartships through non-watertight doors, flooding the passageway and S.D. stores A-310-1A on the port side to about the same depth. Torpedo workshop A-310-1AE flooded to a depth of one foot. The water in these compartments was eventually cleared by plugging the fragment holes and using submersible pumps and bucket brigades. In S.D. stores A-310-1A, many loose papers hampered the unwatering process by intermittenly clogging the strainers of the submersible pumps. 20mm clipping room A-308M and 20mm magazine A-309M also flooded to a depth of one foot. Fragment holes in these compartments were plugged and the water removed by a bucket brigade. As reported in reference (f), small arms magazine A-307M flooded to the waterline through fragment holes. Underwater sound room A-421C flooded completely through watertight hatch 3-59-1 in passageway A-310-1A, which was not properly secured. These two compartments were not unwatered until drydocking. The fragment holes in aviation bunk room A-207-1L on the second deck above the waterline, were not plugged properly and resulted in some flooding during later attacks when a list developed.

16. After reaching the open sea, CHINCOTEAGUE was attacked by four planes at 0805. All bombs fell clear and no damage resulted. The enemy planes withdrew and the vessel returned to the bay to fuel planes. At 1020, the ship weighed anchor and left the bay. At 1120,

enemy planes were again contacted and at 1145, the first bombing run took place. All bombs fell clear.

17. Five minutes later, a second attack developed. In this attack, the vessel was struck by a small general purpose bomb with a short delay in the fuze. The bomb pierced the superstructure deck between frames 81 and 82 about 18 inches inboard of the port deck edge, and continued through the main and second decks, traveling almost vertically downward and slightly inboard. After piercing the second deck, the bomb was deflected aft by bulkhead 81 and detonated in the after engine room at about frame 84, just forward of and between the two diesel main engines. The inner bottom was ruptured, but the shell of the vessel was not pierced. Foundations and piping in the vicinity of the detonation were demolished. An 8-inch suction line, supplying cooling water to the main propulsion diesel engines was ruptured. The engine room flooded to the overhead. The port side of bulkhead 81 was badly buckled and ruptured and bulkhead 80 was distorted and punctured. The second deck above the engine room was bulged up a maximum of 16 inches over the detonation. Other effects of the blast were noted in damaged access and ventilation trunks. The rapid flooding of the after engine room and other material damage resulted in loss of power to the port shaft and rendered useless other important auxiliaries. CHINCOTEAGUE remained at sea following this attack, maintaining a speed of 10 knots by the forward engines. The flooding resulting from No.3 bomb caused the vessel to settle and trim by the stern, placing the second deck aft of amidships below the waterline. Compartments C-201L and C-202L began to flood slowly through the ineffectively plugged fragment holes. This flooding reduced the stability of CHINCOTEAGUE to a negative value and a list to starboard developed. This resulted in increased flooding in C-201L and C-202L and caused water to enter aviation bunk room A-207-1L.

18. At 1420, of the same afternoon, three bombers dropped numerous bombs which bracketed the ship. One bomb detonated about 15 feet from the port side at frame 65. The detonation dented a large area of shell plating between frames 54 and 74. The plating was neither ruptured nor pierced by fragments. The main area of indentation extended from about 2 feet above the waterline to about 5 feet below with less indentation extending up to the main deck. The column of water also deluged the topside, doing damage to equipment. Shock broke electrical equipment and gages in the forward engine room. At this point, the forward main engines stopped, leaving CHINCOTEAGUE dead in the water.

19. At 1450, with CHINCOTEAGUE dead in the water, a single plane made another attack. No damage resulted, as the bombs fell about 200 yards abeam. At about 1800, the eleventh and final attack was made, but the enemy planes were driven off by air cover which had been provided in the meantime. CHINCOTEAGUE at this point

had lost all power, was flooding slowly in many compartments, and was listing to starboard.

20. All available men were pressed into service to control the flooding. With no power available, only the gasoline handy billy pumps could be used. These were augmented by extensive bucket brigades. These were not enough, and despite all efforts, the water continued to gain. Later that night, it was discovered tha t the flooding in the forward engine room could be held below the level of the floor plates and an attempt was made to regain power. The generators were successfully started, and the main engines were put into commission. At 2350, the vessel got underway.

21. About one hour later, THORNTON (AVD11) arrived and transferred additional handy billy pumps to CHINCOTEAGUE. These pumps, along with the electric submersible pumps now in operation, were of considerable help in keeping even with the flooding. During the night, two electrical fires started in the forward engine room and were extinguished with CO_2.

22. At 0230, on 18 July, the inboard (No. 2) main engines began to overheat and black smoke was emitted from the stack. At 0245, it was decided to investigate the engine. It was not desirable to stop both main engines simultaneously since all starting air had been exhausted and it would have been impossible to restart them. The procedure followed in picking up the THORNTON small boat two hours previously, had been to place the engines in idling position and then dump the oil from the hydraulic clutch, thus taking power off the propeller shaft. The same procedure was followed in investigating the overheating of No. 2 engine. When the load was removed, however, the engine began to speed up. The throttle was closed with no apparent effect. No. 2 engine picked up speed rapidly and within 30 seconds, had reached a dangerously high speed. No. 1 engine was secured, and the engine room abandoned with No. 2 engine racing out of control. The runaway engine started a fire. An effort was made to smother the fire by closing all access openings and at the same time foam generators were set up. THORNTON came alongside, hoses were connected to her fire mains and foam poured into the compartment. The fire was fought until 0545, when the last of the foam was expended. The compartment was then battened down and all intakes plugged. The fire at this time appeared to be localized, but still smoldering. The after bulkhead of I.C. Room A-310-2C was kept cool by spray from a gasoline handy billy pump.

23. At 0740, the tow line was broken because of a submarine contact THORNTON resumed the tow at 0939 and continued until 1217, at which time the list had increased to a point where the tow had to be dropped. Flooding contined to gain despite the efforts of the crew. The stern had settled and the list was variously reported as 12 to 18 degrees starboard. Orders were given to lighten ship. Torpedoes, heavy machinery,

winches and other gear on the starboard side were jettisoned. Apparently, as the result of a radio request to Espiritu Santo, additional pumps were flown in by a patrol plane. These eventually removed much of the free surface. THORNTON again came alongside at 1304 to furnish power for submersible pumps and remained until the following morning. During the night of the eighteenth, CHINCOTEAGUE remained dead in the water with THORNTON alongside. JENKINS (DD447) and TREVER (DMS16) acted as anti-submarine screen. Pumping and bucket brigades continued without stop.

24. Heavy seas forced THORNTON to cast off on the morning of 19 July. The tug SONOMA (AT12) came alongside at 1113 with additional pumping equipment and took CHINCOTEAGUE in tow, arriving at Espiritu Santo at 0825 on 21 July. After temporary repairs to make the hull watertight were accomplished, CHINCOTEAGUE was towed to Navy Yard, Mare Island, arriving 4 September, 1943. All battle damage was repaired and many authorized alterations completed. The vessel is now back in service.

SECTION III - DISCUSSION

A. Types of Bombs

25. From fragments recovered, the bomb which struck CHINCOTEAGUE has been identified by the U.S. Navy Bomb Disposal School, Washington, D. C., as a Japanese Type 99, No. 6. This has a total weight of 63 Kg. (138.4 pounds) and contains an explosive charge of 32 Kg. (70.4 pounds) of picric acid. It has a machined case which has caused some authorities to classify it as a semi-armor-piercing bomb. However, the percentage of explosive weight is 50.8, which places it in the U.S. general purpose category. The bomb passed through three decks totaling 13/16 inches in thickness, pierced a door frame and detonated some 25 to 30 feet from the point of initial impact -indicative of a short delay, of the order of .025 - .030 seconds, in the fuze. The fragment damage from the two bombs which landed a short distance from the starboard side, was consistent with that which would be caused by bombs of the same size as that which hit the ship. Their fuzing was such as to cause detonation a short distance below the surface of the water.

26. Bomb No. 4 is reported to have detonated below the surface of the water about 30 feet from the port shell of the vessel. The references estimate this to have been a 500-pound bomb. The damage to the side of the vessel indicates that the bomb was probably smaller and closer to the shell. There is no evidence of fragment attack, an indication that the fuze was set with a short delay which caused detonation below the surface. The indentation of the shell consisted of two portions. The deeper of these extended from frames 60 to 70 and from the waterline to about 7 feet below the waterline. The maximum

indentation seems to have occurred at about bulkhead 65. Above this area, a region of shallower indentation extended to the main deck. This is clearly shown in photo 12. The position of the deeper indentation indicates that the bomb detonated about 3 or 4 feet below the surface. The area of indentation was quite small, thus placing the detonation fairly close to the vessel. The damage was of the order of that caused by small charges fairly close to the hull. The area of shallower indentation above the waterline and the reported damage to bridge equipment is clearly a result of the accompanying water geyser. This is still another sign that the detonation occurred quite close to the hull. The evidence thus indicates that this bomb was one of the 63Kg. type and that it detonated a short distance below the surface, not far from the hull.

27. When bombs Nos. 1 and 2 detonated close to the surface about 50 feet from the ship, some fragments with a trajectory over the surface of the water pierced shell plating below the waterline. Apparently, that portion of the hull was exposed above the surface of the water while the ship was rolling or heeled in a turn. The plating penetrated was light, 3/10 to 1/4-inch medium steel. Although bomb No. 4 landed closer to the ship, its detonation was sufficiently deep beneath the surface and still far enough away to prevent fragment penetration. The behavior of the fragments from these bombs was consistent with the damage caused by a bomb of a similar size and type which detonated upon impact with the main deck of CHESTER (CA27)*. In that case, several fragments traveled a horizontal distance of over 100 feet: through the 1/4 and 3/16-inch medium steel bulkheads of the wardroom pantry to dent the 1/4-inch forward bulkhead of the wardroom.

28. On vessels of the same class as CHINCOTEAGUE, the shell plating in way of the gasoline tanks is somewhat heavier than the shell in other locations in order to provide a margin for corrosion. A 1/2-inch doubler (some of the ships have STS), was installed over the shell in way of these tanks for fragment protection. It is notable in the case of CHINCOTEAGUE that although the bomb fragments made many indentations in the HTS doubler, the shell itself was not penetrated.

B. Structural Damage

29. Reference (f) states that the bomb which struck the ship detonated "just above the inner bottom" between frames 85 and 86. Careful study of the references and photographs indicates that the point of detonation probably was somewhat higher, possibly just above the engine room floor plates. This estimate is based on the facts that the damage to the inner bottom and foundations was sharply localized (Photos 7 and 8) and has the appearance of having been caused by large fragments rather than blast. The effects of blast are evidenced by the bulging of the second deck (Photo 10), the distortion of bulkhead 81 and the indentation of the panels of the inner bottom forward of the disrupted area

---

* Buships War Damage Report No. 10.

(Photo 8). Bulkheads 81 and 80 were also punctured by fragments. These facts tend to place the center of detonation somewhat higher than reported. Possibly the bomb tumbled after penetrating the second deck and was nose-up when detonation occurred. In any event, the structural damage was somewhat less than would be expected normally from a bomb of this size.

C. Machinery Damage

30. Machinery and electrical damage from bombs Nos. 1 and 2 was caused entirely by flooding with the exception of degaussing cables which were cut by fragments in several places. Damage to the machinery in the after engine room, caused by the bomb which hit the ship, was not extensive, considering the location of the detonation.

31. The engineering casualty in the forward engine room occurred at a critical time. It resulted in a serious fire and the loss of all power when power was urgently required to provide pumping capacity. The cause of the casualty is not clear. The rapidity of events and the subsequent fire make an analysis of the evidence difficult. A study of the case, however, reveals the following facts and probabilities.

32. The flooding of the after engine room left the mobility of the vessel dependent upon the two 1600 h.p. Fairbanks-Morse diesel engines geared to the starboard shaft. The operation of these engines was further complicated by the fact that all starting air had been expended. Although not specifically reported, presumably some casualty to the air system prevented the replenishment of the air supply. This made it imperative that the engines not be stopped simultaneously for any reason, since they could not be started again. After operating satisfactorily for about three hours, the port (inboard) engine began to overheat and it was noticed that an abnormal amount of lubricating oil was being used. The temperature of the exhaust, normally about 600°F, was found to be 800°. About 150 gallons of lubricating oil disappeared in approximately 15 minutes, indicating a probable failure in some portion of the lubricating oil system as a result of bomb No. 4. Smoke from the stack appeared to be thick and black. The exact condition of the engine could not be observed since all gages had been damaged. After twenty minutes it was decided that it was dangerous to operate the engine further. Both engines were brought to slow speed and the hydraulic clutch on the port engine dumped, releasing the load. The engine began to pick up speed immediately. The throttle was closed with no apparent result. The governor and overspeed trip did not operate. The engine reached a dangerously high speed in 30 seconds. Cylinder relief valves blew open, the indicator card cocks blew off and black smoke poured into the engine room. The engine room was abandoned and all hatches secured with the engine racing at high speed. The fuel oil shut-off valve was not closed

due to the speed of events and because it was believed that the engine was running away on lubricating oil rather than diesel oil. Reference (h) states that the hydraulic clutch was not reconnected because " it was felt that the engine would be damaged by a sudden increase of load upon it". The engine finally stopped when the pistons seized. According to reference (f), the cylinder liners were so badly warped that a 90-ton jack was necessary for the removal of the pistons at Mare Island.

33. After the fire caused by the runaway engine was extinguished, an inspection of the engine revealed that the blower which supplies the engine with scavenge air had two inches of oil in the bottom of the casing. A more complete inspection upon arrival at Mare Island disclosed two important points. First, an examination showed that the fuel control rod which operate the fuel injection pump control racks had elongated, due to heat, and as a result, ten of the fuel injection pump control racks were open from one-third to full when the throttle was closed. The fuel injection pumps near the throttle end were closed, while those farther away were open by amounts which increased as the distance from the throttle increased. Second, it was discovered that the air intake filter to the blower, which is horizontal, was severely clogged with foreign matter. The filter, upon inspection, was so heavily clogged that water would not "pour" through it. Furthermore, it had been bellied down into the intake pipe by the excessive vacuum created between the screen and the blower.

34. It is evident that the detonation of bomb No. 4 shook down foreign matter onto the filter. It is not probable that the air filter was as completely clogged at the time of the casualty as was reported, since a considerable amount of air would have to be available for the engine to overspeed. It is more probable that the air filter was sufficiently clogged so as to seriously reduce the supply of air to the engine. The first result of this constriction would be incomplete scavenging of the cylinders and some incomplete combustion of the fuel charge. This incomplete scavenging was undoubtedly the cause of the initial overheating of the engine.

35. Subsequent events make it seem quite probable that the scavenging air being supplied to the cylinders was laden with more or less atomized lubricating oil from a source in the blower. It is unusual for partially atomized lubricating oil entering through the scavenge ports to operate a diesel engine. If, however, a small amount of diesel oil, with properly timed injection, is injected into the cylinder, the lubricating oil will burn with the diesel oil, providing additional power. It is believed that such was the case in the subject casualty. The condition of the fuel control rods described in paragraph 32 has been advanced to explain the existence of diesel injection with the throttle closed. It cannot be stated positively that the expansion of the fuel control rods occurred during the overheating of the engine and before the load was removed, since this condition might have been a result of the severe fire which followed.

Indeed, the position of the fuel control rods in the engine militates against this assumption, since they are not located adjacent to any hot surface. The heat required to expand the fuel control rods the necessary amount approaches that of an oil fire. No fire was reported in the engine before the casualty. It is more reasonable to believe that the shock produced by bomb No. 4 caused the sticking or jamming of a number of fuel control racks. These racks are actuated positively by the control rods in opening, but work against a spring when the throttle is closed. Those racks which were jammed or stuck would merely compress the springs, rather than close. The expansion of the control rods during the ensuing fire would effectively mask the original condition of the racks.

36. The rapidity with which the engine reached a dangerous speed and the clouds of black smoke emitted, prevented an appraisal of the cause of the casualty by the operating personnel. As a result, the engine room was evacuated immediately to prevent loss of life. Upon studying the facts, many of which were not available to the operating personnel at the time, it is evident that the engine probably would have stopped if the fuel oil shut-off valve had been closed. This would have removed the timing influence of the diesel injection, as well as the diesel oil supply itself. There is no service experience which indicates that a diesel can reach dangerous speeds burning lubricating oil alone.

37. In addition, the surest way to halt a runaway engine is to put it under load. Probably no vital damage to the machinery would have been caused by the refilling of the hydraulic clutch as was feared by the operating personnel. In any event, the damage incurred could hardly have been greater than that which resulted from allowing the engine to run away.

38. The governor and overspeed trip, which are designed to prevent overspeeding of the engine, operate to close the throttle. The devices were powerless to prevent the engine from running way in this instance, since the throttle had already been closed by hand and it was obvious that the source of fuel was not controlled by the throttle. In reference (g) it was recommended that an air shut-off device be provided to prevent overspeeding when fuel is being supplied, independent of the throttle. Past experience with diesels indicates that such a device is not particularly effective on large engines. Inasmuch as this type of casualty is rare and the closing of the fuel oil shut-off valve or the re-engaging of the load will prevent its occurrence, such a device appears to be unnecessary.

D. Fire

39. Fires occurred at the starboard gasoline fueling station on the main deck, in bedding in compartments C-201L and C-202L, and in No. 1 motor whaleboat as a result of fragments from bombs Nos. 1 and 2. These fires were isolated, confined and extinguished in

twenty minutes. The gasoline fire was extinguished by the use of hose lines equipped with three-position, all purpose nozzles. Non-automatic fixed fog nozzles, installed in B-202L, C-201L, and C-202L to protect the gasoline pump rooms and the gasoline tanks below, were used in extinguishing the bedding fires.

40. Non-automatic fixed fog sprinkler systems such as those which were used to extinguish the bedding fires in C-201L and C-202L are not installed for the purpose of actually extinguishing a fire. The intended purpose is to permit sprinkling to be carried out progressively from one compartment to another, in the event of a major conflagration, starting with a tenable compartment and working toward the origin of the fire. Sprinkling in each compartment should be continued only long enough to insure that it is tenable when entered. Fixed fog sprinkler systems have certain limitations which should be recognized:

(a) The system will control the surface flame in ordinary combustibles such as dry stores, bedding, and clothing, but will not of itself completely extinguish a deep-seated fire in these materials until the compartment is more or less completely flooded - not only a lengthy process, but also one which introduces an unnecessary amount of water inside the ship.

(b) There is a possibility that the extent of such a system may defeat its intended purpose. There may be some segregated sections of the fire main in which the pumping capacity is not sufficient to supply an adequate amount of water to parts of the fixed fog sprinkler system, as well as to vital hose lines which may be in use at the same time.

(c) The possibility of rapidly creating large, wide areas of free water. In cases of reduced stability, the resultant free surface effect may further jeopardize the safety of the ship.

(d) The possibility of impairment of watertight integrity due to inadvertently leaving off caps of hose connections of the fixed fog installations, subsequent to periodic cleaning of these systems with compressed air.

41. No fire resulted from the direct hit. The fire in the forward engine room which followed the overspeeding of No. 2 main engine was brought under control with difficulty and apparently burned itself out. The source of the fuel which fed the fire was not reported, but presumably was diesel oil. The engine room was abandoned when the inboard main engine raced out of control. As a consequence, the fire, which probably could have been extinguished by CO_2 at the outset if personnel had been in the engine room, presumably gained fifteen or twenty

minutes headway before active measures were taken to combat it. This would be sufficient time for a fire to heat the exposed structure to the point where the fuel would be re-ignited after the actual flames had been snuffed out. In addition, the fire parties were at a disadvantage in fighting the fire from outside the compartment, as there are few convenient openings into an engine room. The fire was fought by introducing foam through second deck openings of the engine room. This was not particularly effective, as much of the oil on the surface could not be reached and continued to burn. The difficulties experienced in extinguishing this fire are typical of those which will be experienced with oil fires in engineering spaces which are not immediately taken in hand.

E. Stability, Flooding and Damage Control

(All Plates)

42. The flooding suffered by CHINCOTEAGUE resulted in a stability condition which threatened the survival of the vessel. Although the sequence of flooding of the various compartments is established by the time of the respective bomb hits, the length of time each compartment remained flooded and the total flooding existing when the ship reached its maximum list, are not precisely known because of the overlapping of measures taken to control the situation. The reported behavior of the vessel, however, provides strong clues to the determination of the unreported elements.

43. The drainage facilities were adequate to handle a moderate amount of flooding. The main drain was served by two electric-driven fire and bilge pumps, with a capacity of 375 g.p.m each, one located in each engine room (see Plate II). At the time of the damage, there were on board five portable electric submersible pumps at 200 g.p.m. each and two gasoline handy billy pumps at 60 g.p.m. each. It is assumed that these were all available for use. Exclusive of the gasoline handy billy pumps, a total pumping capacity of about 263 tons per hour was provided.

44. The condition of the vessel before damage has been reported completely. The drafts before damage were 12 feet 0 inches forward and 14 feet 7 inches aft. This corresponds to a displacement of about 2,890 tons, which is 155 tons over the full load displacement as given in the Inclining Experiment Data. The metacentric height (GM) in this condition is 3.2 feet (neglecting free surface in intact ship's tanks).

45. Flooding first occurred at 0738 on 17 July, due to fragment damage from bombs Nos. 1 and 2. As shown in Plate II, two hold compartments, A-421C and C-415E, were flooded completely through access hatches on the platform deck which were not securely dogged. Seven compartments on the platform deck were partially flooded (A-307M, A-308M, A-309M, A-310-1A, A-310-2C, C-6V and C-307-1E). About 168 tons of water were taken aboard in these spaces, the new drafts

after damage being about 13 feet 0 inches forward and 15 feet 2 inches aft, corresponding to a displacement of 3,058 tons. Freeboard at the lowest point (frame 125) was reduced from about 8 feet 4 inches to 7 feet 7 inches. As a result of the free surface due to partial flooding, th GM was reduced to about 1.6 feet. It appears, then, that directly after the first attack stability characteristics were such that a moderate amount of additional flooding could be absorbed without placing the vessel in in jeopardy.

46. A little over 4 hours elapsed between the first attack and that in which a direct hit was received. During this interval, measures were taken to stop the flooding and remove the damage water.

47. At least four compartments were not emptied and remained flooded until the vessel was drydocked. These were A-307M (on the first platform), A-421C, C-6V and C-415E (in the hold). Although the amount of water in three of these spaces was small, the free surface in A-307M was sufficient to reduce GM by about 0.4 feet. Water in the refrigerator space on the platform deck between bulkheads 113 and 121 was drained into stuffing box compartments C-413E and C-414E from which it was pumped overboard using the main drain. On the other hanc water on the platform deck in the spaces between frames 54 and 65 was removed eventually by bucket brigades, and submersible and handy bill pumps. Possible, unwatering here could have been accomplished by opening the hatch at frame 60 port which leads down to compartment A-420A (see Plate II). This latter space likewise has an outlet to the main drain.

48. As a result of the direct hit at 1150, the after engine room flooded to the overhead through the 8-inch cooling water suction line. The shaft alleys flooded, due to water from the after engine room leaking through the shaft glands in bulkhead 97. The forward engine room was flooded to the level of the floor plates by water coming through cab stuffing tubes, a hole where a 1-1/2-inch line was knocked loose and three small splinter holes on the port side of bulkhead 80. Tank B-4W flooded to the level of the after engine room through a rupture in bulkhead 81 port. As the ship sank deeper in the water, compartments A-207L, B-202L, C-201L and C-202L on the second deck flooded to the waterline.

49. About 663 tons of water were taken aboard as a result of the direct hit. The corresponding displacement was about 3,721 tons. The estimated drafts after this attack were 15 feet 2 inches forward and 18 feet 3 inches aft, the freeboard at frame 125 being reduced to about 4 feet 10 inches in the upright condition. The drafts of 11 feet forward and 16 feet aft, reported in reference (f), are obviously in error, since these drafts correspond to a displacement only 50 tons greater than the intact displacement.

50. Shortly after the direct hit, the vessel assumed a heavy starboard list, variously reported as 12 to 18 degrees, putting the main deck edge a few inches above the water. A study of the flooding (see Plate II) indicates that it was largely symmetrical. A small amount of off-center flooding, however, did exist (chiefly in A-207-1L), the resultant moment being about 50 tons-feet to starboard. This small moment alone does not account for the large list. No displacement of large machinery weights occurred. Free surface was present in four large, wide compartments on the second deck, as well as in several smaller spaces. Consequently, the situation following the direct hit can be identified definitely as one of negative GM with a small amount of unsymmetrical flooding. Paragraph 4-17 of FTP170-B states that this condition of negative stability should be suspected whenever heavy list is accompanied by small off-center flooding and extensive free surface. Such was the case with CHINCOTEAGUE. The ship was in a dangerous state, and her ability to remain upright and survive was dependent upon the rapid application of proper corrective measures.

51. Had unwatering been completed and fragment holes above the second deck been adequately plugged prior to the direct hit, calculations indicate that GM after the hit would have had a positive value of about 2.1 feet. This includes the correction for free surface in B-1 and B-202L. List probably would have been negligible. However, free surface still present in A-307M reduced GM to about 1.7 feet. In addition, free surface occurring in ineffectively plugged compartments C-201L and C-202L further reduced GM to the extent that shortly after the direct hit, GM had a negative value of about (-)0.4 feet. The ship heeled over to that angle of list where the shape of the hull was such as to restore positive stability characteristics.

52. Although the fragment holes remaining after the first attack in way of certain of the second deck compartments presented a definite hazard in case of list or further sinkage, efforts to plug or cover them over with a mat during the period between the first two misses and the direct hit, were unsuccessful. The first attempt to plug these holes was made from the outside. The Commanding Officer reported that when the vessel was underway, the plugs worked loose and fell out because of the action of the sea. In those holes (below the second deck) which were plugged from the inside, the plugs remained effective. The Commanding Officer considered that the attempts to plug holes from the outside were ill-advised.

53. CHINCOTEAGUE, after the second attack, was unstable at angle of heel less than about 12 to 18 degrees. Initial efforts to right the ship were based on removing the water by means of gasoline handy billy pumps and bucket brigades. However, progress was slow, and on the morning after the direct hit, the list still was varying between 12 and 18 degrees. The order was given to lighten ship. Torpedoes, heavy machinery, winches and other heavy gear were jettisoned from the starboard, or low side. About 12.75 tons were jettisoned, producing 150 tons-feet of moment. While this weight removal was in process, the pumps supplied by plane were rigged and proved capable of supplying the additional capacity necessary to remove a great deal of the free surface.

54. The attempts to unwater the ship were undertaken under great difficulties, among which were intermittent loss of power, a large angle of list, firefighting and the necessity of maintaining battle stations under enemy air attack. It is not surprising, then, that these efforts were prolonged. A compartment must be almost "dried out" if it is to have a markedly beneficial effect on stability. With stability difficulties, it is well to remember that half-way measures are of little avail. In all cases, every effort should be made to unwater completely all partially flooded compartments. With limited manpower and facilities available to cope with flooding in many compartments, the priority of which to unwater first must be considered. Wide or off-center spaces should be attended to first, as was done in this case, after the first attack with the compartments on the platform deck between frames 54 and 65.

55. The resultant moment produced by the unsymmetrical flooding was small, only about 50 tons-feet. When applying corrective measures, it is safer to treat a borderline case like this is, as one of negative GM with symmetrical flooding, concentrating first solely on improving the stability characteristics. Quoting paragraph 4-16 of FTP170-B,"........ this situation causes a list which cannot be corrected except by improving stability. Efforts to remove such a list by pumping liquids overboard or from one tank to the other will result in an approach towar the upright in a normal fashion, until at some angle short of the upright position, the ship will suddenly lurch to a larger angle on the opposite side....... Any attempt to correct the list under these conditions, except by improving GM, is dangerous and will lead to a heavy lurch and possible capsizing, to the other side." ERIE* capsized after injudicious transfer of weights and liquids while the vessel was unstable. It was fortunate that the total of weights jettisoned from CHINCOTEAGUE was small and that pumping efforts were effective in restoring the stability of the vessel before jettisoning could cause further trouble. The jettisoning of weights to improve stability is often a slow and tedious process, compared to the elimination of free surface from partially flooded compartments. When it is resorted to, it should be carefully supervised. Chapter 4 of FTP170-B contains a very complete discussio of these points.

F. Conclusion

56. In spite of extensive damage and flooding, CHINCOTEAGUE's personnel succeeded in saving their ship. This achievement is all the more remarkable in view of the comparative inexperience of the crew. Only about a month had elapsed from the time the ship left San Diego upon completion of post shakedown repairs, until this action occurred.

* Buships War Damage Report No. 31.

57. This case is an apt illustration of the varied types of casualties that may confront a ship as the result of war damage. It also serves to emphasize that the cumulative effect of several incidents, each of which in itself may be comparatively insignificant, can definitely jeopardize a ship.

Miscellaneous:

Northampton entering the river at Brisbane, Australia, 5 August 1941. Note bow-wave camouflage.

View of port side 5-inch guns on *Northampton* in action against Wotje Atoll in the Marshall Islands 1 February 1942.

Department of the Navy

The Secretary of the Navy
takes pleasure in recognizing the services of:

RADIOMAN THIRD CLASS
SHERMAN E. WALGREN
UNITED STATES NAVY
USS NORTHAMPTON (CA-26)

for participation in

TASK FORCE 16

USS Hornet CV-8	USS Enterprise CV-6
USS Northampton CA-26	USS Vincennes CA-44
USS Salt Lake City CA-25	USS Nashville CL-43
USS Balch DD-363	USS Gwin DD-433
USS Benham DD-397	USS Grayson DD-435
USS Ellet DD-398	USS Monssen DD-436
USS Fanning DD-385	USS Meredith DD-434
USS Sabine AO-25	USS Cimarron AO-22

with Submarines, Pacific Fleet

USS Thresher SS-200	USS Trout SS-202

On the occasion of the 50th anniversary of the Second World War, it is appropriate that we take time to reflect on the unique and daring accomplishments achieved early in the war by Task Force 16. Sailing westward under sealed orders in April 1942, only four months after the devastating raid on Pearl Harbor, Task Force 16, carrying sixteen Army B-25 bombers, proceeded into history. Facing adverse weather and under constant threat of discovery before bombers could be launched to strike the Japanese homeland, the crews of the ships and LTC Doolittle's bombers persevered. On 18 April 1942 at 1445, perseverance produced success as radio broadcasts from Japan confirmed the success of the raids. These raids were an enormous boost to the morale of the American people in those early and dark days of the war and a harbinger of the future for the Japanese High Command that had so foolishly awakened "The Sleeping Giant." These exploits, which so inspired the service men and women and the nation live on today and are remembered when the necessity of success against all odds is required.

DEPARTMENT OF THE NAVY • UNITED STATES OF AMERICA

John H. Dalton
Secretary of the Navy

15 MAY 1995
Date

THE IMAGE OF RANK

AN ADMIRAL...
Leaps tall buildings in a single bound, is more powerful than a locomotive, is faster than a speeding bullet, walks on water, and gives policy to God.

A CAPTAIN...
Leaps short buildings with a single bound, is more powerful than a switch engine, is just as fast as a speeding bullet, walks on water if the sea is calm, and talks to God.

A COMMANDER...
Leaps short buildings with a running start and a favorable wind, is almost as powerful as a switch engine, is faster than a speeding B-B, walks on water in an indoor swimming pool, and talks to God IF a special request is approved.

A LT. COMMANDER...
Barely clears Quonset Hunts, loses tugs-of-war with locomotives, can fire a speeding bullet, swims well, and is occasionally addressed by God.

A LIEUTENANT...
Makes high marks when trying to leap buildings, is run over by locomotives, can sometimes handle a gun without inflicting self-injury, can dog paddle, and talks to animals.

A LIEUTENANT JG...
Runs into buildings, recognizes locomotives two out of three times, is not issued ammunition, can stay afloat if properly instructed, and talks to water.

AN ENSIGN...
Falls over doorsills when trying to enter buildings. Says: "Look at the Choo-Choo," wets himself with a water pistol and mumbles to himself.

A CHIEF...
Lifts buildings and then walks under them, kicks locomotives off the track, catches speeding bullets in his teeth and chews them up, and freezes water with a single glance. HE IS GOD!

The apprentice seaman and the cat, 1940

District of Equatorius
REALM OF NEPTUNE

I HEREBY CERTIFY that I have duly and properly served the within subpoena on the herein named person on board the U. S. S. NORTHAMPTON, in sufficient time previous to the crossing of the Equator by said vessel, to permit the defendant to prepare an ample defense to such charges as appear herein.

Davy Jones, Scribe. Peg Leg, Deputy.

In the Royal Court

OF THE REALM OF NEPTUNE
IN AND FOR THE
District of Equatorius

The people of the Realm of the Deep

VS

SHERMAN ELIAS WALGREN

SEAMAN FIRST CLASS

Of the U. S. S. Northampton

SUBPOENA

Filed July 21, 1941 A. D.

Davy Jones, Scribe

Peg Leg, Deputy

IN THE ROYAL COURT OF THE REALM OF NEPTUNE
In and for the District of Equatorius

The People of the Realm of the Deep
Versus
All Landlubbers of the U. S. S. NORTHAMPTON

To SHERMAN E. WALGREN SEA/1 U. S. Navy,

It having been brought to the attention of His Royal Highness, NEPTUNUS REX, Supreme Ruler of the Deep, through his trusty shellbacks, that a ship manned by a crew who have not acknowledged the sovereignty of the Ruler of the Deep, has transgressed on his domain and thereby incurred the Royal displeasure.

Be it known: To ye all that His Most Royal Highness, NEPTUNUS REX, Supreme Ruler of all mermaids, sharks, crabs, pollywogs, timmonogs, and other denizens of the deep, will, with his Secretary and Royal Court, meet in full session on board the offending ship NORTHAMPTON in Latitude 0° 0' 00", Longitude 165° 50' 00" W., at 9:00 o'clock in the morning of the 21st day of July, A. D. 1941 to examine into your fitness to be taken into the citizenship of the deep and to hear your defense on the charge of:

EATING POGI BAIT IN FRONT OF SHELLBACKS AND FAILING TO SHARE SAME TO SAID SHELLBACKS, CALLING DAVY JONES NAMES NOT BEFITTING THE STATUS OF ONE SO ROYAL. THESE AMONG MANY OTHERS TO NUMEROUS TO MENTION.....

It is therefore ordered and decreed that the above named man present himself before the Royal Court at the time and place mentioned under penalty of eternal pickling.

By order of the Court:
for His Majesty

Given under my hand and seal this 21st day of July A. D. 1941.

Davy Jones, Scribe

Peg Leg, Deputy.

Letters to the Editor, Los Angeles Times,
Times Mirror Square, Los Angeles, CA 90053

ment being humanitarian in spirit. Justice is more important than technicalities of international law and compassion is absolutely necessary in such an extreme case as this. If this child is returned and tortured or killed, the inadequate reaction of our government will be to blame!

ROBERT BEEBE
Idyllwild

Pappy Boyington

Your story about the death of Pappy Boyington (Part I, Jan. 12) called him "the oldest active Marine pilot in the war." He was not even the oldest pilot in the Black Sheep Squadron. Fred Avey was.

We who were members of the Black Sheep Squadron bitterly resent the constant reference to the pilots as "ragtags" and "rejects." The fact is that the Black Sheep Squadron was formed in Espiritu Santo at the suggestion of the assistant wing commander, Gen. James T. Moore (not Boyington) because an additional fighter squadron was needed in combat.

The 28 pilots who comprised the squadron for our first combat tour included, besides Boyington, eight pilots with South Pacific combat experience and a total of 14½ Japanese planes to their credit, including three transfers from the RCAF and two who had been instructors. Not one was a ragtag, brawling fugitive from court martial.

That crummy TV show which described the Black Sheep as drunken brawlers who had to be rescued from court martial by Boyington does a disservice to a fine group of young men who performed in the best tradition of the Marine Corps.

FRANK E. WALTON
Colonel, USMCR (Ret.)
Honolulu

Congratulations on the excellent article "A HUD Roadshow Raises Questions of Conflict" (Part I, Dec. 27). As the president of American Federation of Government Employees Local 476 which represents Housing and Urban Development Department headquarters employees in Washington, D.C., I appreciate the thorough reporting of Times staff writer Claire Spiegel.

The present federal fair housing law does now provide an enforcement mechanism for HUD. The Department of Justice can enforce the federal fair housing law in "pattern and practice" cases but Justice has been reluctant to do so under the Reagan Administration.

HUD employees send housing discrimination cases to the Justice Department recommending enforcement action and are seldom informed what action, if any, Justice has taken.

HUD has estimated that as many as 2 million cases of housing discrimination occur annually. In metropolitan areas, black families seeking to buy stand a 48% chance of encountering discrimination and blacks renters stand a 72% chance of encountering discrimination. Clearly, a federal fair housing law with an enforcement mechanism inside HUD is needed.

Such a law was again proposed during 1987. It would have provided for administrative law judges who could have issued cease and desist orders and awarded damages in housing discrimination cases. The Reagan Administration did not actively support this bill and the National Assn. of Realtors opposed it.

I whole-heartedly agree with your editorial "Pierce's Traveling Circus" of Dec. 30. (U.S. Housing Secretary Samuel) Pierce should take his fair-housing roadshow to the White House and convince the Reagan Administration to actively support a federal fair housing law with teeth.

BARBARA DAVIDSON
President
American Federation
of Government Employees
Washington, D.C.

30 January 1988

Dear Mr. Walgren,

Thank you for your comments about "ONCE THEY WERE EAGLES." Coming from one such as you who was out there, makes it more meaningful.

Regarding your question as to whether or not it was pilots from the Black Sheep Squadron who gave you air cover on 16 July 1943, it could not have been a Black Sheep since we were not formed until 7 September. It COULD have been one of the pilots from the replacement pool at Espiritu Santo who was later assigned to the Black Sheep when they were formed.

However, if they were F4Us from Santo, they were flown by Marine pilots because the Navy was not flying Corsairs.

Thanks, too, for sending along your nostalgic "SAILING HOME." I guess we all felt that way when we headed for home.

Best regards,

Frank Walton

Lewis Thomas

From: "Perry Ustick" <pustick@mchsi.com>
To: "Albert Mayer" <wythare@pe.net>
Cc: <ByTheChance@aol.com>; "Lewis Thomas" <tom26@whro.net>; <efkca@attglobal.net>; <himselfbob@prodigy.net>
Sent: Tuesday, August 19, 2003 2:16 AM

AL Mayer, USS Northampton,Ca26

Thanks for the article by Capt Ray Schultz in the Cruiser/Sailor's Assoc. magazine of the account of the Jap Fighter attack on Mickey Reeves and Fred Covington with Radioman John Melton and Bob Baxter in their two SOCS' on December 7th at the Island of Niihau West of Oahu. I have the original official Confidential report written by Mickey Reeves of the attack. It differs somewhat from Schultz's article, but not significantly. If I can find the report I'll send you a copy. Again thanks a lot.

You know I flew into Pearl in the back seat on the 8th with Anderson as his radioman. What an experience to see the devastation along Battleship row. There was so much fire, oil , and small boats we had to land over at West Locke and taxi about three miles to get back to Pearl. We tried to go ashore at Ford Island and a guy in a 'T' shirt came running down and yelled at us to go back to the ship at Anchorage 16 about 300 yards from the stern of the Arizona which was afire. What a night. We spent all night on an 'all hands evolution' loading supplies and ammunition. We got underway before dawn and went out of Pearl heading West to chase the Japs. By that time they were well on their way to the Homeland. I don't remember exactly, but I remember they said we had 9 torpedoes shot at the Task Force before we got back to Pearl. Didn't you come aboard when we got back? I remember you and I standing at the rail on the well deck looking at the Battleships that were afire and capsized as we sortied to go out to the Marshall/Gilberts Wotje Island Bombardment. I remember you and I talking about the men trapped in the capsized Oklahoma. I also remember that I was one scared Ensign when we sortied on the 9th to chase the Japs. I was so scared that I was afraid to go to my bunk in that room with the other 18 Ensigns. My bunk was on the Starboard bow next to the ship's skin, over a tank full of 115/145 fuel. I couldn't eat or sleep for at least two days and I was totally exhausted, both mentally and physically. I envied the Catholics who had their prayer beads and faith in the Almighty. I was an Episcopalian in name only,(but not a very religious one). After two days I became a 'Fatalist' and said "to hell with the torpedoes, if one hits me that will be it!" and that was the first night I fell exhausted on my bunk and slept all night. When I woke up I was a new man.

I guess each one of us has a story to tell of our experiences during those first terrible days after the Pearl Harbor attack.

Again thanks for the Article.

Regards,

Perry Ustick

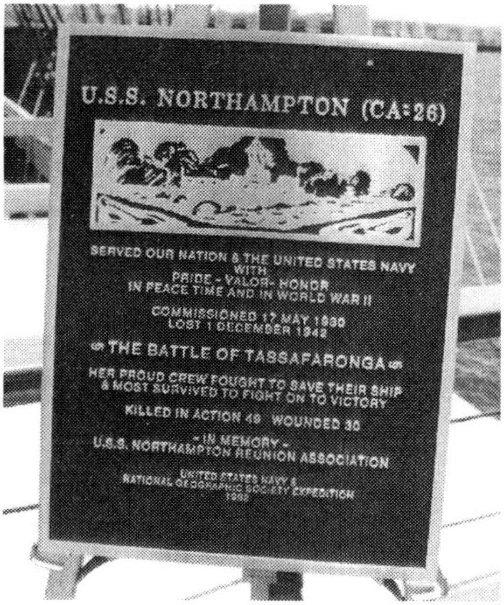

National Cemetery in Northanpton, MA
Memorial Service 2002

Sail Easy showing air crews the radio antenna that is lowered in flight.
VP73 Minneapolis 1949

My airplane in Korean War. Lt. Hollingsworth, Pilot. Gibbons RDO 2/c other radioman. This happened in Dutch Harbor, Alaska when I was in the hospital in Bremerton, WA. Lost brakes, in a ditch off runway.

Russ Lee & Freddy Lehman. I designed paint job and the number 9. Freddy painted it. This was taken after I was in the Navy.

Shim, Bob Berdahl and Nick Natchcas, Feb. 1981

Sail Easy at Task Force 16 ceremony at Alameda, CA
For recognition of participation on
Doolittle Raid, May 1942
USS Hornet CV12

Chincoteague reunion in Portland, OR, 2004
Memorial for our lost shipmates, Frank Murfy, Chairman

Koopman radioman with me on Nora, Sail Easy, Rev. John Soloverdt,
Ed Pouliet & Don Ericson. We joined the Navy together. 2002

Reciting definition of the Pledge of Allegiance in St. Louis. Nora reunion, 2000. Bob O'Malley next.

Grass in backyard in Arcadia, CA
Checker board and grass cut by
Sherman Walgren

Two love birds.

*Sail Easy with 1930 1/3 HP John Deere.
I made the wagon. From cousins farm
In Minnesota.*

Sail Easy, Northampton, MA
National Cemetery, 2002

45th Reunion
U.S. NAVY SQUADRON

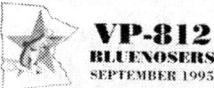

VP-812
BLUENOSERS
SEPTEMBER 1995

3 Days & 4 Nights of Indc
Plus Many Hours for

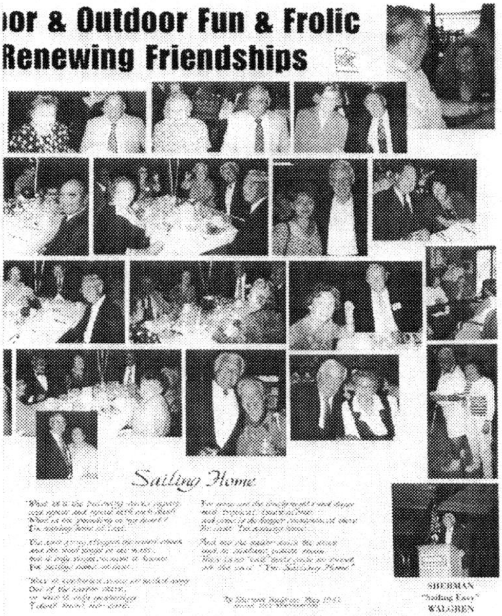

or & Outdoor Fun & Frolic
Renewing Friendships
Sailing Home
SHERMAN
"Sailing Easy"
WALGREN

VP-812 BLUENOSERS
A NON-PROFIT ORGANIZATION
MINNEAPOLIS, MINNESOTA

CBS Radio Program Script:

CLIENT: WM. WRIGLEY JR. CO. **CBS** WRITER

PROGRAM TITLE "THE FIRST LINE" - EPISODE # 106 - REVISION # 3

FEBRUARY 10, 1944 THURSDAY

CAST

PRODUCTION	ANNOUNCER	BILL	QUARTERMASTER
	NARRATOR # 1	HOBBS	DAWSON
ANNOUNCER	NARRATOR # 2	BOB	TALKER # 2
		LOOKOUT	CROOK
REMARKS	TONY	OFFICER	SELLERS
	HANK	OFFICER # 2	WEBB
70 Copies - Sheppard	CHIEF	TALKER	
	VOICE (BULL HORN)	VOICE	

MUSIC:	FANFARE
NARR #2:	Wrigley's Spearmint Gum presents....the First Line!
MUSIC:	"ANCHORS AWEIGH" - - UP AND DOWN BEHIND.
NARR #2:	Of all our Navy ships which fight so gallantly and brilliantly against the enemy in the First Line....there seems to be some which are selected by destiny to be tried up to and beyond the limit of endurance. It is the story of such a ship that we bring you tonight..
MUSIC:	FANFARE
NARR #2:	The story of the USS Chincoteague, a seaplane tender in the Navy of the United States....
MUSIC:	FANFARE
NARR #1:	And to tell the epic story of the Chincoteague, the man who commanded her in her time of greatest peril....Commander Ira E. Hobbs, United States Navy....
MUSIC:	FANFARE
NARR #1:	Listen then to this dramatic story of your Navy....fighting in the First Line.
MUSIC:	PLAYOFF

OPENING

ANNOUNCER: This story of courage and tenacity which you will hear in just a moment is one of hundreds of brilliant achievements of our fighting Navy men. The makers of Wrigley's Spearmint Gum bring it to you so that you may get a vivid, true-to-life picture of how these men perform in action. Thus, we try to make these First Line programs serve a useful wartime purpose - as Wrigley's Spearmint Gum itself is doing for millions of busy, alert American people. By helping to relieve nervous tension - keeping the mouth and throat moist - and making hard work seem a bit easier and pleasanter - that familiar little package of Wrigley's Spearmint Gum is serving a real need today. Now - as an added wartime service - this popular, helpful product brings you - The First Line!

MUSIC: BRIDGE #22 to B.G.

NARR #1: Ladies and Gentlemen, it is our pleasure to present Commander Ira E. Hobbs, United States Navy. Commander Hobbs....will you tell us something about your ship, the Chincoteague....her size and the number in her crew....and something of the kind of work she does...?

HOBBS: (IN PERSON) Let's take your questions in order....First.... the Chincoteague....a little longer than a football field and about 35 feet wide....

NARR #1: Not a large ship then....

HOBBS: No, not a large ship....only a little larger than a destroyer. ....There are about 250 officers and men in the crew and the job of the Chincoteague is the same as that of any seaplane tender....to provide a floating base from which seaplanes may be re-fueled and repairs affected. Tenders are to seaplanes, what land bases are to other planes.

NARR #1: Except, of course,....that ship like yours move about....

HOBBS: Yes. Tenders are used for advance bases....the seaplanes come to us for servicing and re-arming. We carry spare parts for minor repairs....playing mother hen to a brood of patrol-planes keeps us preetty busy....

NARR #1: We can understand that. And on the day about which you are going to tell us....the Chincoteague was out in the Pacific, was she not....?

HOBBS: It was last July that we had our trial by fire....The Chincoteague, with its complement of reserve officers, and a crew of which only 50% had ever been to sea, was anchored in a bay off one of the Pacific Islands, an island which the Japs

HOBBS: (CONTINUED) were still hoping to take back. It was evening. The sea and the jungle and the sky were bleeding into the soft, neutral shades of night. Those of the crew who were off duty, took their ease (fading) in the comparative coolness of the deck.

SOUND: GENTLE WASH OF WAVES. OCCAISIONAL OFF-STAGE VOICES.

TONY: (COMFORTABLY) You know what this reminds me of, Hank.... looking in toward the island....?

HANK: Uh-uh....

TONY: It's like summer-time in Wisconsin....We've been fishing over on Three-mile lake all day and we're just getting home....

HANK: (MATTER-OF-FACT) That jungle in there's a lot different from the Wisconsin woods....

TONY: Sure....sure....but at night it doesn't look so different.... (DREAMY) We've got a nice catch....and a few minutes after we get to shore we'll have a big fire going and the....

HANK: Big Fire! (SCORN) Want the Japs to spot you?

TONY: Aw....Hank....I mean....if this <u>was</u> Wisconsin, we'd have a fire and cook our own suppers out in the open...

HANK: Nothing wrong with the chow on the Chincoteague.

TONY: (DISQUIETED) Aw....you haven't got any imagination, Hank.

HANK: Sure I have....but when you talk about fires, I can imagine just what would happen if the Japs spotted us. ....Us with a cargo of high octane gas, bombs and torpedoes for those PBY's ....Don't talk about fire to me. It gives me the Willies just thinking of it....How about hitting the sack? We'll have to re-fuel those PBY's in the morning, and that'll keep us plenty busy.

TONY: Sure....I'm bushed tonight anyway....and....(PAUSE)

DISTANT PLANE ENGINE

TONY: What's that....?

HANK: There's a plane up there somewhere....

TONY: Coming nearer, too....Well....if we can't see him....the chances are he can't see us....

HANK: Maybe it's one of our own planes....

TONY: Maybe....Huh....sounds as if it's right above us....

(BOTH STARTLED BY FLARES AS THEY LIGHT UP SCENE)

SOUND: VOICES IN BACKGROUND

HANK: (EXCITED) Flares, Tony....that guy's dropping flares....

TONY: Look how light it's getting....We're in plain sight.... Chief....what's up?

CHIEF: (FADING IN) What's up? Huh....that's a Jap reconnaissance plane up there....Dropped enough flares to light up the whole harbor....trying to give their bombers a target....

TONY: Will we be bombed tonight...do you think?

CHIEF: I don't know....

VOICE: (BULLHORN) All hands....general quarters....

HANK: But we'll be ready for 'em if they do come in....Come on, Tony....Maybe we'll get a chance at one of 'em with our machine guns....

NARR #1: The crew of the Chincoteague stood ready for any attack which might develop. Slowly the flares drifted down....while the Jap plane hovered in the sky....out of range and out of sight ....On the bridge, one of the officers said to the Captain....

BILL: It doesn't look like they mean to attack us tonight, Captain...

HOBBS: (ACTOR) No....if they were coming they'd have been over us by now. I have an idea this is purely reconnaissance, and that monkey up there is taking pictures...It's not tonight we need to worry about....It's tomorrow....(ASIDE)....Bob....

BOB: Yes, Captain....

HOBBS: How many PBY's will be ready for servicing in the morning?

BOB: We're expecting to take care of more than a dozen....

HOBBS: Very well, then. Commander Gardner....let's get the work underway as early as possible in the morning....I have an idea tomorrow will be our busy day!

MUSIC: BRIDGE TO B.G.

NARR #1 Before dawn the next morning found the Chincoteague the center of great activity....From her tanks into the tanks of the seaplanes, flowed the precious gas and oil which was to sustain them on their missions for the day. Some of the pilots had returned to their planes....Other were still aboard the Chincoteague when....

LOOKOUT: Enemy planes off port quarter....about 8000 feet.

HOBBS: Sound battle stations....

SOUND: HORN

VOICE: (BULLHORN) All hands....man battle stations....

SOUND: PLANES COMING IN HIGH ABOVE

OFFICER: There they are , Captain....They're staying up there....That's pretty high, sir, for accurate bombing. Are we going to slip our anchor and get out to sea...?

HOBBS: No....we still have some of our pilots aboard. And I don't want to run out on our planes....See that the pilots are put back aboard their planes....

OFFICER: Yes, sir...

OFFICER#2: There come their bombs, sir...

HOBBS: What poor shots they are.... Those bombs won't even land in the bay....

SOUND: BOMBS EXPLODING AWAY. KEEP IT BEHIND.

OFFICER: They landed in the jungle. Captain....They weren't even close ....And the bombers are going away....

HOOBS: They don't give up that quickly. They'll be back....We may not have to wait long....Complete servicing our planes...

OFFICER #2: Yes, sir....

HOBBS: Friedman....

TALKER: Aye, sir.

HOBBS: Ask communications radio for fighter protection....a couple of....

TALKER: Just a moment, sir....Mr. Crook reporting now....(PAUSE) AYE, aye, Mr. Crook....Cap'n....Mr. Crook say there's a big fight going on and no fighters are available at this present time.

HOBBS: That's going to make it harder....We'll have to take care of ourselves until the big push is over and some fighters can be spared to take on those Jap bombers! Only one thing to do.... Work fast....Maybe we can be out to sea before the Japs return....

MUSIC: BRIDGE TO B.G.

NARR #1: Every man on the Chincoteague worked at top speed....worked against time. Quickly fuel lines were passed to the seaplanes alongside....Working with machine-like precision, their job was completed....

(SOUND OF SHIP IN BACKGROUND)

SOUND: UP

VOICE: Slip anchor....

SOUND: RATTLE OF CHAIN AS ANCHOR IS SLIPPED....

HOBBS: Quartermaster....

QUARTER: Aye, sir....

HOBBS: Right full rudder....steady on course two - two - zero.

QUARTER: Rudder is full right, sir.

HOBBS: All engines ahead full....

SOUND: BELLS AS SIGNAL IS GIVEN.

SOUND: SHIP IS NOW UNDER WAY. VOICES IN BACKGROUND.

TALKER: Captain....

HOBBS: Yes....Friedman....

TALKER: Lookout reports nine enemy bombers approaching from 185....

HOBBS: All hands to general quarters!

SOUND: BATTLE STATIONS ARE SOUNDED. (BACKGROUND OF VOICES)

OFFICER: They're coming in low, Captain....

HOBBS: This will be the first action for some of our gunners.... Now we'll see how well they remember their training....

SOUND: PLANES IN CLOSE NOW. SWELL UP BEHIND LINES....

HOBBS: Damage control parties, stand by. We'll have to work fast if we're hit....or the Chincoteague is likely to go up like a torch....

OFFICER: Yes, sir....We're ready....

OFFICER #2: Here they come....

HOBBS: Commence firing....

VOICES: (TAKE IT UP) Commence firing....

SOUND: A.A. AND MACHINE GUN ROAR....

OFFICER #2: They're right over us....and they aren't dropping on us....

HOBBS: They're making a dummy run....lining us up for the sure kill... (PLANES HAVE FADED NOW) Don't relax....They'll come in again and this time they'll let us have it....(FADES)....Maybe we can make the Chincoteague hard to hit....Left full rudder - all engines ahead - flank!

(ALL SOUND DOWN FOR SHORT TRANSITION....THEN BRING UP PLANES AGAIN AS THEY COME IN....GUN FIRE ALSO)

HOBBS: Here they come....Now....right full rudder....

QUARTER: Rudder in full right, sir!

(PAUSE)

SOUND: BOMBS DROPPING NEARBY.

OFFICER: (TENSE) They're missing, Captain....they're missing....

HOBBS: Now left full rudder....

QUARTER: Rudder is full left, sir!

SOUND: EXPLOSIONS CLOSE BY.

HOBBS: That one was too close. Ascertain if we have been damaged....

TALKER: That last bomb dropped less than fifty feet astern, sir.... minor splinter damage about the fantail, sir....

HOBBS: Have the damage repaired as quickly as possible. ....We'll continue out to sea and we can be mighty thankful we escaped so lightly....All engines ahead....standard....

QUARTER: All engines all ahead standard, sir!

MUSIC: BRIDGE TO B.G.

NARR #1: That was only the beginning of the trial of the Chincoteague. The Japs had her spotted and, although the skipper of the Chincoteague knew that to venture again into the harbor meant certain attack and the possibility of turning the ship into a flaming torch,....he gave the order....

MUSIC: TRUMPET FLARE TO B.G.

HOBBS: We're going back into the harbor. Those planes need the gas and oil in our tanks in order to carry out their missions. ....(FADE) Come right to course zero - nine - zero to take us into the harbor!

NARR #1: Gallantly....the Chincoteague returned to the harbor and to her job of refueling the seaplanes waiting there....As night closed its protective arm over them....the men of the Chincoteague sighed deeply, knowing that with the dawn the Japs would return for the kill....

MUSIC: UP....AND SEGUE TO

SOUND: PLANES COMING IN.

NARR #1: Then....morning and the Jap bombers again....

SOUND: PLANE ROARS IN.

TONY: (YELLS) It's gonna be close....Duck, mates....get down.

SOUND: BOMB EXPLODES.

HANK: That was <u>too</u> close....

TONY: Here comes another....Look! They're coming in waves....

SOUND: PLANES ROAR IN AND SOUND OF EXPLODING BOMBS.

NARR #1: On the bridge, the captain estimated the chances for survival....

HOBBS: (AGAINST SOUND) If we stay in the harbor....they've got us where they want us....We'll be sunk for sure. We've got to get out to sea! (CALLS) Slip anchor....All engines standard Left full rudder....(FADE ON VOICES REPEATING ORDERS)

MUSIC: SNEAK & B.G.

NARR #1: Not once....but three times was the gallant little Chincoteague attacked by enemy bombers before it could make the mouth of the harbor. That made four attacks....and she was still afloat....and save for minor damage from splinters ....and in miraculously good condition....

SOUND: PLANES ROAR IN AND BOMBS EXPLODE. BATTLE SOUND THIS WHOLE SCENE.

NARR #1: It was in the fifth attack that the Chincoteague suffered her first serious damage....

TALKER #2: After repair station reporting, sir....That last bomb started a fire down there. Gasoline lines ruptured....Raw gas is being fed to the flames....They're having a tough time, sir.... The flames are driving the damage control party out of the compartment.

HOBBS: That's our danger....If that fire gets out of control....the Chincoteague is gone....

TALKER #2: The valves seem to have been jarred open, sir....some place the damage control party can't reach....

BILL: I know where that is, Captain....You have to crawl in on top of the tanks to get at the valves....They're pretty well hidden back there....but I know where they are....

HOBBS: Can't you show someone, Bill?

BILL: That'd be hard to do, Captain. But I could get in there and find them....I'm sure. I know that section of the ship....

HOBBS: You know the whole ship better than any manaboard, Bill. But you're the navigator....

BILL: Captain....My navigation won't be of much help if that fire gets out of control....As long as that raw gas is being fed through those open valves....the fire will spread....May I go, Captain....?

HOBBS: All right, Bill....and good luck....(ASIDE)Notify damage control that Mr. Wilson is on the way....(FADE) Tell them to give whatever help he needs....

NARR #1: Far down in the hold of the Chincoteague....in a world of tanks and pipes and valves....where a spark in the wrong place would send the Chicoteague and all aboard her into eternity in one blinding flash....Bill Wilson made his way through the darkness towards the open valves....Members of the damage control party waited....tensely....grimley....

(PAUSE)

(WE'RE IN HOLD....SOME ECHO)

HANK: (TENSE) Why don't he come back....? He's has plenty of time....

CHIEF: Shut up....that's a slow job....squeezing over the tops of those tanks....getting way back in there....

HANK: Maybe he's caught....Maybe he can't go any further....Maybe he can't find the valves....Maybe they ain't where he thought they'd....

CHIEF: Quiet, you!

HANK: I was just thinkin'....

CHIEF: All right....think but....don't talk!

HANK: The nerve of that guy....crawling back in there....If we were to get hit by a bomb now....he wouldn't have a chance....

TONY: We haven't got much of a chance if he doesn't turn those valves off....Listen to those guys fightin' the fire in the next compartment....It must be getting worse....

CHIEF: Look, you guys....if anyone can find those valves, it's Mr. Wilson....

HANK: But he's been gone so long....Maybe....

TONY: Shut up....listen....

(PAUSE)

CHIEF: (THRILLED) That's him....He's comin' back....Here....stand by to give him a hand....How about it, sir....Did you get to them valves?

SOUND: METALLIC SOUND AS BILL CRAWLS OUT OF MAZE OF PIPES.

BILL: (FADING IN....STRAINING) Yeah....I found them....

CHIEF: Did....did you manage to turn 'em off....

BILL: (WEAKLY) Notify the bridge....the valves are turned off..

(MUFFLED CHEERS FROM MEN)

CHIEF: (THRILLED) Hear that, you guys...I told you he'd do it. He knows this ship like he knows his own mother...Come on....give him a hand...(FADING) Get him oughta this smoke...Get him up on deck so he can get some air...

MUSIC: BRIDGE TO B.G.

NARRATOR #1: Perhaps it isn't fair to single any one man out as being particularly brave. Every man on the Chincoteague did his job unflinchingly. If he hadn't....well....there was a much worse trial coming....and there's no telling what might have

NARRATOR #1: (CON'T) happened....for again, the Chincoteague turned and went into the harbor to serve its brood of patrol planes. After them....raging to the attack came the Jap bombers....

SOUND: (ROAR OF PLANES BEHIND....PUNCTUATE NEXT LINES WITH EXPLODING BOMBS)

NARRATOR #1: For the sixth time....bombs dropped around her....and now the Chincoteague was being hit....

OFFICER: (OVER SOUND) All but three planes serviced, sir....

HOBBS: (ACTOR) Then we'd better get out to sea again....They're making it too hot for us....

SOUND: FADE OUT

NARRATOR #1: The sixth attack and the Chincoteague reeled....recovered and went on....the seventh....and then relentlessly came attack number eight.

SOUND: (WE'RE ON BRIDGE. PLANES ARE COMING IN)

OFFICER: Here they come...five of them....

OFFICER #2: And they're low....coming right out of the sun....

OFFICER: Our gunners can't see them....

HOBBS: ......I don't see how they can miss us this time.... Here they are....This is going to be a bad one...They're dropping....

(SLIGHT PAUSE)

SOUND: (A JARRING EXPLOSION)

OFFICER: We're hit....

HOBBS: That was a direct hit on our after deck....

OFFICER #2: Sounded like a delayed action bomb....

TALKER: It's the after engine room, sir....It's knocked out....We can't expect any power from there, sir!

HOBBS: Do what you can to get our after engines working....We'll need thm....Mr. Tugman....

DAWSON: Yes, Captain....

OFFICER: We're in a bad way, Captain....Most of our life boats have been wrecked....our hull is riddled with splinters....and we've still got some fire below decks....

HOBBS: I know that....and one engine room out of commission. I realize our position....but we're still afloat....Remember that.... we're still afloat. I don't know how....but we are!

MUSIC: UP AND DOWN

NARRATOR #1: Commander Hobbs, was that the end of the bombing attacks?

HOBBS: (SELF) It was on the next attack that the Chincoteague suffered paralyzing damage. A near miss put our forward engine room out of commission....and there we were.....dead in the water....without power, without pumps, without lights.... and night was drawing near.

NARRATOR #1: Did you consider abandoning ship, Commander?

HOBBS: The struggle seemed tough and there was the ever present danger of an explosion which would kill every man aboard....but to abandon ship would have been the easiest way out. I knew without asking that every man aboard wanted to stay and fight to make good the forlorn hope that we could bring the Chincoteague through....so the order to abandon ship was not given.

OFFICER: Captain....

HOBBS: Yes....What is it, now....?

OFFICER: The forward engine room is flooding....We've had to stop work on the engines because of the water....

HOBBS: It's bad enough to have some of the compartments flooded....but the engine rooms...We've got to keep the water down somehow....

HOBBS: (CONT'D) The work on the engines must go on....Take every man who can lift a bucket and form a bucket brigade....Use the gun crews.... use everyone....it's our only chance....bucket brigades....

OFFICER: Yes, sir....(FADING) Here....you men....this way....get buckets and follow me....

NARR. #1: And so your crew formed a bucket brigade, Commander?

HOBBS: (SELF) Yes, they did. They were the greatest, toughest bunch of fighting men I've ever seen. Those Navy men, exhausted after hours of fighting fire and water, drew upon their last remaining strength.

NARR. #1: Did every one take part, Commander?

HOBBS: Every available man....Down at the bottom of the brigade I could hear the voice of Lt. Griffith, our paymaster.

SOUND: SPLASHING OF WATER AND RATTLE OF BUCKETS.

VOICE: (UNISON) Heave....take it away....Heave....take it away....(KEEP THIS GOING BEHIND)

CHIEF: (PANTING) That's the spirit, men....We're getting ahead of it....(JOINS IN UNISON) Heave....take it away....Hank....watch the kid....he's gonna cave....

TONY: I won't cave, Chief....

CHIEF: You'd better go up on deck....The surgeon has moved sick bay up there....

TONY: I'm all right, Chief....Lemme stick....

CHIEF: Okay....if you think you can make it....(TAKE UP CHANT)

VOICE: Get the water down a couple of more inches, men, and maybe the pumps will be able to hold it there. (CHANT ACCELLERATES) (FADE IT....THEN BRING IT BACK WITH SOUND OF PUMPS)

CHIEF: (TIRED) What time is it, Tony?

TONY: Must be nearly midnight....

HANK: How they coming on the engines....?

TONY: Now that the water is under control....they're working fast.... We'll have power pretty soon....But it's awful up on deck.... The deck's so hot you can't walk on it....I don't know how they're standing it....What a bunch of gurys....Bein' able to take it - - and keep goin'....

CHIEF: Okay....okay...it's worth it...if we can just save the Chincoteague....just so we save her...(FADE) Keep at those pumps....keep going....

HOBBS: (SELF) ....It was after midnight before we got power....before we got under way hoping to be out of range of the Jap bombers by morning....It was at this time that another tender, the Thornton, arrived and formed an anti-submarine screen.... But it was only a few hours before we received bad news from the destroyer....

SOUND: (ON DECK AT NIGHT. WASH OF WAVES)

HOBBS: Yes, Webb....what is it?....

TALKER #2: Engine room sir....fire's broken out....

HOBBS: Fire? In the engine room?

TALKER: They may be able to check the fire but they can't stop the flooding....We're filling up, sir....The pumps can't hold it....

HOBBS: Very well....Call all hands and have them throw all heavy gear overboard....Everything....(FADING) Overboard....

OFFICER: (FADE IN) Captain....Captain Hobbs....

HOBBS: (ACTOR) Yes....what is it?

OFFICER: We've only got two feet of free board, sir. If we go down just two more feet our decks will be under water....

HOBBS: Two feet, eh?

OFFICER: That's all....sir.

HOBBS: Looks bad....About all you can say is....we're still afloat.... (MUTTERING AS TO SELF) Is there a chance of bringing the ship and crew through....?

OFFICER: Beg pardon....what did you say, sir...?

HOBBS: I was just thinking....wondering....(SIGHS) I had hoped never to give the order to abandon ship....but I can't gamble the lives of all these men against the forlorn chance that something will save the Chincoteague and all in her....So...I guess we'd better....

(PLANE ENGINE FADING IN ....AWAY)

(INTERRUPTED BY)

OFFICER: Captain....listen....listen....what's that?

HOBBS: It's a plane....

OFFICER: And not a Jap....I know it isn't....not that engine....Captain.... maybe....maybe it's

SOUND: (PLANE FADING IN)

CROOK: (THRILLED) There's a PBY landing out there....it's one of ours... That's a PBY and she'll have pumps aboard. They were ordered by Commodore Kendall to bring them to us.......

HOBBS: Good....Perhaps he'll send us some fighter planes, too.

CROOK: (GLEE) Yes, sir...that's what I thought...sir....

HOBBS: Maybe we'll have some fighters out here to work on those Japs

CROOK: If they come back this afternoon....(PLEASED) We have a chance.

HOBBS: Mr. Crook....We're not going to go down those two feet....that PBY's got pumps for us...and more on the way, eh Mr. Crook?

CROOK: Yes, sir....We can use plenty of them.

HOBBS: Keep lightening the ship until those pumps can be put to work.... (FADE) Now we've got a chance.

MUSIC: BRIDGE TO B.G.

HOBBS: (SELF) It was a race then....a race to stay afloat. The other tender returned from a depth bombing attack on an enemy submarine a gave us a hand....and then....at sunset....came the 11th attack of the Jap bombers....

SOUND: PLANES AND BOMBS

HOBBS: (SELF) The Thornton was alongside and I called over to her skipper, Commander Sellers....

HOBBS: (ACTOR) Sellers - better cast off. You'll be able to fight your ship better.

SELLERS: (OFF) No - we'll stand by. We're here to help you and we'll stay here until we're sure there's nothing that can be done to save the Chincoteague....

HOBBS: Thanks....we'll need all the help we can get.

OFFICER: It looks bad, sir....We can't take any more damage and stay afloat....This time they'll get us....Our list is 18 degrees to starboard.

HOBBS: I'll admit....we're in for it....unless....(THRILLED) do you see what I see?....

OFFICER: Where?....

HOBBS: There....Up there, coming in over the Japs....

OFFICER: Those are Marines Corsairs....

HOBBS: Corsairs....our own planes....four of them....

OFFICER: Look at them come down on those Japs....

HOBBS: The Japs see 'em....Look....they're turning....

CROOK: And they're jettisoning their bombs....trying to get away.... (PRAYERFULLY) Come on, you Corsairs....Come on, you Marines! I'll fight anybody up to 200 pounds whoever makes a crack about the Marines!

OFFICER:	Now....they've got the Japs where they want 'em.... They're firing....(YELLS OF GLEE FROM ALL) Two of the Japs....in flames....going down....
CROOK:	That other one isn't going to get away, though.... Here comes another Corsair....
HOBBS:	And that Jap's gone. No wonder the Japs call our Corsairs "Whistling Death." Three up....three down.... We'll have fighter protection now.... (GLEE SUBSIDES SLOWLY) Well, gentlemen....we aren't so bad off. We're two feet out of the water....and righting our list. A lot of fuel has burned below decks....but there's a lot more in our tanks that hasn't burned.... The Japs have bombed us eleven time but we're still afloat.... Gentlemen.... the Chincoteague is going to come through....!
MUSIC:	UP AND OUT
NARR.:	And did the Chincoteague make port, Commander Hobbs?
HOBBS:	(SELF) Indeed she did.... It took quite a while....but she made it.
NARR.:	And you were all pretty tired after that experience weren't you, sir?
HOBBS:	Oh....I suppose so....when we took time to think about it.
NARR.:	How long were you on the bridge, sir....?
HOBBS:	I think it was in the neighborhood of 60 hours.
NARR. #1:	And no sleep in that time....?
HOBBS:	None....but it was no harder for me than for the other officers and the men of the Chincoteague. Every man had his job to do.... and every man did it. I couldn't single out men for particular mention....because it would simply be a roll call of the Chincoteague's crew.

NARR. #1: You're proud of that crew of the Chincoteague, aren't you, Commander Hobbs....?

HOBBS: I certianly am. I shall always remember them with the deepest affection and admiration.

NARR. #1: Commander Hobbs, one of our CBS engineers was an officer aboard your ship. His name is Milt Korf.

HOBBS: Oh, yes, I remember Korf well. He did a splendid job of maintaining communications. And when I go to sea again....I should like to have with me the same bunch of men....in my opinion the finest bunch of men....that ever went to sea.

NARR. #1: And what has become of the Chincoteague, sir....?

HOBBS: She's gone back to sea again. The spirit of the men is the spirit of the Chincoteague. There is still work to do....and the Chincoteague will do her share.

NARR. #1: Thank you, Commander Ira E. Hobbs for your thrilling and inspiring story....

MUSIC: FULL TO B.G.

NARR. #1: Friends....it is ships like the Chincoteague and men like those about whom you have heard tonight....that make up your Navy. Men and ships who never quit....but who press on and on....through every adversity....until final victory is assured. And all America gives its praise....its thanks and its support to the Navy....as it fights....in the First Line!

MUSIC: UP AND OUT

- 22 -

CLOSING

ANNOUNCER: Yes, today and every day millions of loyal Americans are giving their support to the Navy and to our other splendid fighting forces throughout the world. In factories and offices - on farms and in homes - men and women are working hard to make victory come as soon as possible. Naturally we are glad that - under these conditions of extra pressure and activity - many people are finding Wrigley's Spearmint Gum helpful. They find that chewing gum tends to relieve that unpleasant feeling of strain and nervous tension....seems to give them comfort and satisfaction while they're working. Then, too, chewing on a piece of gum keeps the mouth and throat moist - has a refreshing effect when the air is dry or dusty. Hence, the demand for delicious Wrigley's Spearmint Gum is the greatest it has ever been. We want you to know we are doing everything humanly possible to supply you - making as much Wrigley's Spearmint Gum as can be made without sacrificing its famous quality.

MUSIC: UP AND B.G.

NARR. #2: Be sure to listen to the First Line next Thursday evening.... and hear the dramatic story of what happened to a young Coast Guardsman when a tiny Higgins boat on patrol off Guadalcanal met a huge Japanese warship. Next Thursday night...this time....this station....the First Line!

MUSIC: UP AND B.G.

- 23 -

ANNOUNCER: While Navy personnel appeared on this program, the makers of Wrigley's Spearmint Gum do not wish to imply that the Navy endorses our product.

MUSIC: UP AND B.G.

ANNOUNCER: This program has come to you from our Chicago studios in the Wrigley Building.

This is CBS, the Columbia Broadcasting System.